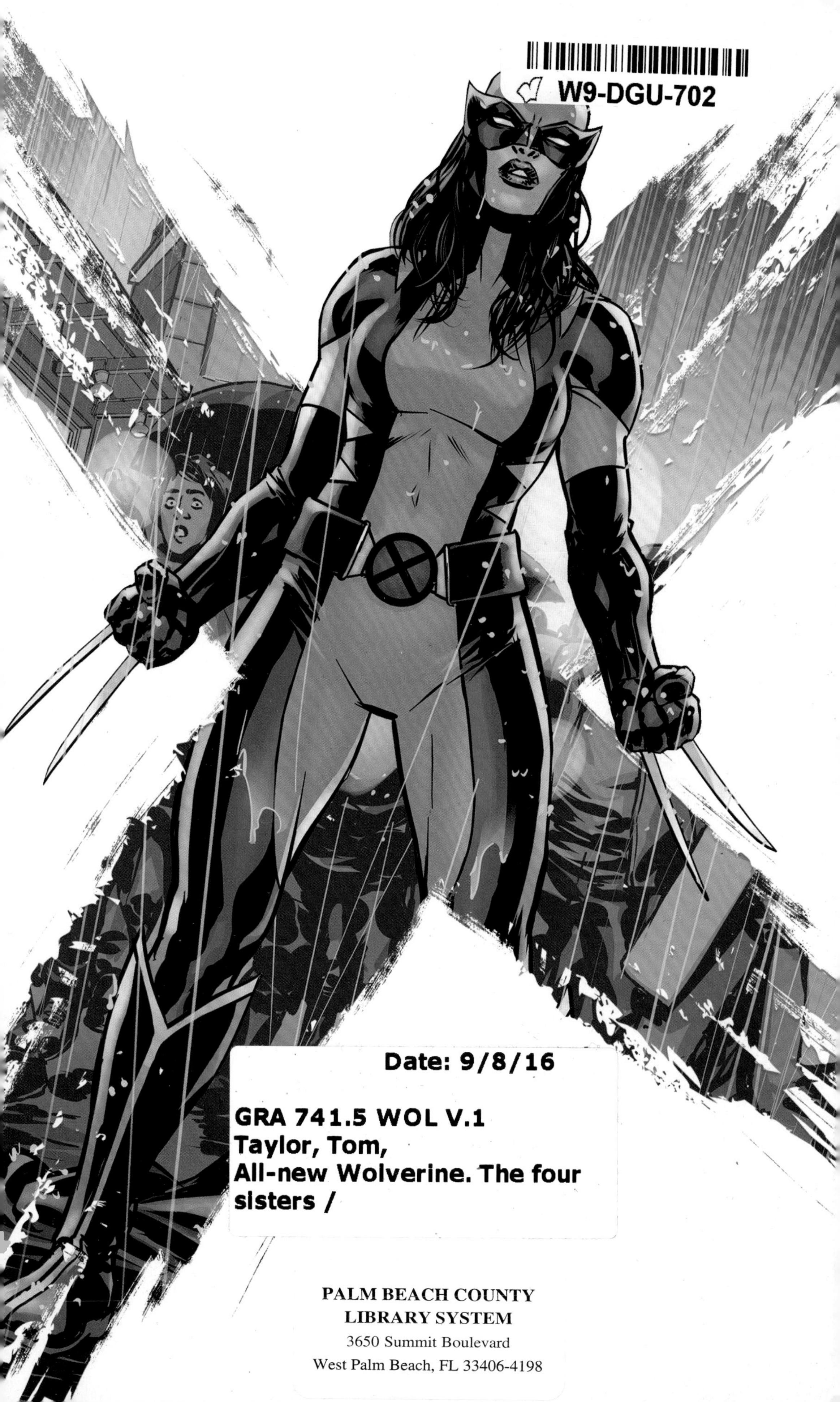

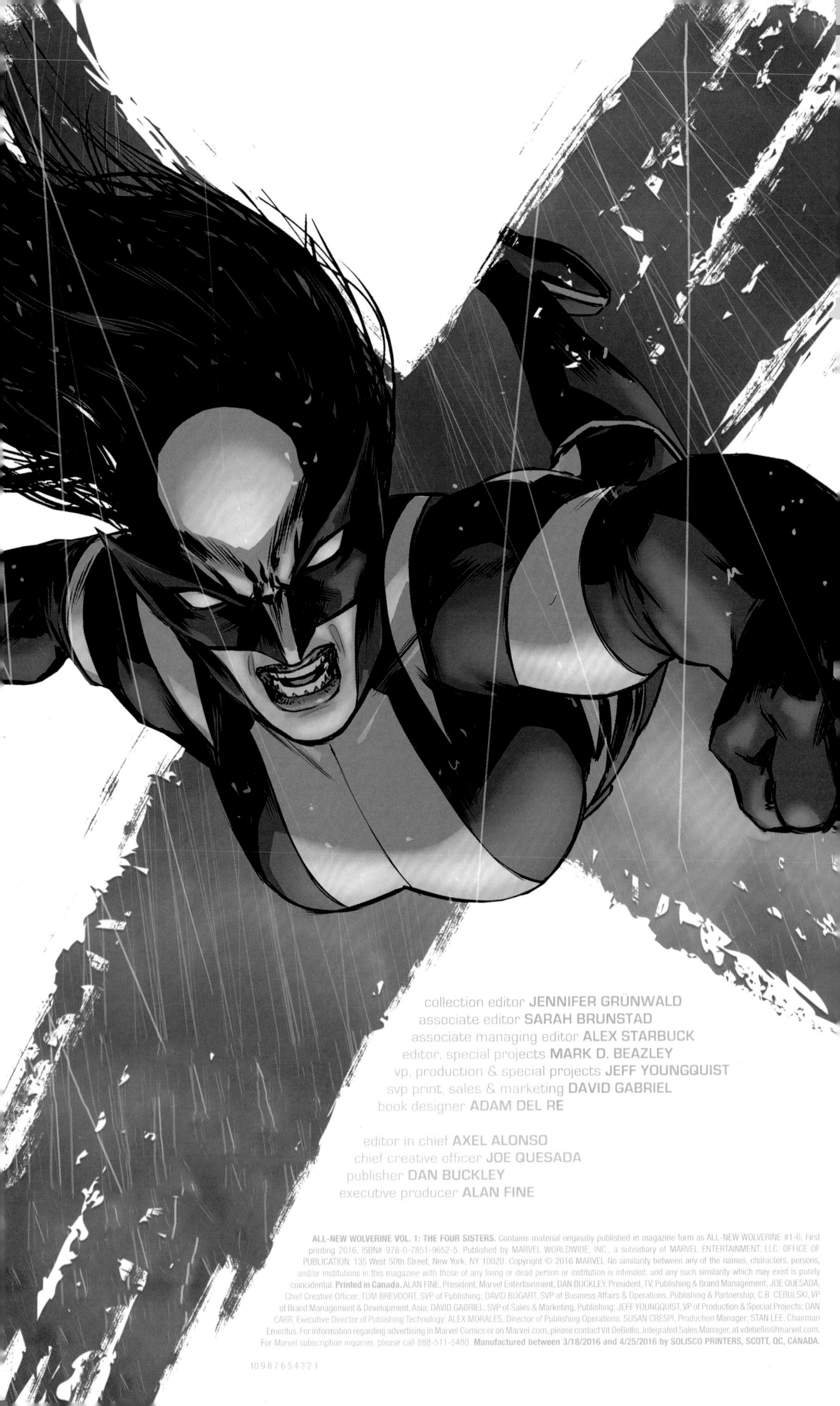

collection editor **JENNIFER GRÜNWALD**
associate editor **SARAH BRUNSTAD**
associate managing editor **ALEX STARBUCK**
editor, special projects **MARK D. BEAZLEY**
vp, production & special projects **JEFF YOUNGQUIST**
svp print, sales & marketing **DAVID GABRIEL**
book designer **ADAM DEL RE**

editor in chief **AXEL ALONSO**
chief creative officer **JOE QUESADA**
publisher **DAN BUCKLEY**
executive producer **ALAN FINE**

ALL-NEW WOLVERINE VOL. 1: THE FOUR SISTERS. Contains material originally published in magazine form as ALL-NEW WOLVERINE #1-6. First printing 2016. ISBN# 978-0-7851-9652-5. Published by MARVEL WORLDWIDE, INC., a subsidiary of MARVEL ENTERTAINMENT, LLC. OFFICE OF PUBLICATION: 135 West 50th Street, New York, NY 10020. **Printed in Canada.** ALAN FINE, President, Marvel Entertainment; DAN BUCKLEY, President, TV, Publishing & Brand Management; JOE QUESADA, Chief Creative Officer; TOM BREVOORT, SVP of Publishing; DAVID BOGART, SVP of Business Affairs & Operations, Publishing & Partnership; C.B. CEBULSKI, VP of Brand Management & Development, Asia; DAVID GABRIEL, SVP of Sales & Marketing, Publishing; JEFF YOUNGQUIST, VP of Production & Special Projects; DAN CARR, Executive Director of Publishing Technology; ALEX MORALES, Director of Publishing Operations; SUSAN CRESPI, Production Manager; STAN LEE, Chairman Emeritus. For information regarding advertising in Marvel Comics or on Marvel.com, please contact Vit DeBellis, Integrated Sales Manager, at vdebellis@marvel.com. For Marvel subscription inquiries, please call 888-511-5480. **Manufactured between 3/18/2016 and 4/25/2016 by SOLISCO PRINTERS, SCOTT, QC, CANADA.**

10 9 8 7 6 5 4 3 2 1

X-23 WAS CREATED TO BE A WEAPON.
For a time, that's all she was. But Laura Kinney escaped that life with the help of the man she was cloned from, the man who became her mentor: THE WOLVERINE. Tragically, the original Wolverine has fallen, and the mantle has been left empty.

Laura will live as Logan's legacy, and she will fight for her brighter future.

She will leave behind her old life and make a new one. She is the...

ALL-NEW WOLVERINE

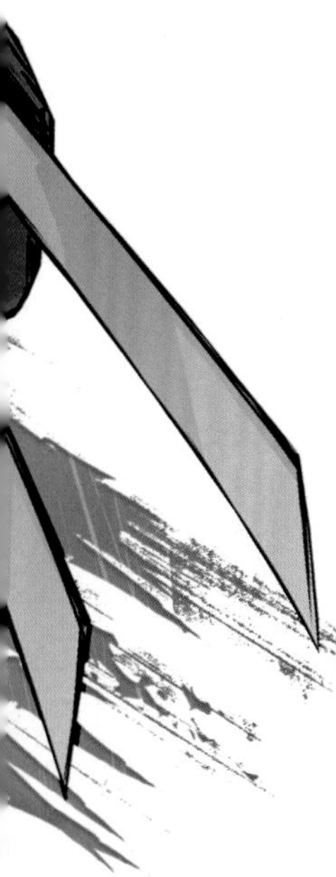

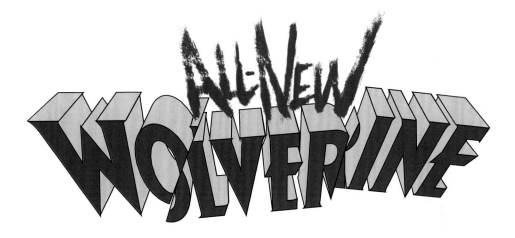

writer
TOM TAYLOR

art
DAVID LOPEZ & DAVID NAVARROT

colorist
NATHAN FAIRBAIRN

letterer
VC's CORY PETIT

cover art
BENGAL

assistant editor
CHRISTINA HARRINGTON

associate editor
DARREN SHAN

editor
MARK PANICCIA

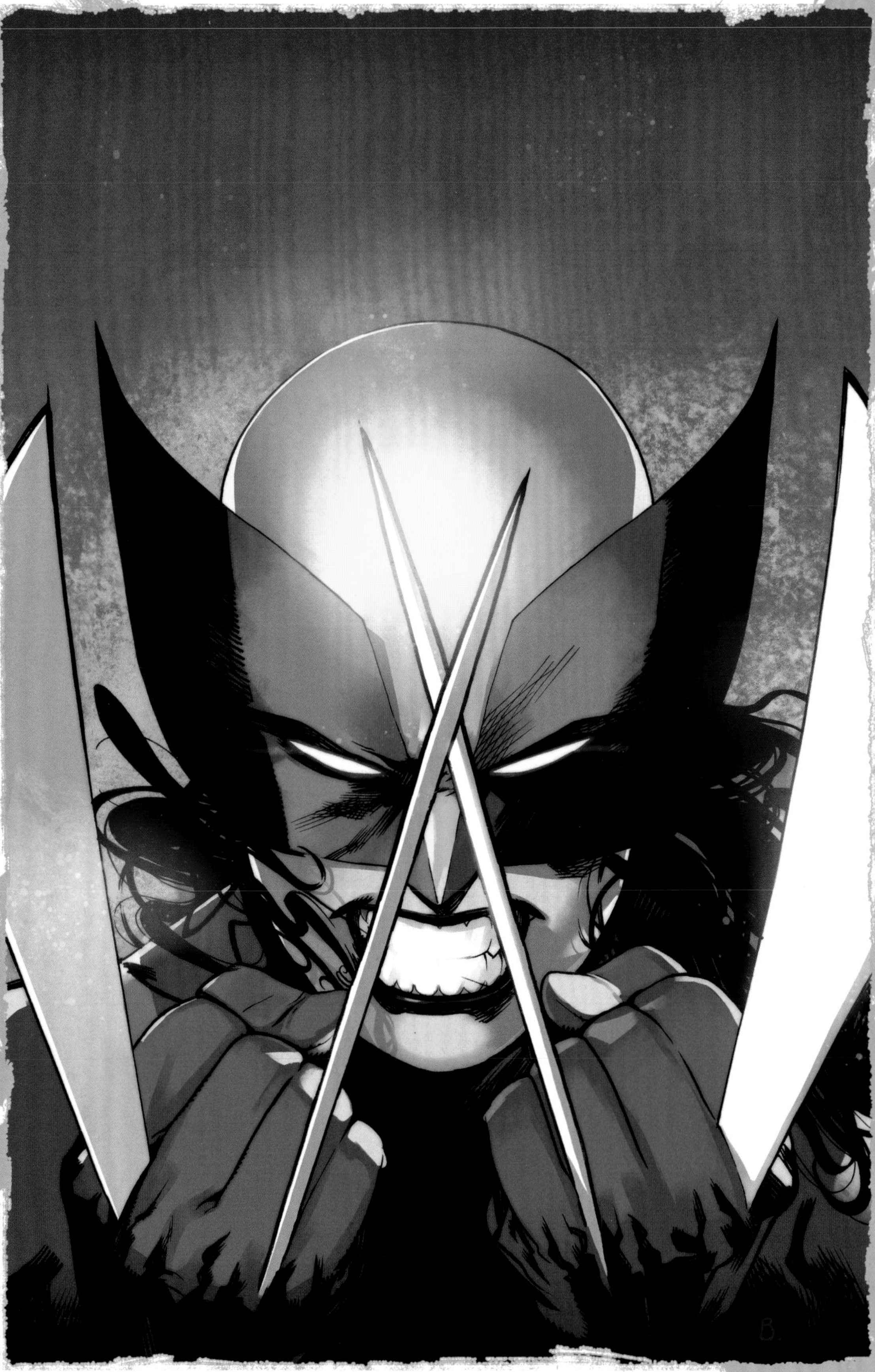

I

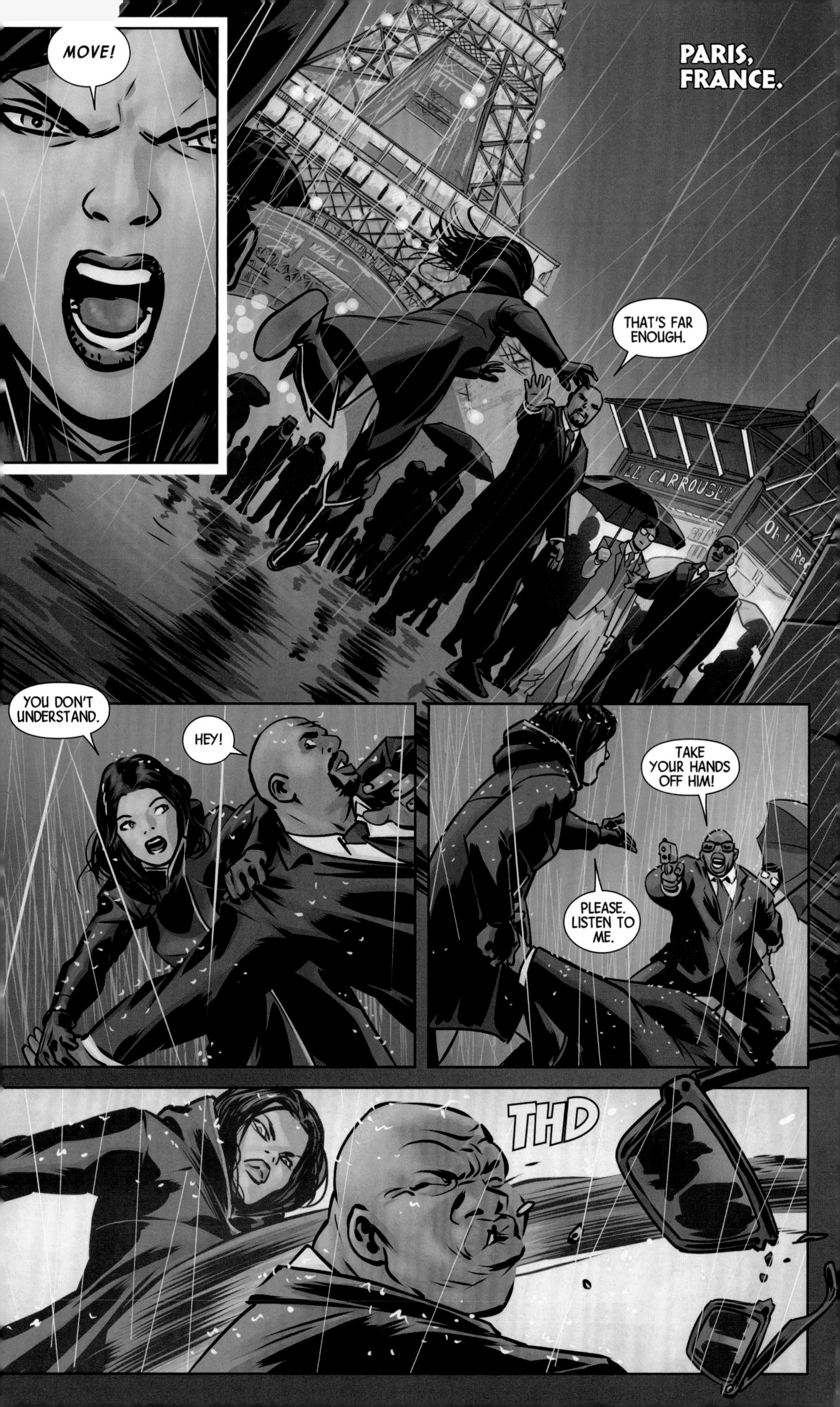

MOVE!
PARIS, FRANCE.
THAT'S FAR ENOUGH.
LE CARROUSEL
YOU DON'T UNDERSTAND.
HEY!
TAKE YOUR HANDS OFF HIM!
PLEASE. LISTEN TO ME.
THD

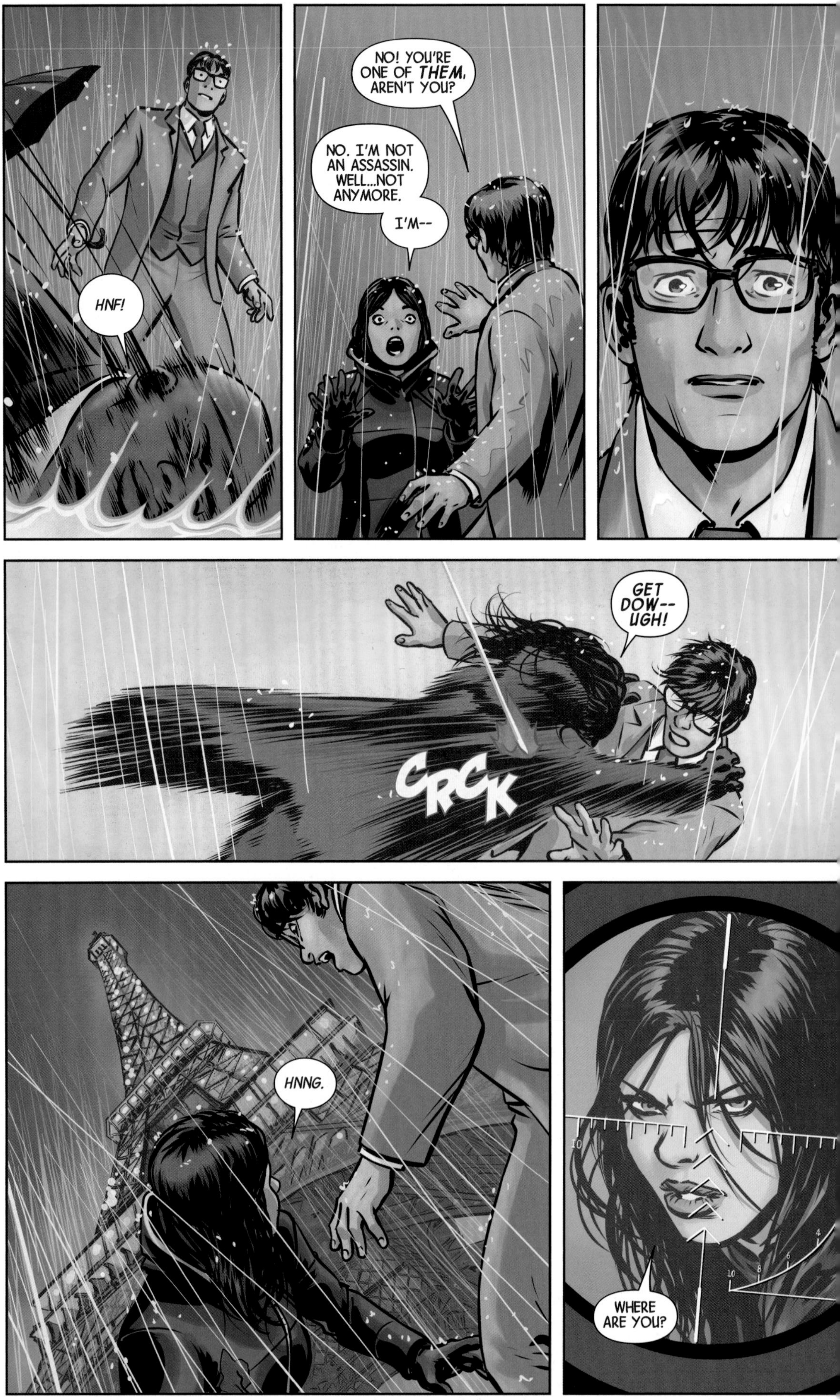
HNF!
NO! YOU'RE ONE OF *THEM*, AREN'T YOU?
NO. I'M NOT AN ASSASSIN. WELL...NOT ANYMORE.
I'M--
GET DOW--UGH!
CRCK
HNNG.
WHERE ARE YOU?

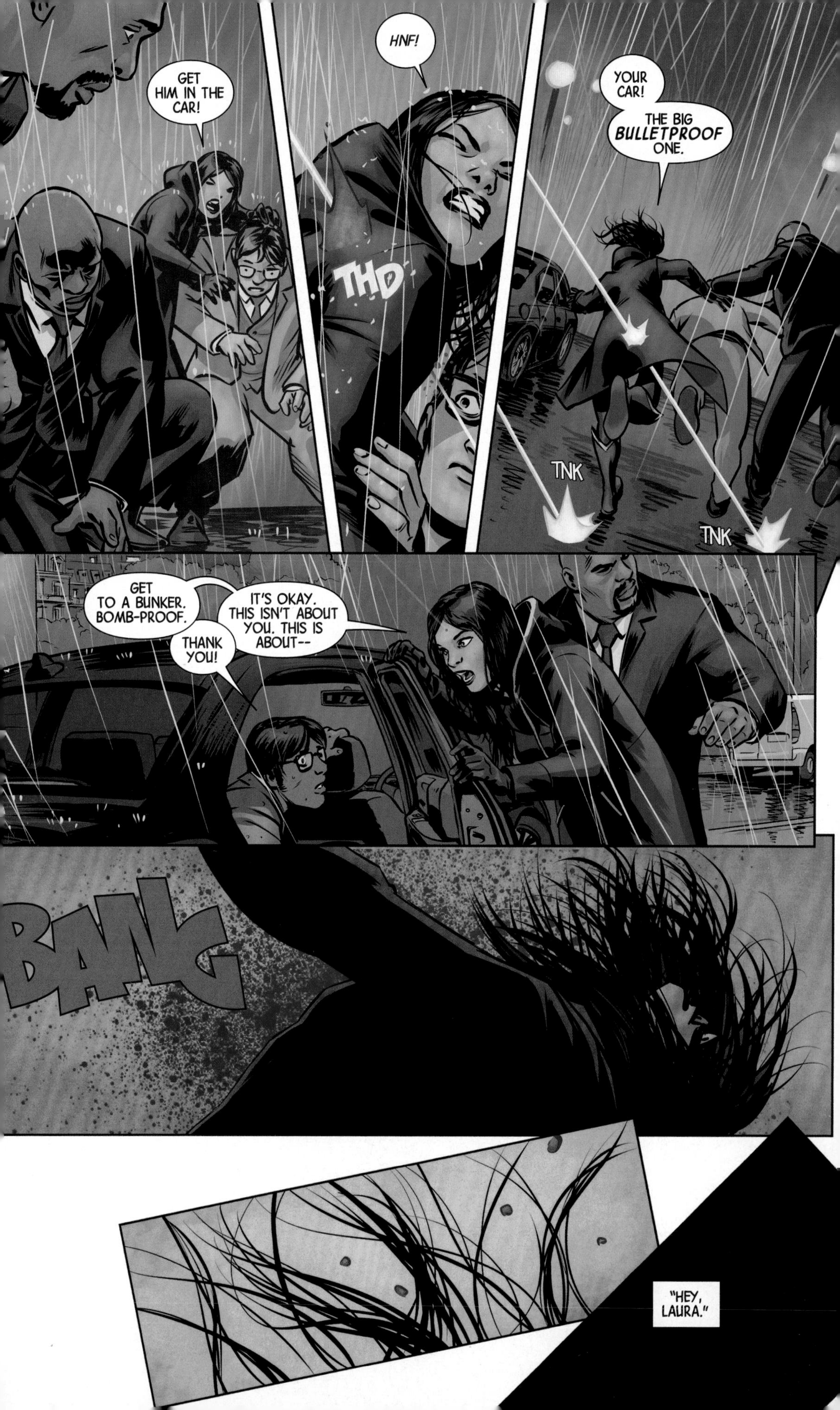
GET HIM IN THE CAR!
HNF!
THD
YOUR CAR!
THE BIG BULLETPROOF ONE.
TNK
TNK
GET TO A BUNKER. BOMB-PROOF.
THANK YOU!
IT'S OKAY. THIS ISN'T ABOUT YOU. THIS IS ABOUT--
BANG
"HEY, LAURA."

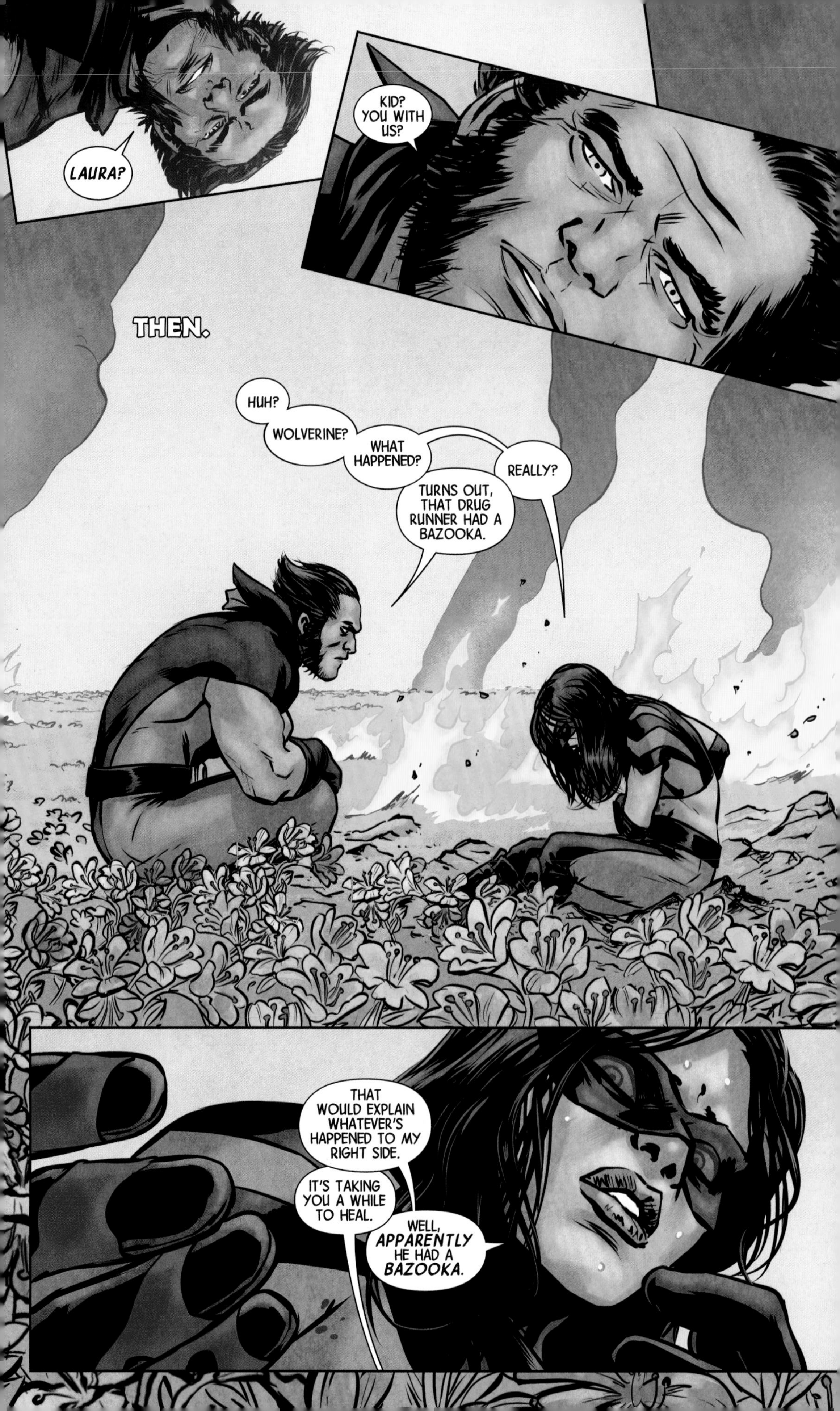

LAURA?
KID? YOU WITH US?
THEN.
HUH?
WOLVERINE?
WHAT HAPPENED?
REALLY?
TURNS OUT, THAT DRUG RUNNER HAD A BAZOOKA.
THAT WOULD EXPLAIN WHATEVER'S HAPPENED TO MY RIGHT SIDE.
IT'S TAKING YOU A WHILE TO HEAL.
WELL, APPARENTLY HE HAD A BAZOOKA.

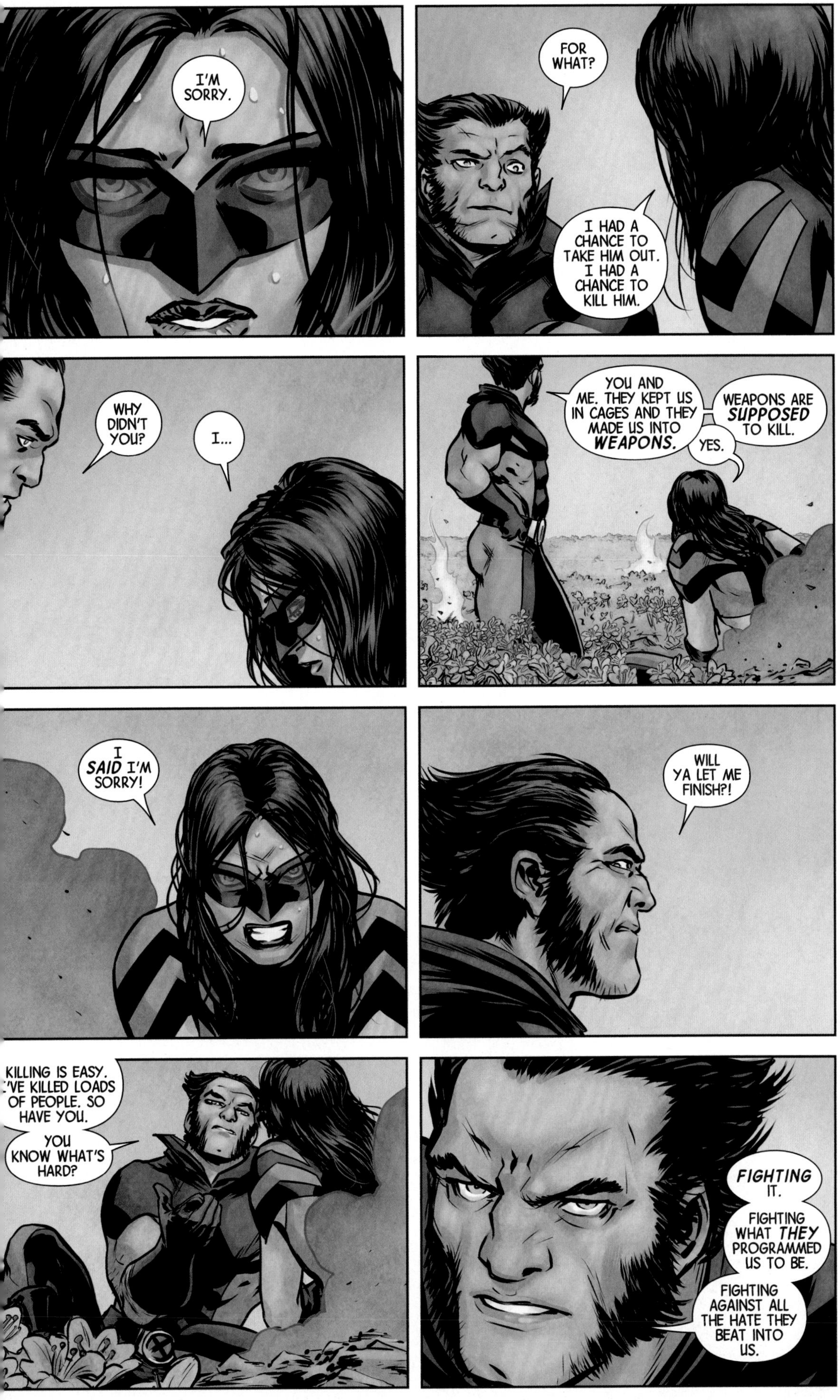
I'M SORRY.
FOR WHAT?
I HAD A CHANCE TO TAKE HIM OUT. I HAD A CHANCE TO KILL HIM.
WHY DIDN'T YOU?
I...
YOU AND ME. THEY KEPT US IN CAGES AND THEY MADE US INTO *WEAPONS.*
YES.
WEAPONS ARE *SUPPOSED* TO KILL.
I *SAID* I'M SORRY!
WILL YA LET ME FINISH?!
KILLING IS EASY. I'VE KILLED LOADS OF PEOPLE. SO HAVE YOU.
YOU KNOW WHAT'S HARD?
FIGHTING IT.
FIGHTING WHAT *THEY* PROGRAMMED US TO BE.
FIGHTING AGAINST ALL THE HATE THEY BEAT INTO US.

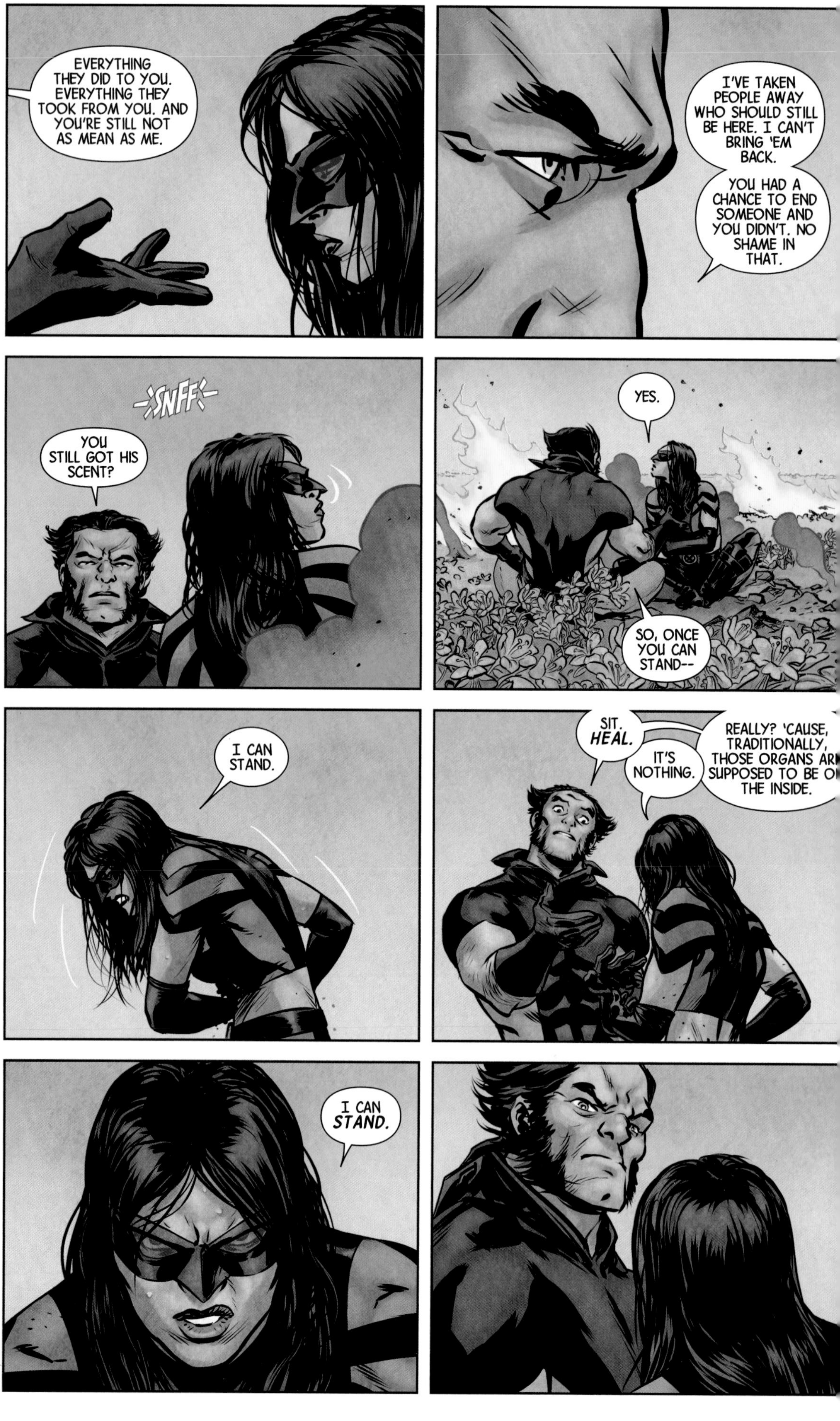
EVERYTHING THEY DID TO YOU. EVERYTHING THEY TOOK FROM YOU. AND YOU'RE STILL NOT AS MEAN AS ME.
I'VE TAKEN PEOPLE AWAY WHO SHOULD STILL BE HERE. I CAN'T BRING 'EM BACK.
YOU HAD A CHANCE TO END SOMEONE AND YOU DIDN'T. NO SHAME IN THAT.
SNFF
YOU STILL GOT HIS SCENT?
YES.
SO, ONCE YOU CAN STAND--
I CAN STAND.
SIT. HEAL.
IT'S NOTHING.
REALLY? 'CAUSE, TRADITIONALLY, THOSE ORGANS AR
SUPPOSED TO BE O
THE INSIDE.
I CAN STAND.

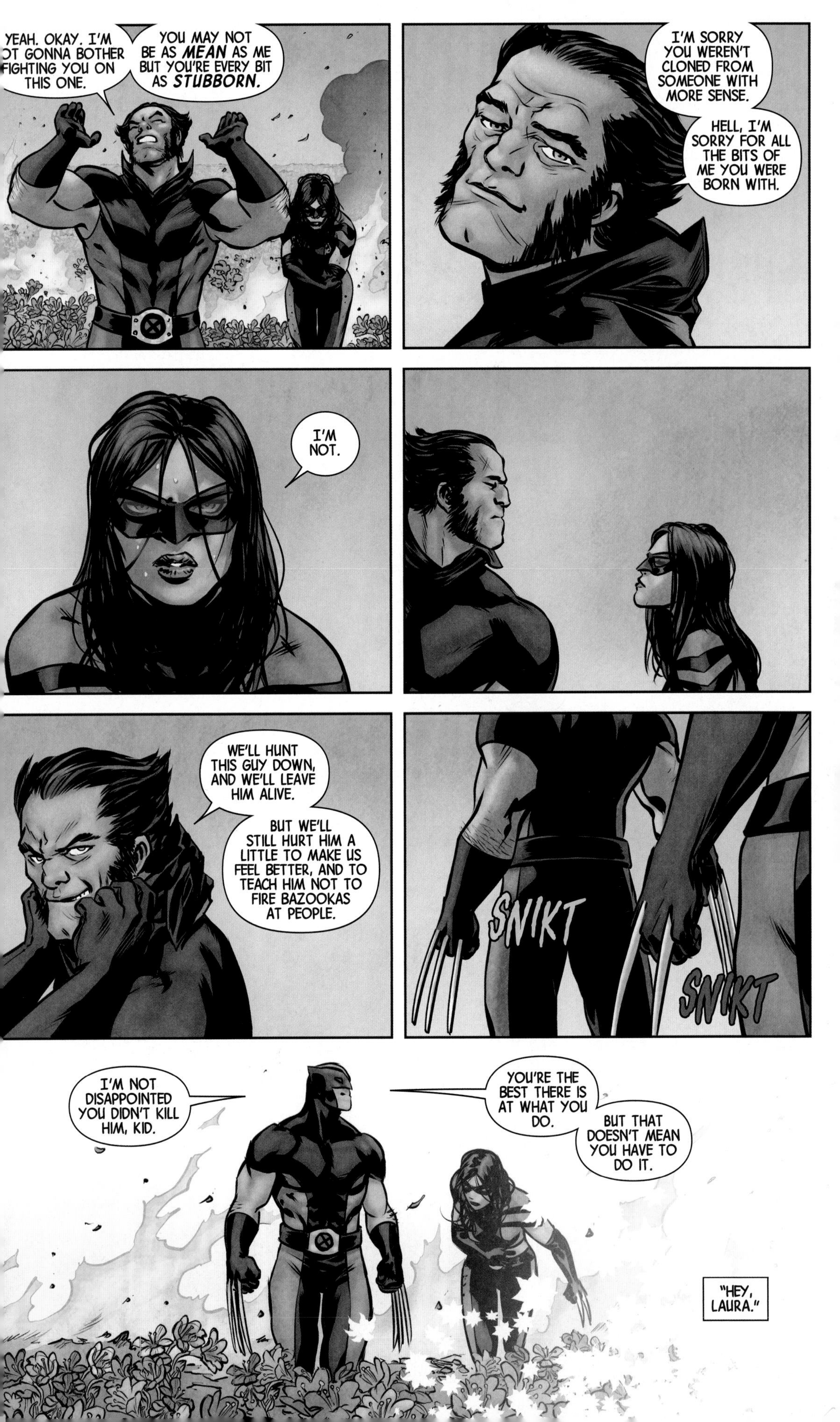
YEAH. OKAY. I'M NOT GONNA BOTHER FIGHTING YOU ON THIS ONE.
YOU MAY NOT BE AS MEAN AS ME BUT YOU'RE EVERY BIT AS STUBBORN.
I'M SORRY YOU WEREN'T CLONED FROM SOMEONE WITH MORE SENSE.
HELL, I'M SORRY FOR ALL THE BITS OF ME YOU WERE BORN WITH.
I'M NOT.
WE'LL HUNT THIS GUY DOWN, AND WE'LL LEAVE HIM ALIVE.
BUT WE'LL STILL HURT HIM A LITTLE TO MAKE US FEEL BETTER, AND TO TEACH HIM NOT TO FIRE BAZOOKAS AT PEOPLE.
SNIKT
SNIKT
I'M NOT DISAPPOINTED YOU DIDN'T KILL HIM, KID.
YOU'RE THE BEST THERE IS AT WHAT YOU DO.
BUT THAT DOESN'T MEAN YOU HAVE TO DO IT.
"HEY, LAURA."

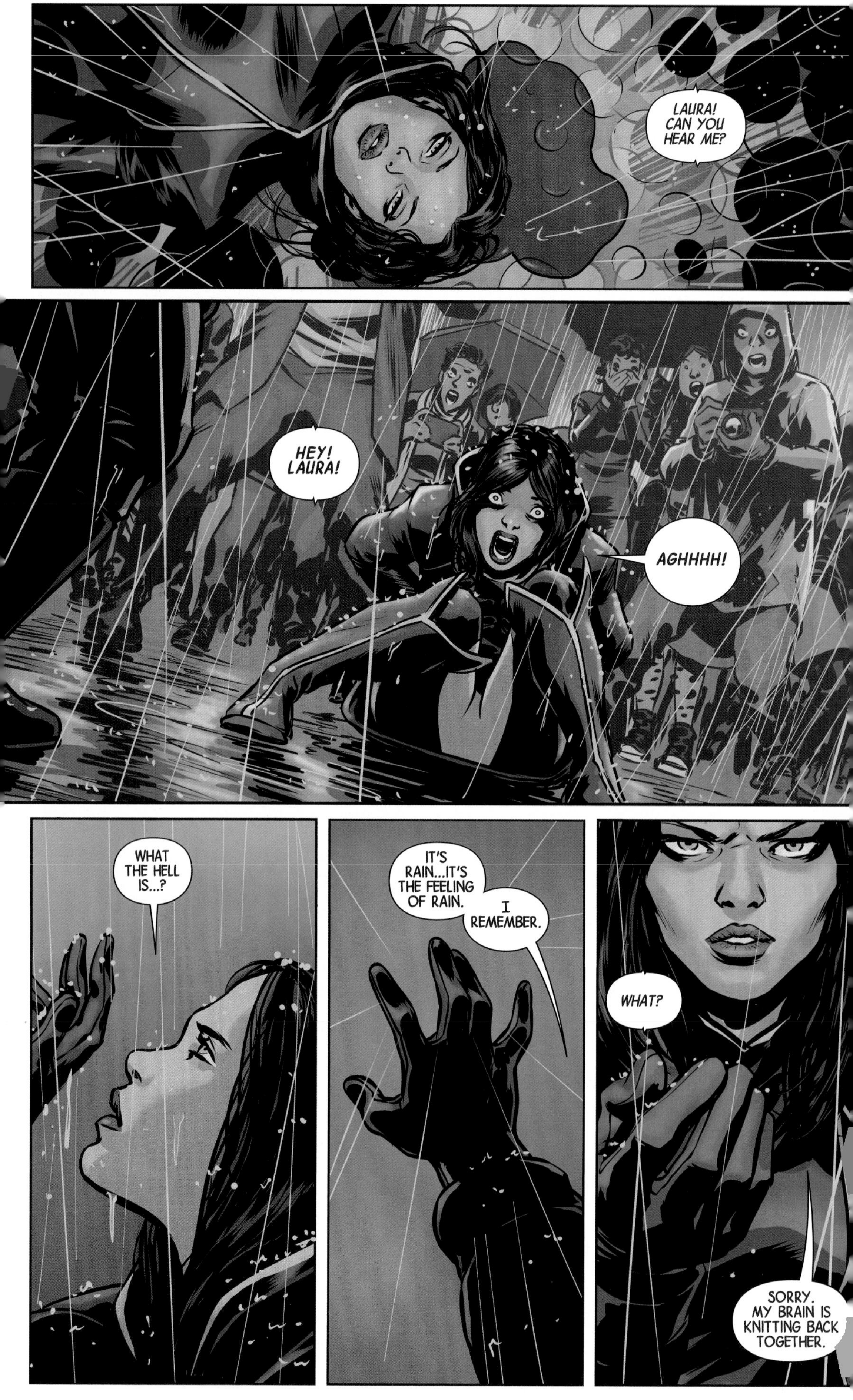
LAURA! CAN YOU HEAR ME?
HEY! LAURA!
AGHHHH!
WHAT THE HELL IS...?
IT'S RAIN...IT'S THE FEELING OF RAIN.
I REMEMBER.
WHAT?
SORRY. MY BRAIN IS KNITTING BACK TOGETHER.

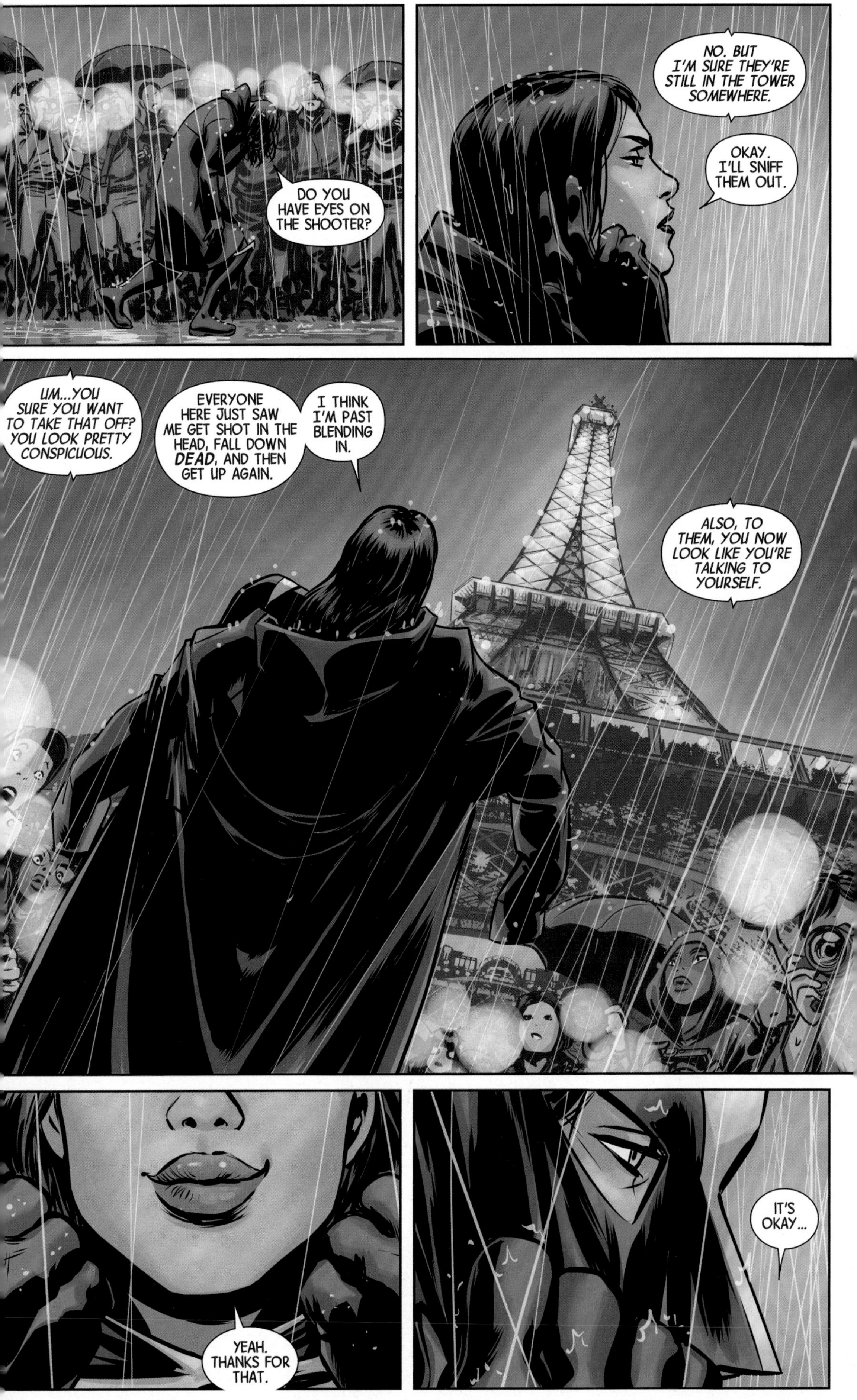
DO YOU HAVE EYES ON THE SHOOTER?
NO. BUT I'M SURE THEY'RE STILL IN THE TOWER SOMEWHERE.
OKAY. I'LL SNIFF THEM OUT.
UM...YOU SURE YOU WANT TO TAKE THAT OFF? YOU LOOK PRETTY CONSPICUOUS.
EVERYONE HERE JUST SAW ME GET SHOT IN THE HEAD, FALL DOWN DEAD, AND THEN GET UP AGAIN.
I THINK I'M PAST BLENDING IN.
ALSO, TO THEM, YOU NOW LOOK LIKE YOU'RE TALKING TO YOURSELF.
YEAH. THANKS FOR THAT.
IT'S OKAY...

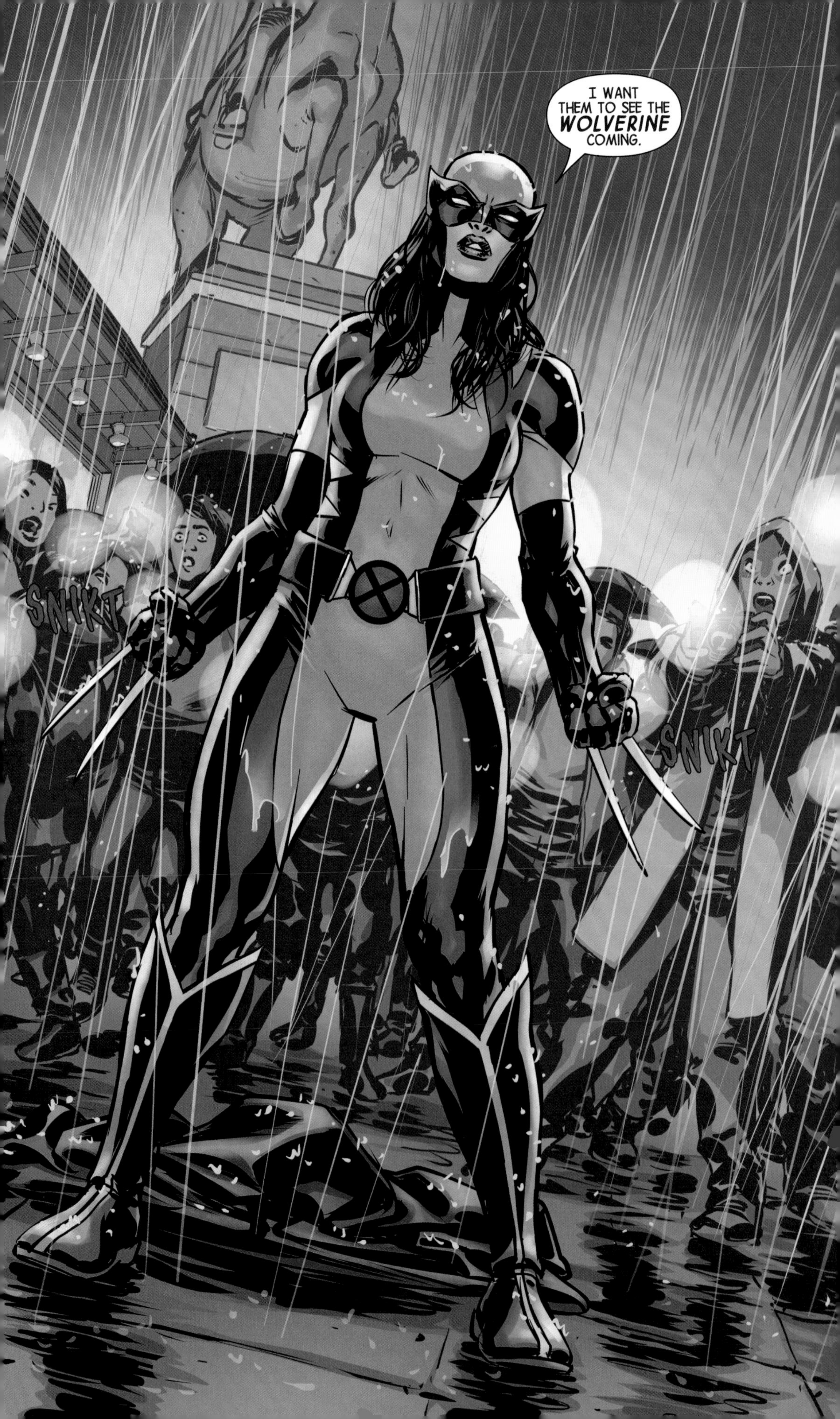
I WANT THEM TO SEE THE WOLVERINE COMING.
SNIKT
SNIKT

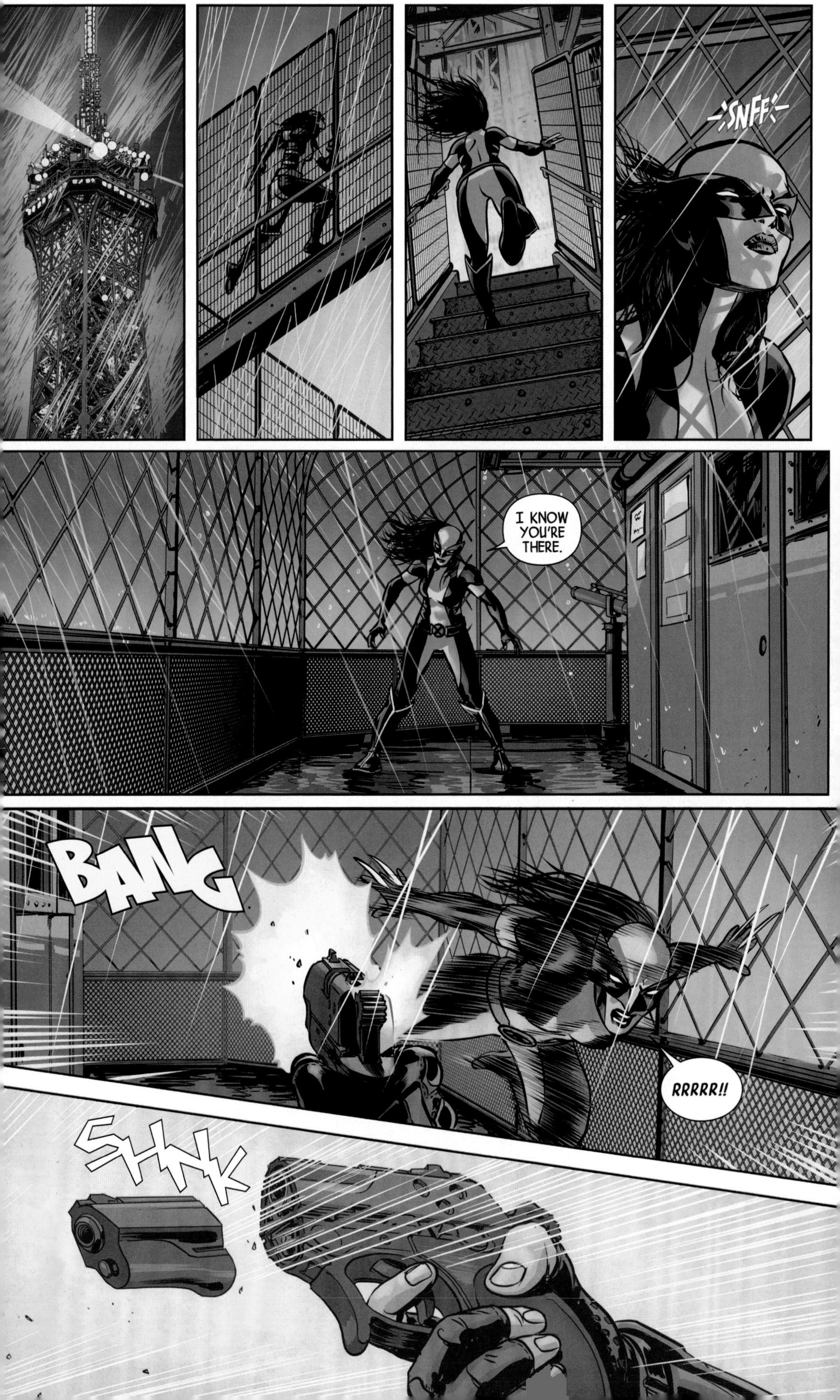
SNFF
I KNOW YOU'RE THERE.
BANG
RRRRR!!
SHNK

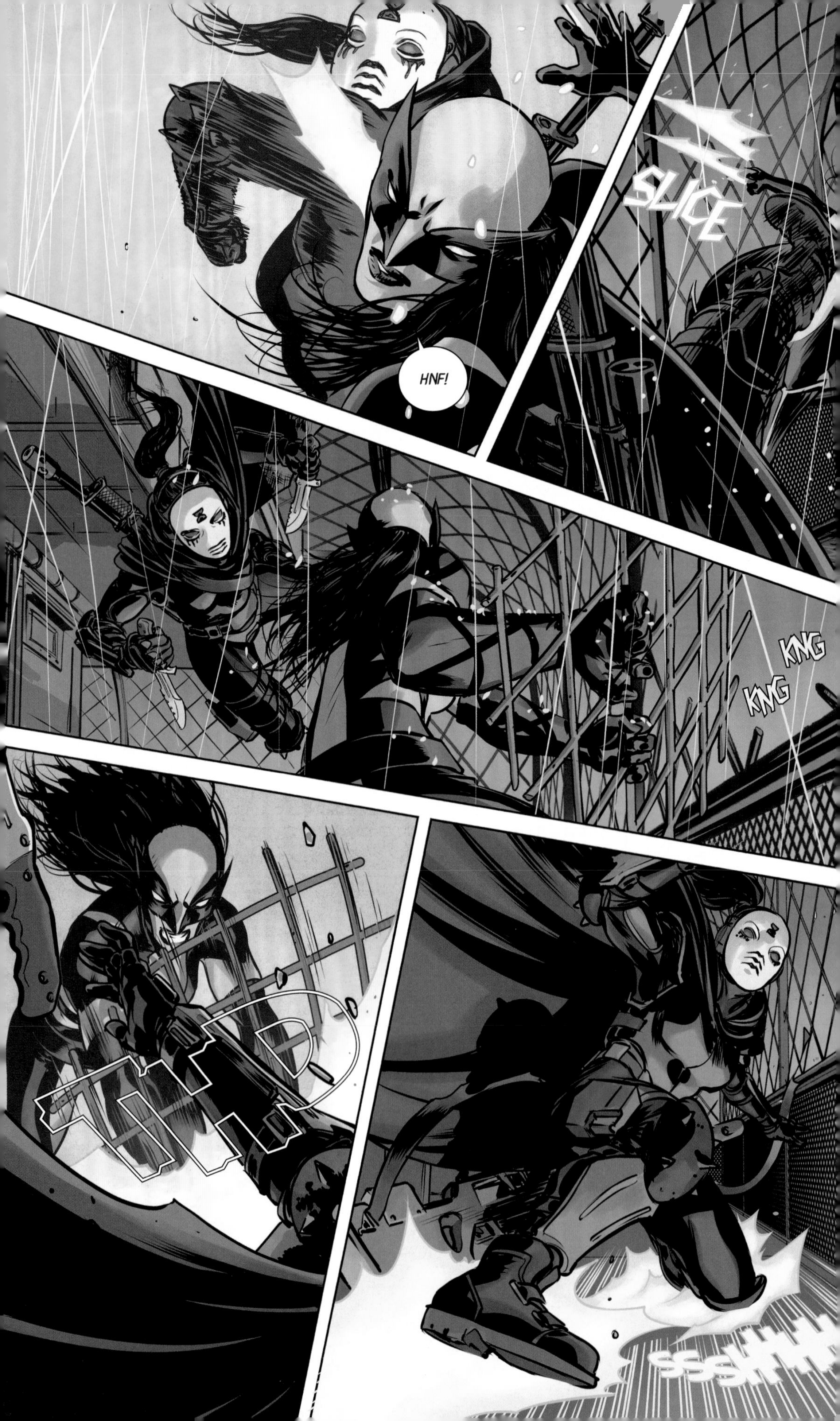

SLICE
HNF!
KNG
KNG
SSSSHHHH

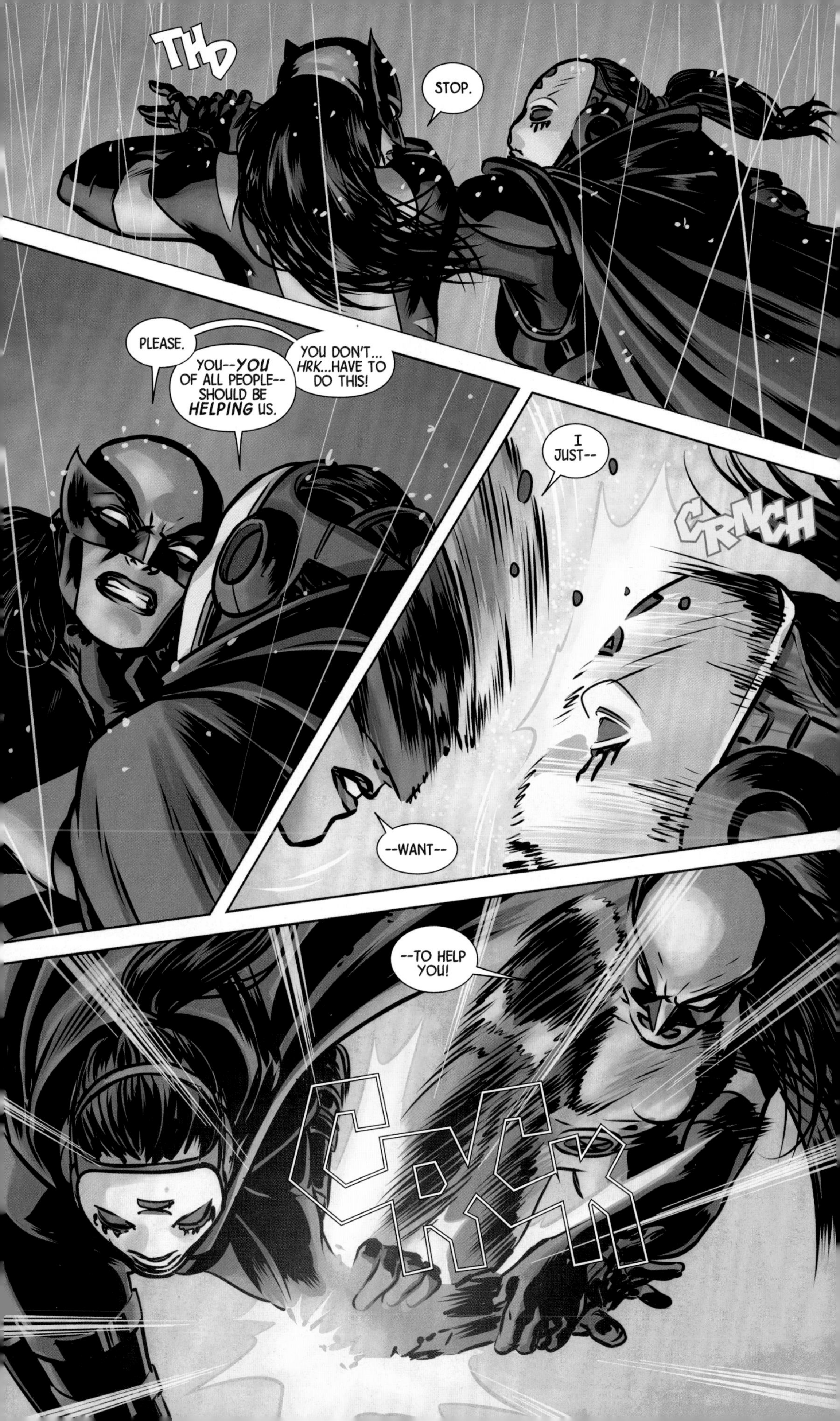
THD
STOP.
PLEASE.
YOU--YOU OF ALL PEOPLE-- SHOULD BE HELPING US.
YOU DON'T... HRK...HAVE TO DO THIS!
I JUST--
CRNCH
--WANT--
--TO HELP YOU!
CRCK

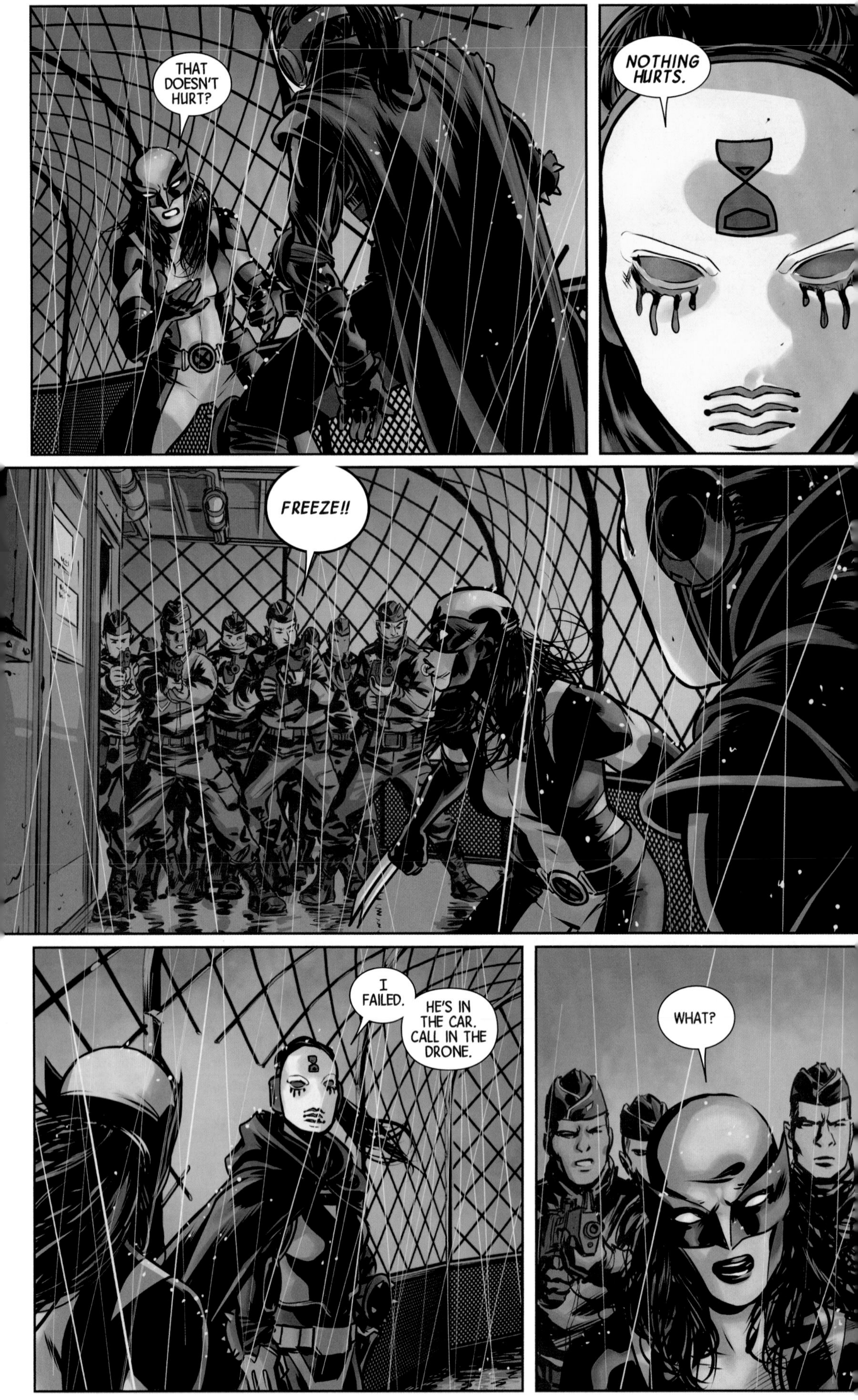
THAT DOESN'T HURT?
NOTHING HURTS.
FREEZE!!
I FAILED.
HE'S IN THE CAR. CALL IN THE DRONE.
WHAT?

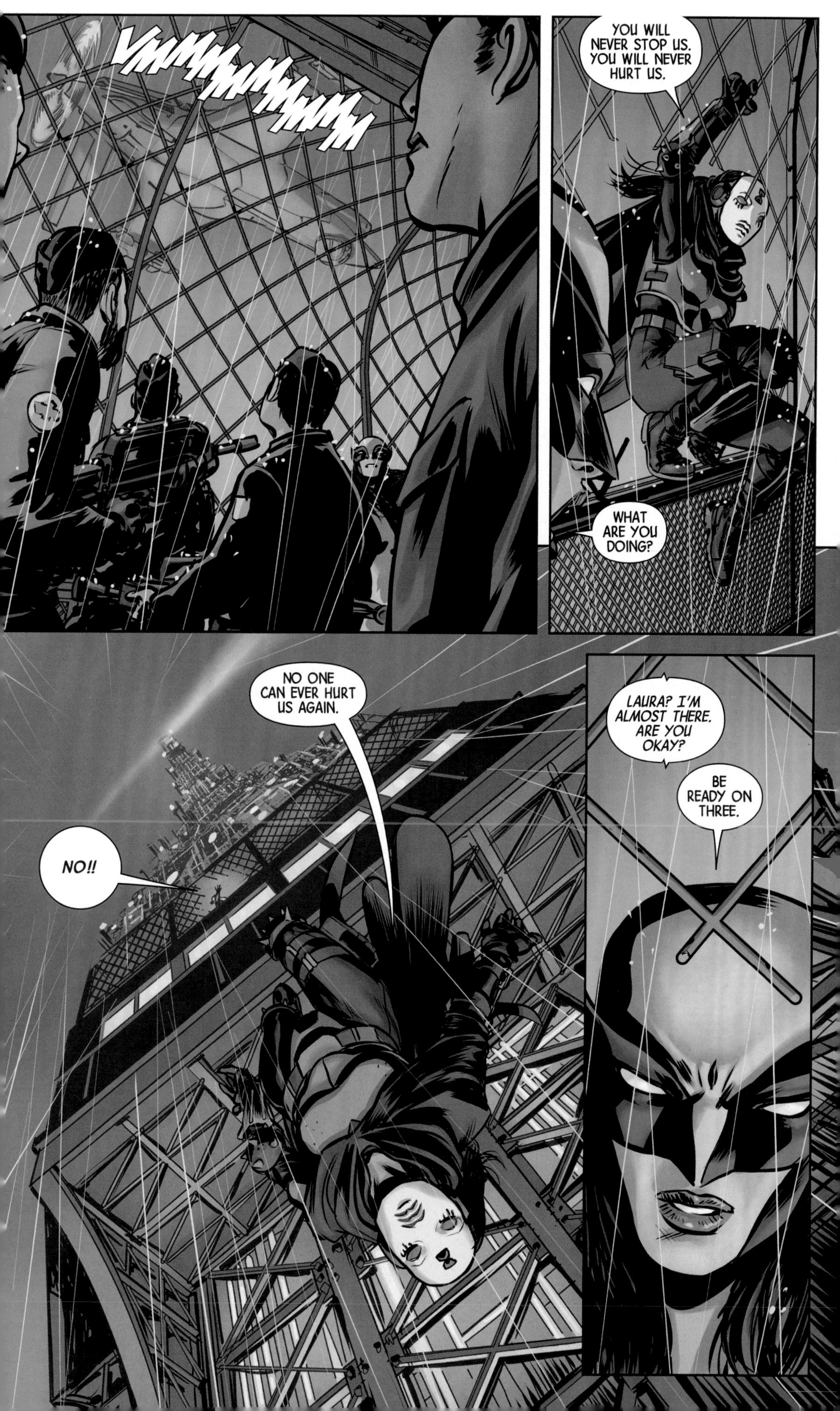
VMMMMMMMMMMM
YOU WILL NEVER STOP US. YOU WILL NEVER HURT US.
WHAT ARE YOU DOING?
NO ONE CAN EVER HURT US AGAIN.
NO!!
LAURA? I'M ALMOST THERE. ARE YOU OKAY?
BE READY ON THREE.

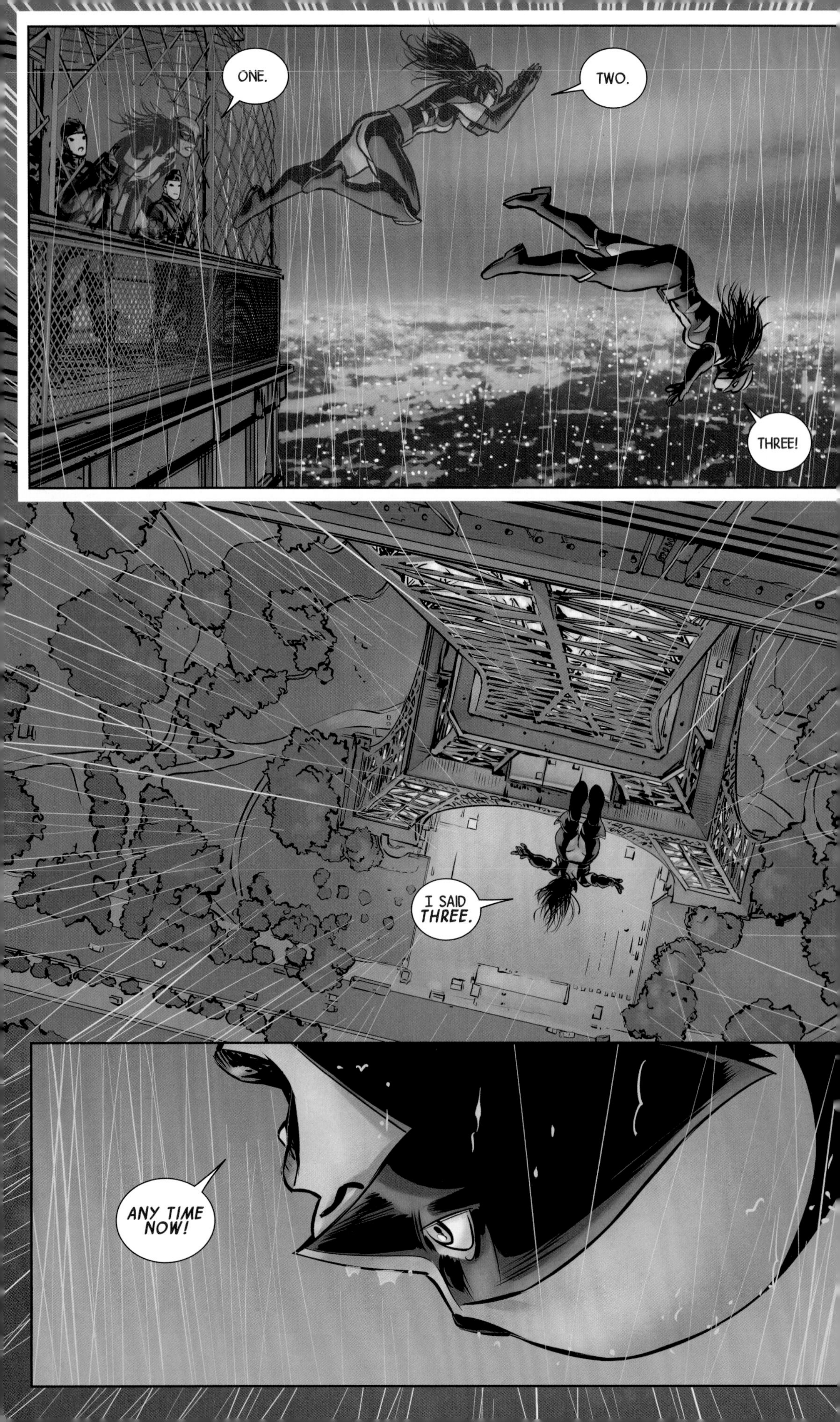
ONE.
TWO.
THREE!
I SAID *THREE.*
ANY TIME NOW!

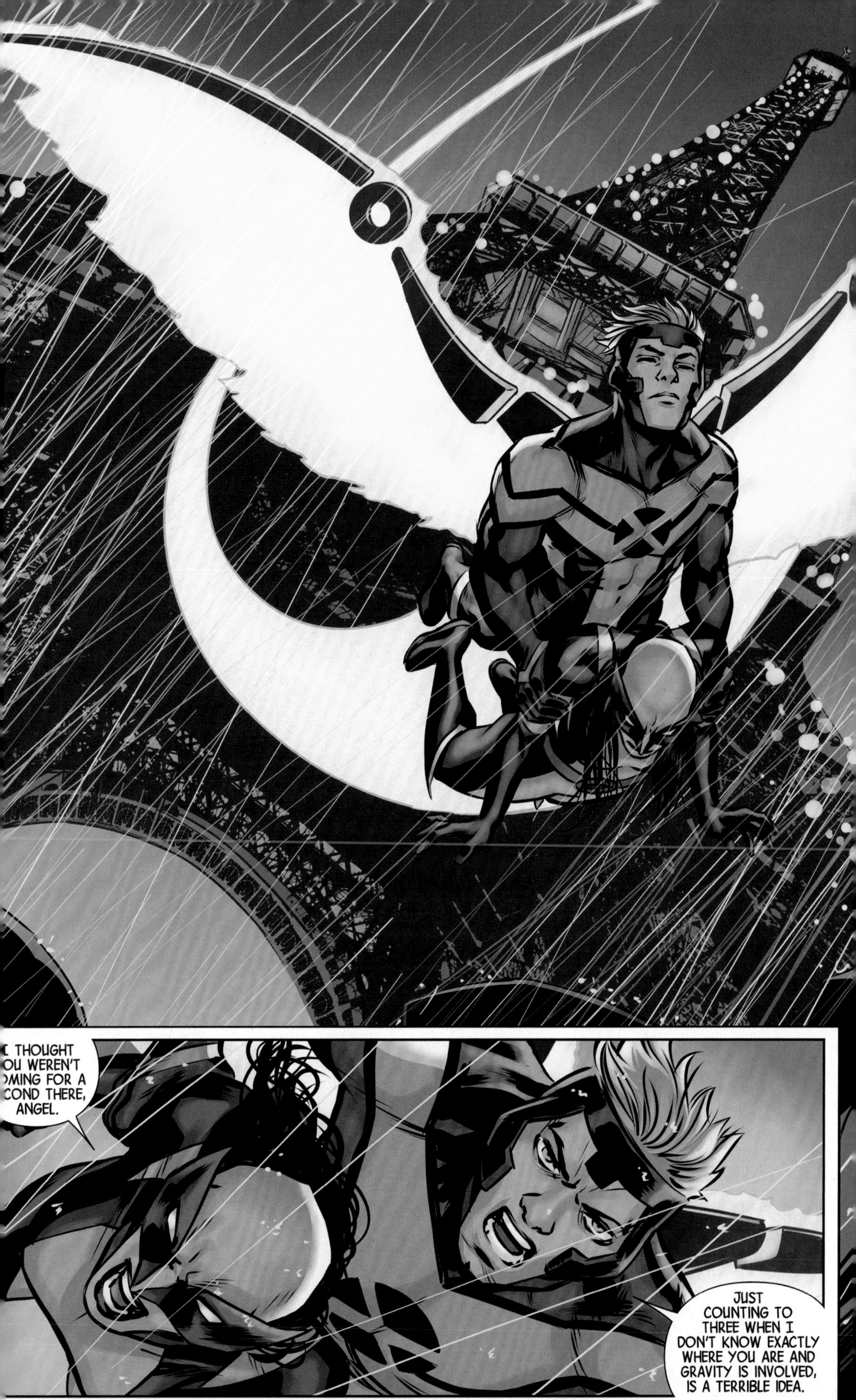

I THOUGHT OU WEREN'T OMING FOR A COND THERE, ANGEL.
JUST COUNTING TO THREE WHEN I DON'T KNOW EXACTLY WHERE YOU ARE AND GRAVITY IS INVOLVED, IS A TERRIBLE IDEA.

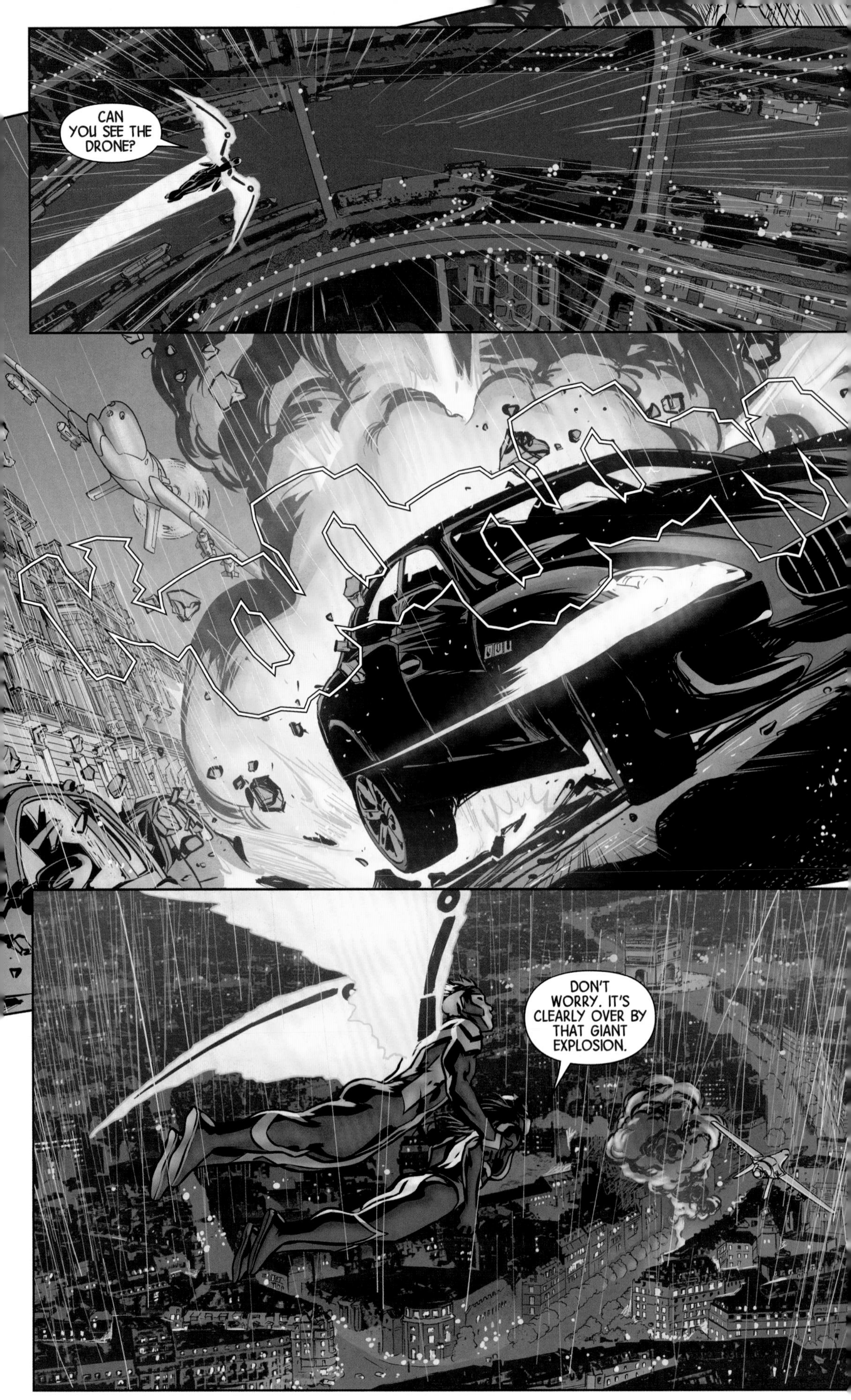
CAN YOU SEE THE DRONE?
DON'T WORRY. IT'S CLEARLY OVER BY THAT GIANT EXPLOSION.

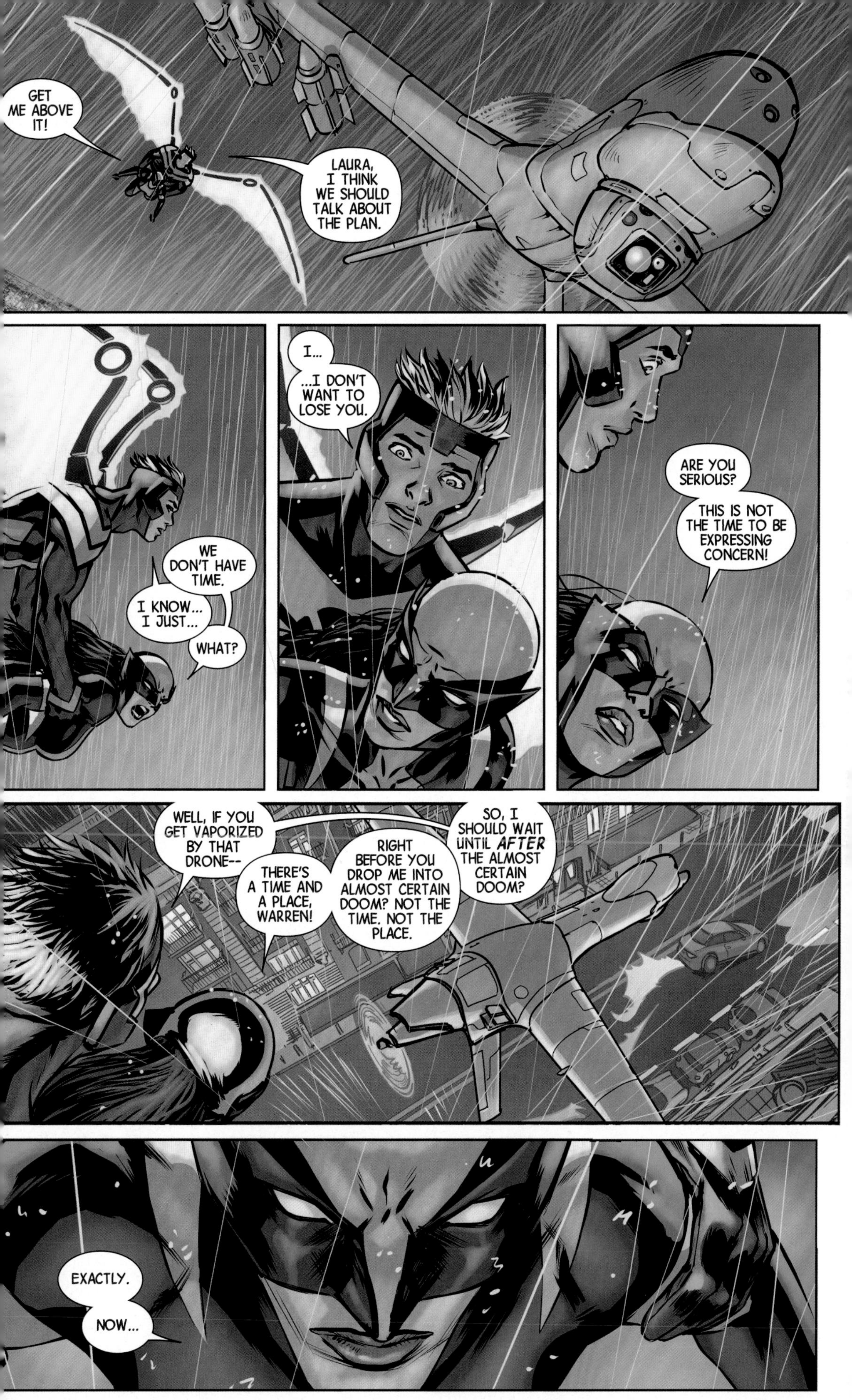
GET ME ABOVE IT!
LAURA, I THINK WE SHOULD TALK ABOUT THE PLAN.
WE DON'T HAVE TIME.
I KNOW... I JUST...
WHAT?
I...
...I DON'T WANT TO LOSE YOU.
ARE YOU SERIOUS?
THIS IS NOT THE TIME TO BE EXPRESSING CONCERN!
WELL, IF YOU GET VAPORIZED BY THAT DRONE--
THERE'S A TIME AND A PLACE, WARREN!
RIGHT BEFORE YOU DROP ME INTO ALMOST CERTAIN DOOM? NOT THE TIME. NOT THE PLACE.
SO, I SHOULD WAIT UNTIL *AFTER* THE ALMOST CERTAIN DOOM?
EXACTLY.
NOW...

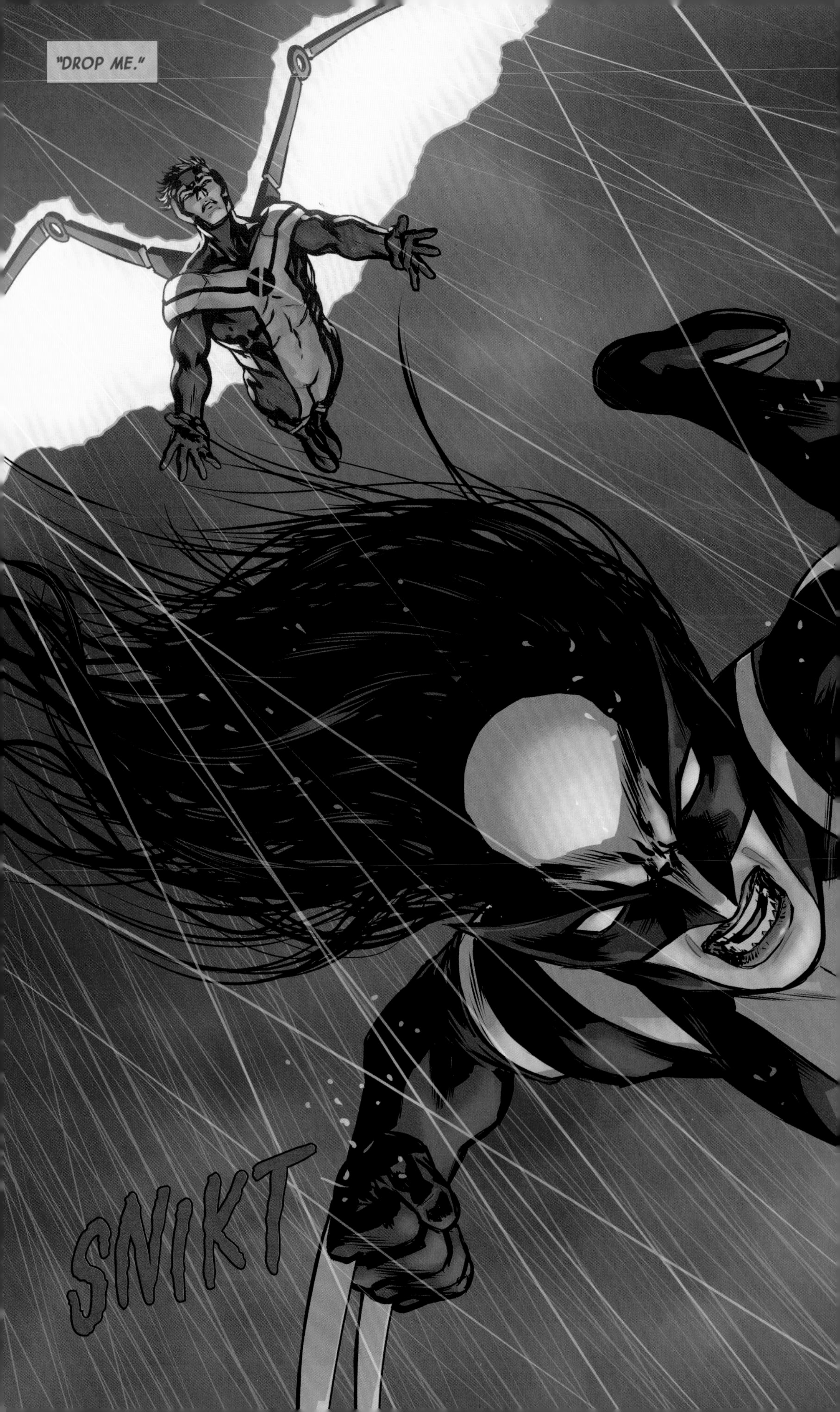
"DROP ME."
SNIKT

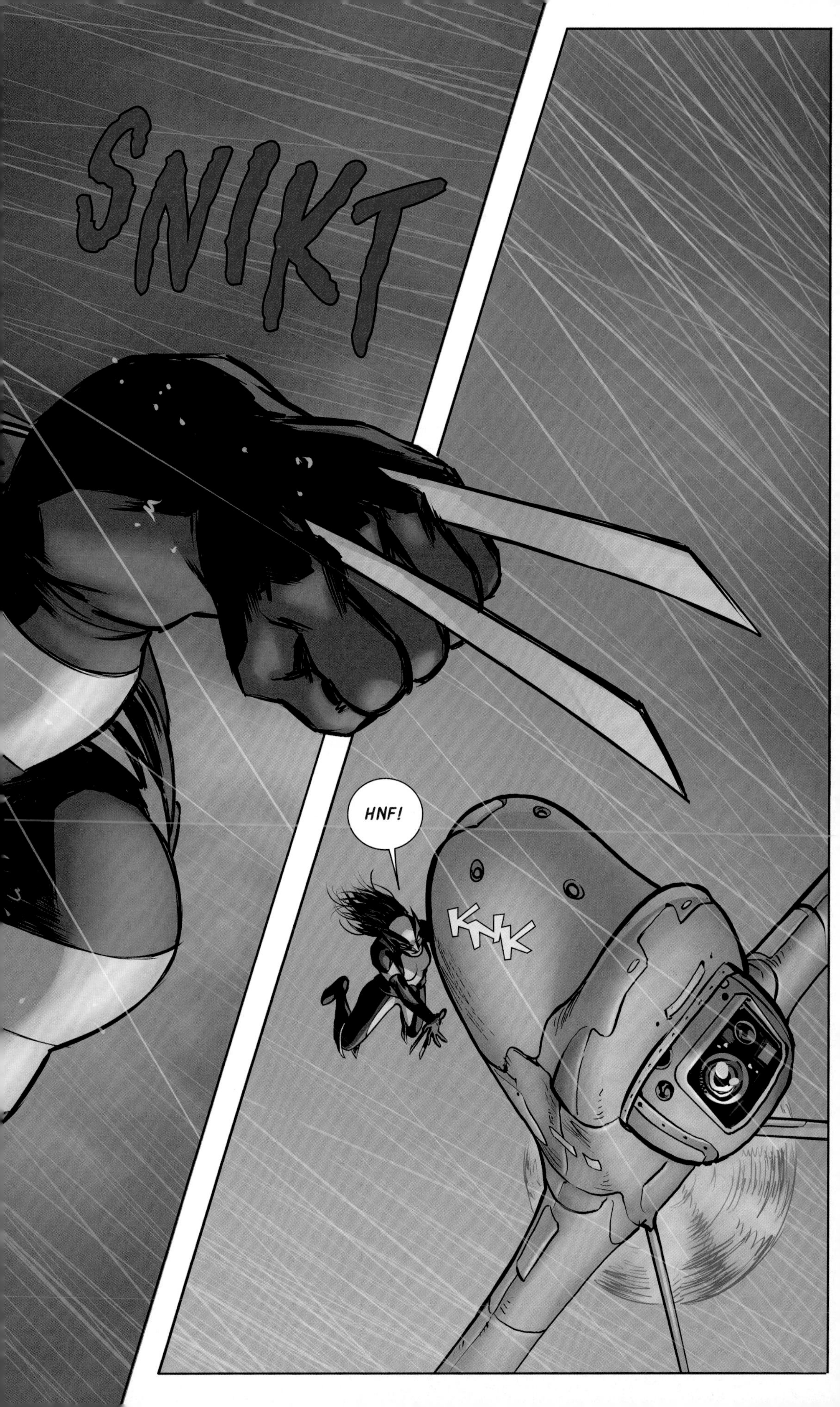
SNIKT
HNF!
KNK

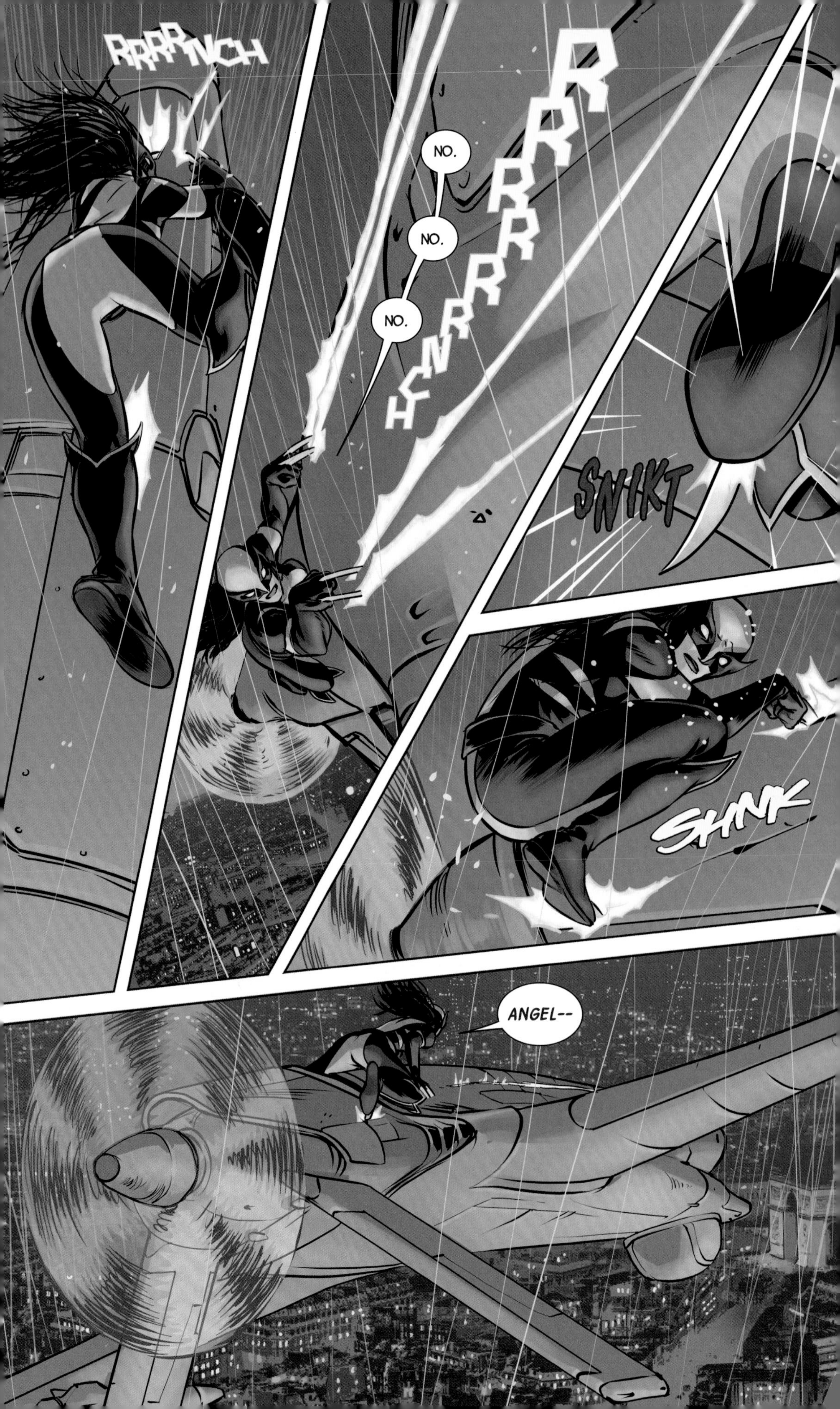
RRRRNCH
NO.
NO.
NO.
RRRRRRRNCH
SNIKT
SHNK
ANGEL--

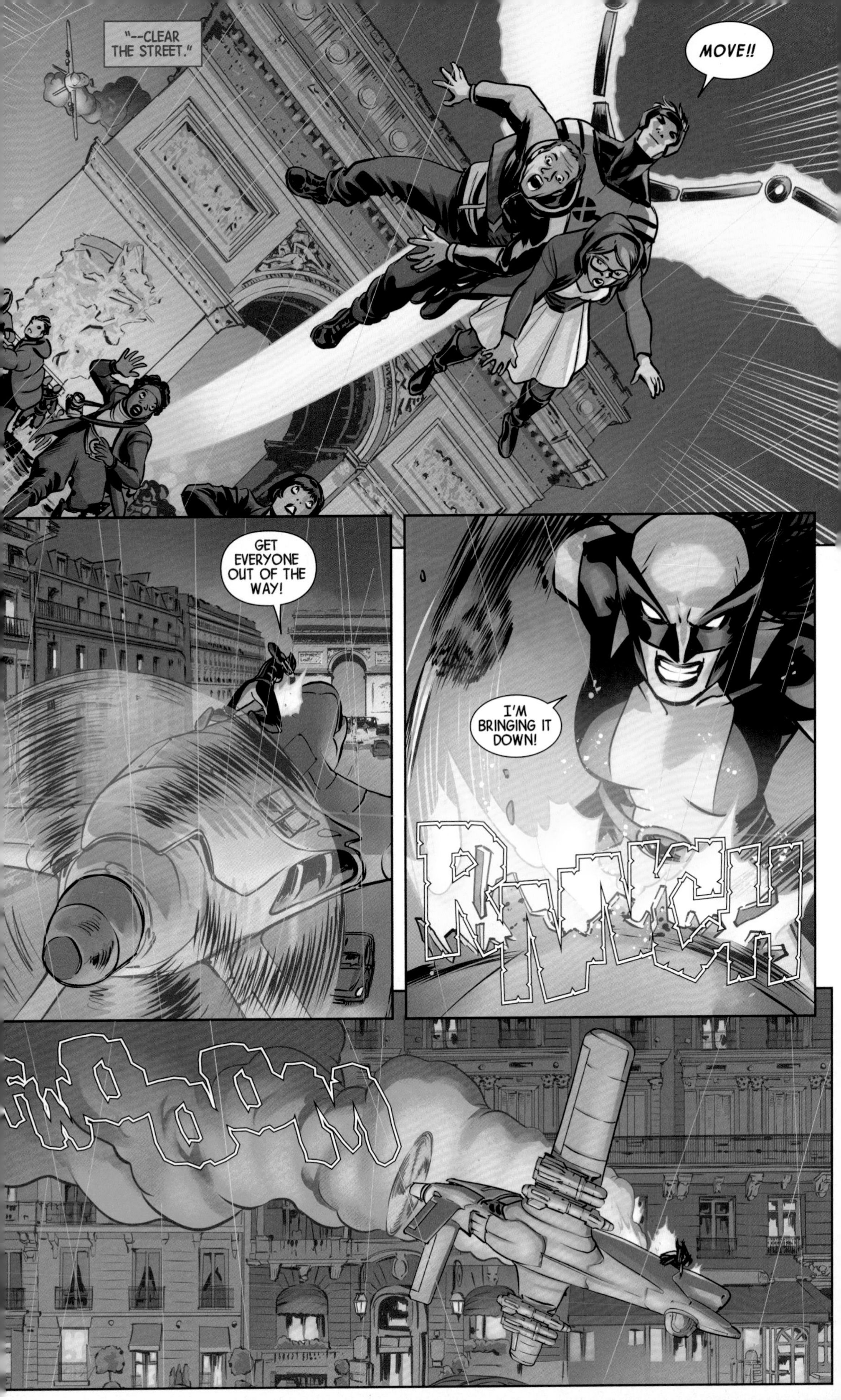

"--CLEAR THE STREET."
MOVE!!
GET EVERYONE OUT OF THE WAY!
I'M BRINGING IT DOWN!
RNNCH

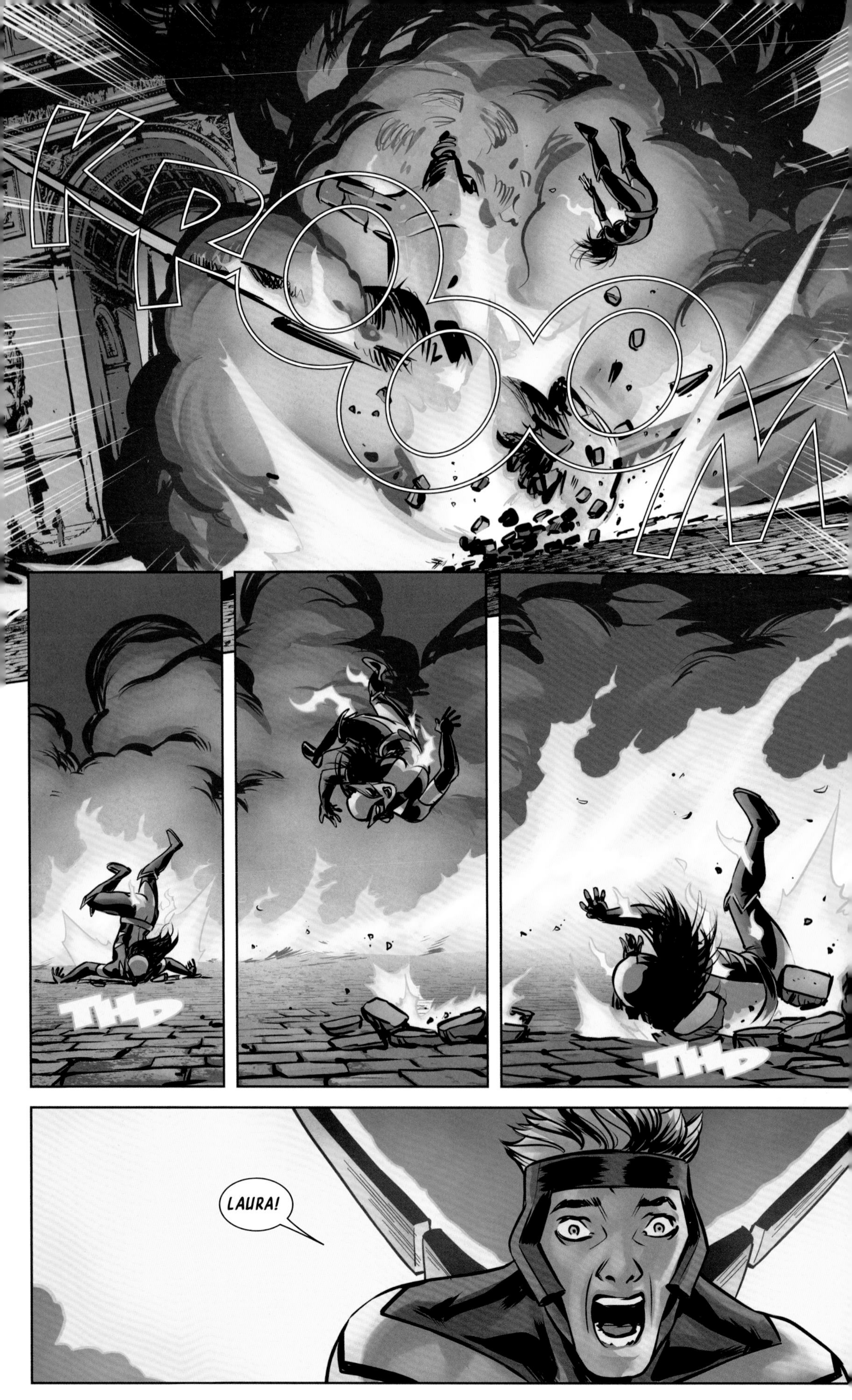
KROOOOM
THD
THD
LAURA!

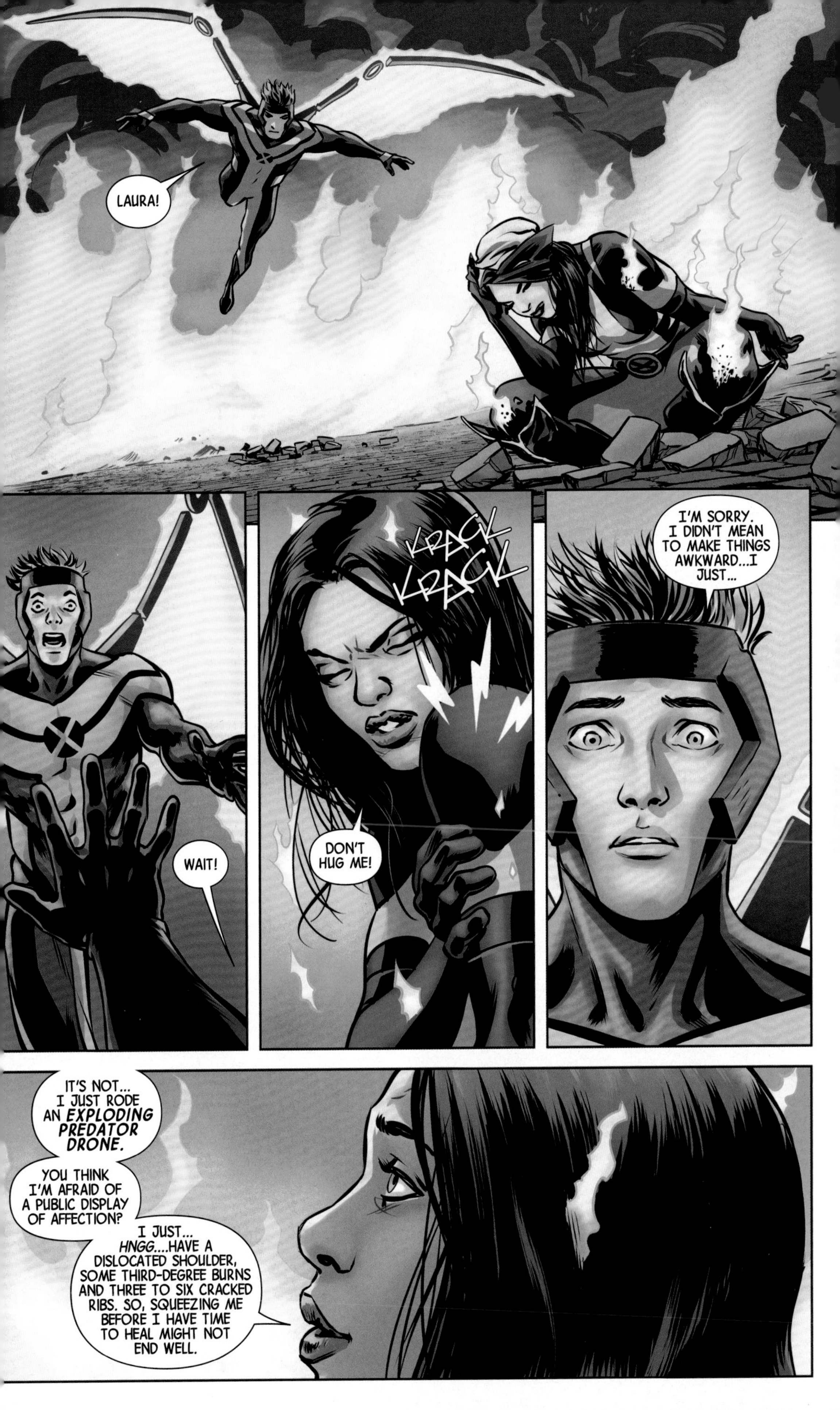
LAURA!
WAIT!
KRACK KRACK
DON'T HUG ME!
I'M SORRY. I DIDN'T MEAN TO MAKE THINGS AWKWARD...I JUST...
IT'S NOT... I JUST RODE AN ***EXPLODING PREDATOR DRONE.***
YOU THINK I'M AFRAID OF A PUBLIC DISPLAY OF AFFECTION?
I JUST... *HNGG*....HAVE A DISLOCATED SHOULDER, SOME THIRD-DEGREE BURNS AND THREE TO SIX CRACKED RIBS. SO, SQUEEZING ME BEFORE I HAVE TIME TO HEAL MIGHT NOT END WELL.

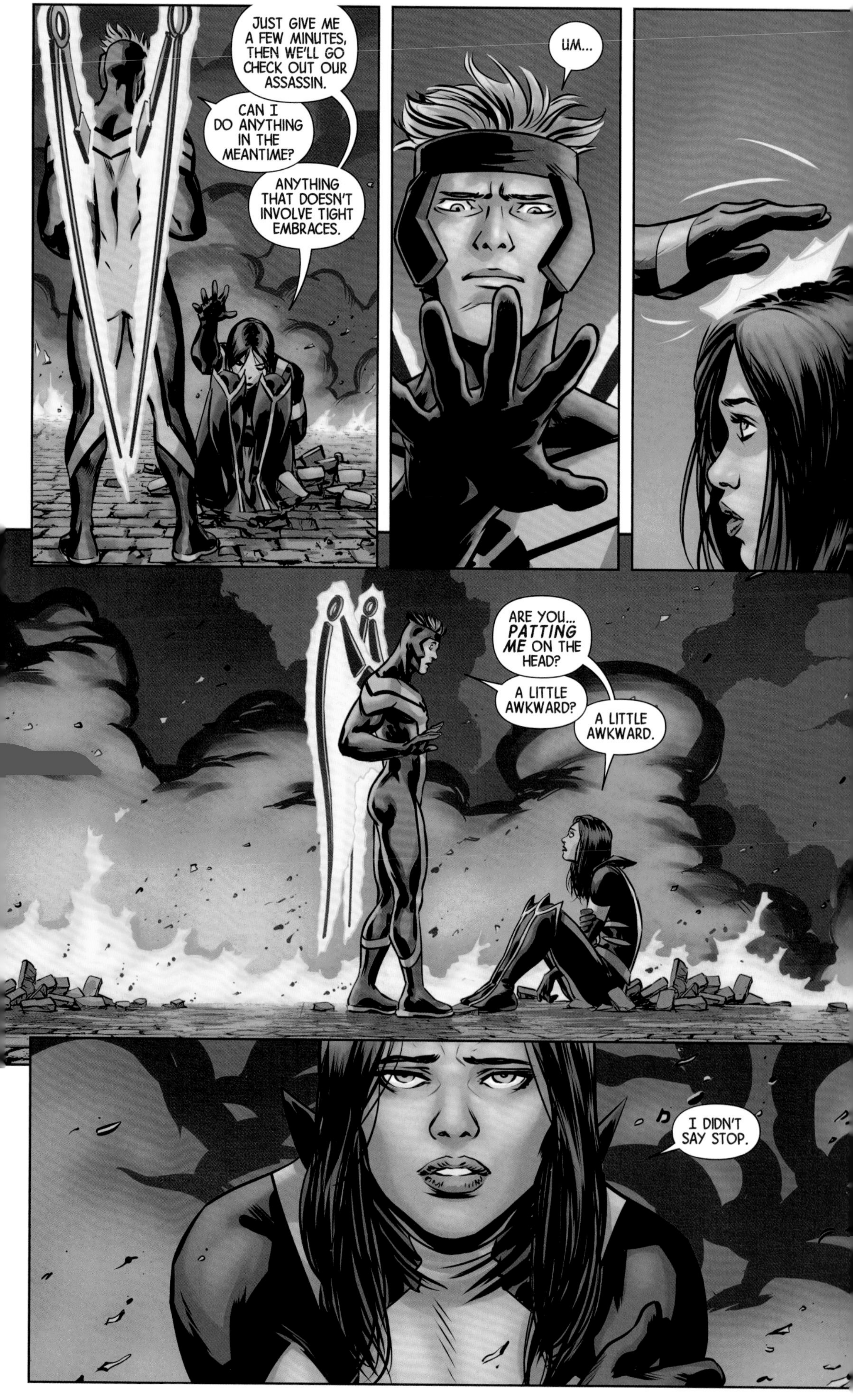
JUST GIVE ME A FEW MINUTES, THEN WE'LL GO CHECK OUT OUR ASSASSIN.
CAN I DO ANYTHING IN THE MEANTIME?
ANYTHING THAT DOESN'T INVOLVE TIGHT EMBRACES.
UM...
ARE YOU... *PATTING ME* ON THE HEAD?
A LITTLE AWKWARD?
A LITTLE AWKWARD.
I DIDN'T SAY STOP.

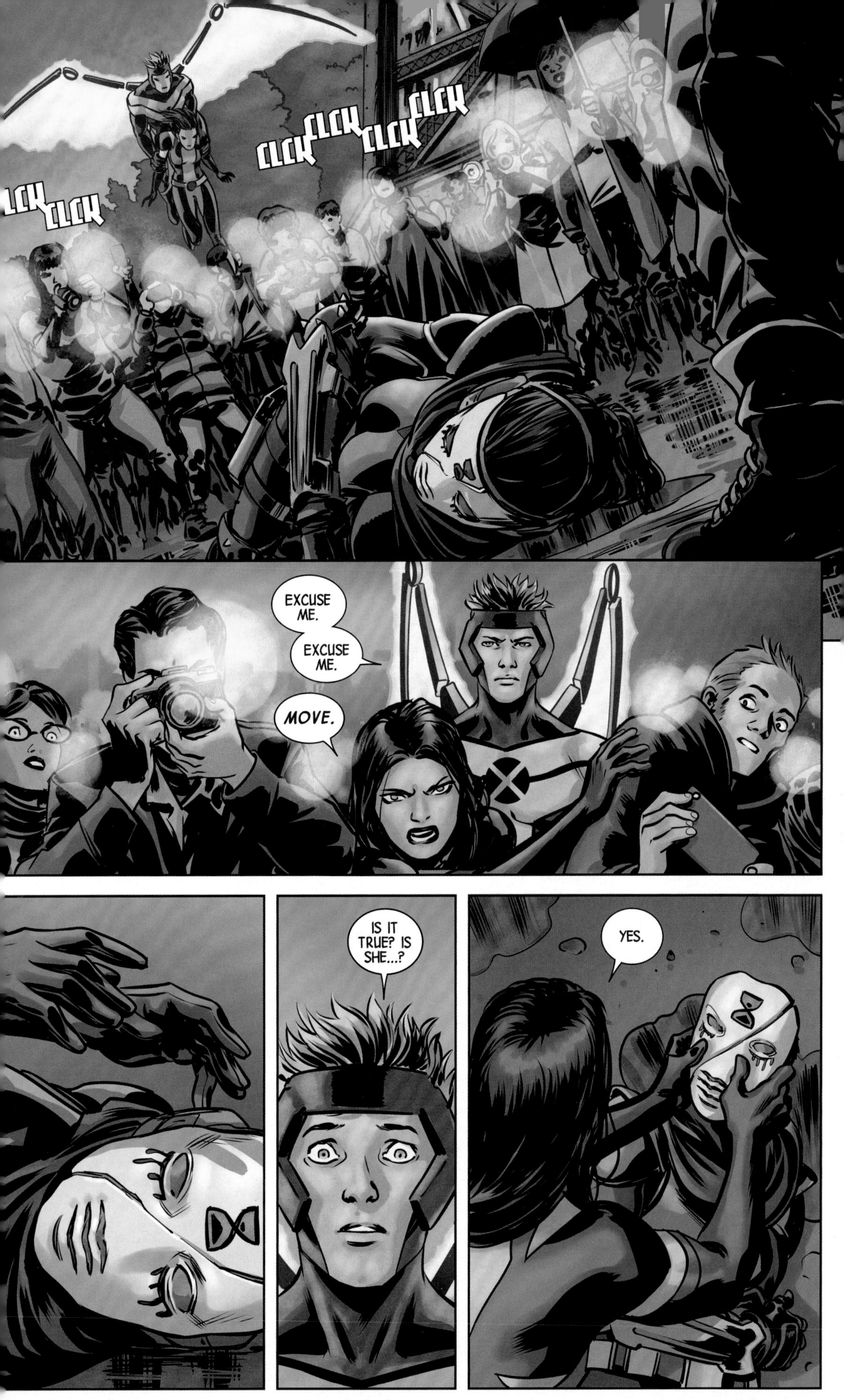
CLCK CLCK
CLCK CLCK CLCK CLCK
EXCUSE ME.
EXCUSE ME.
MOVE.
IS IT TRUE? IS SHE...?
YES.

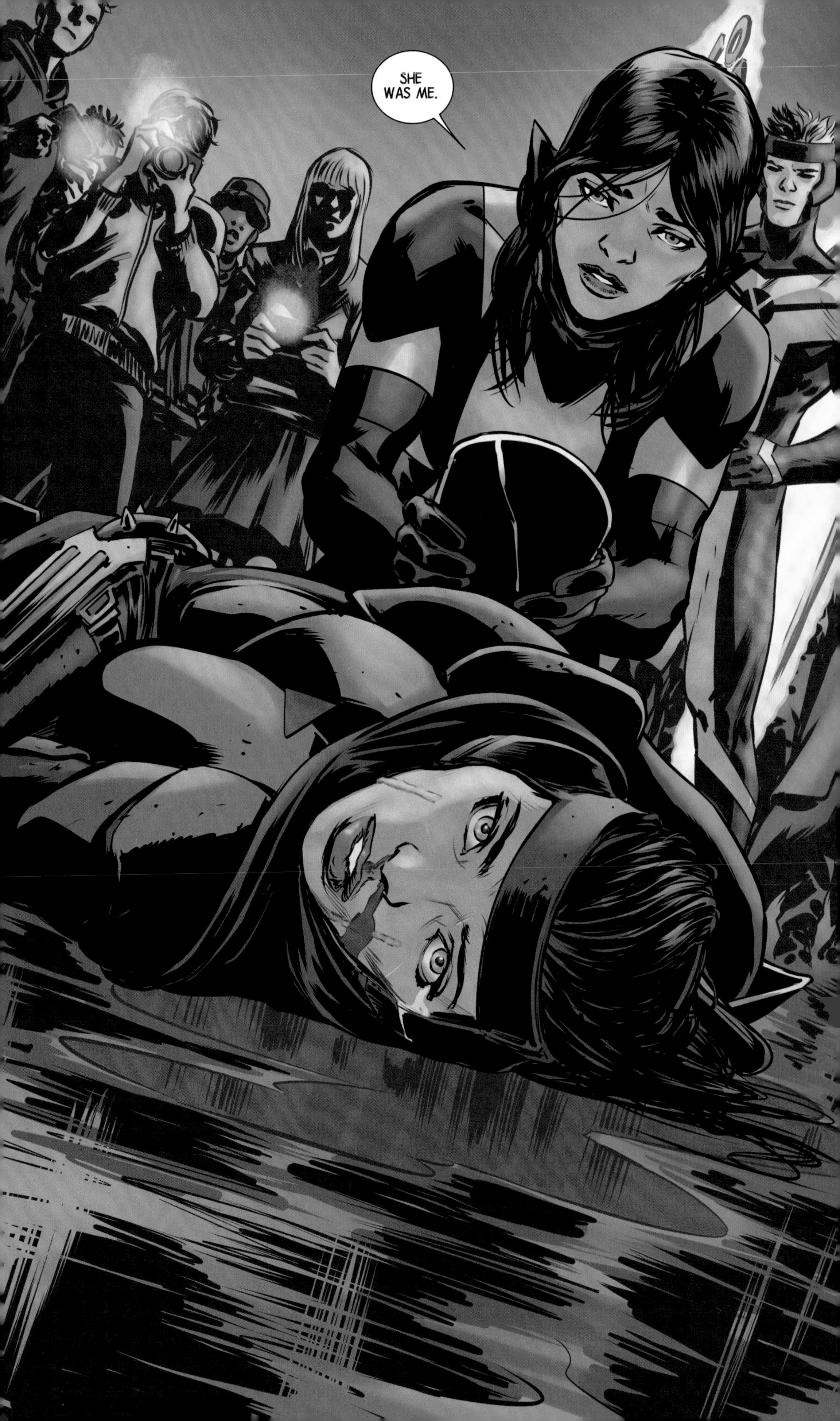
SHE WAS ME.

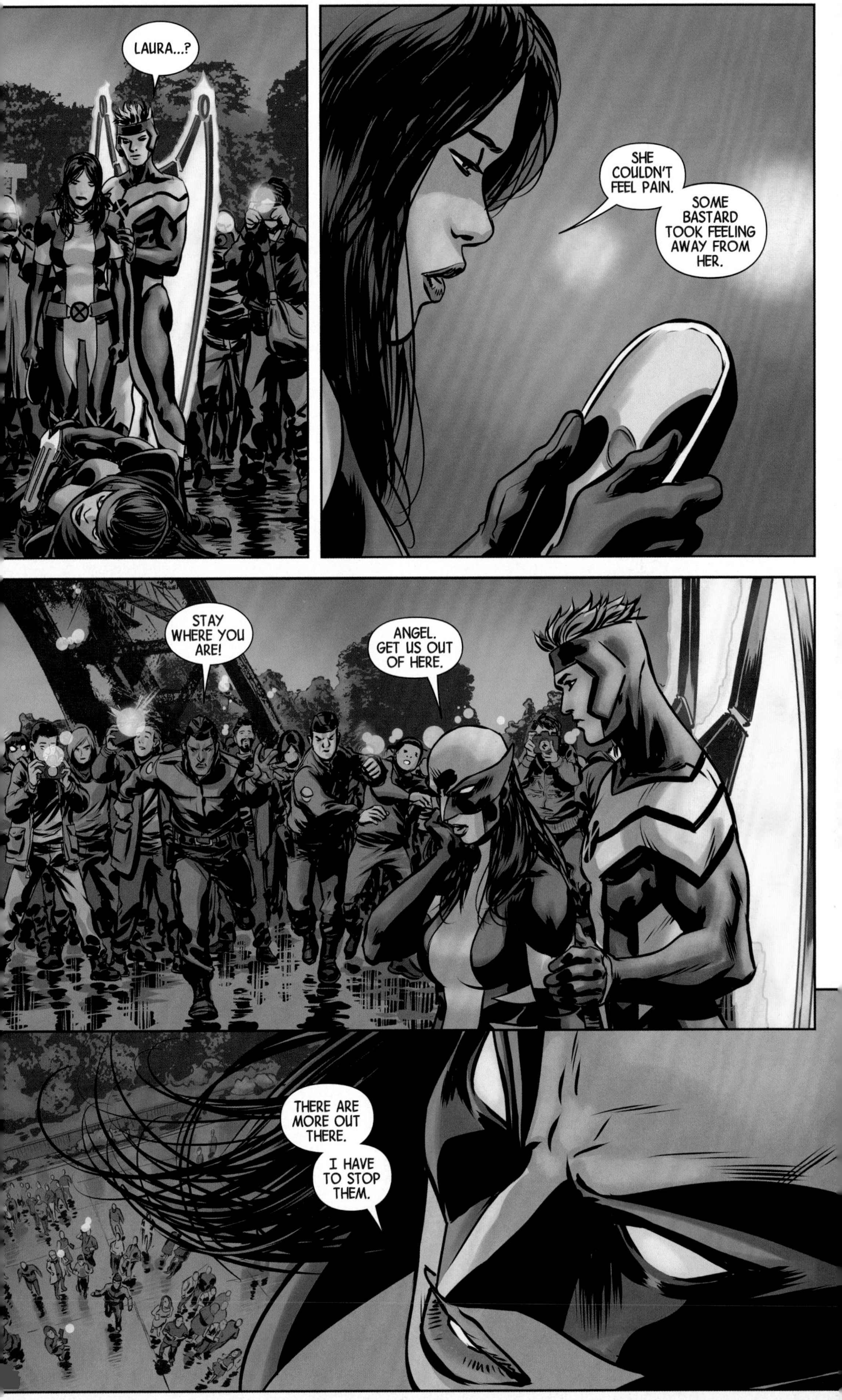
LAURA...?
SHE COULDN'T FEEL PAIN.
SOME BASTARD TOOK FEELING AWAY FROM HER.
STAY WHERE YOU ARE!
ANGEL. GET US OUT OF HERE.
THERE ARE MORE OUT THERE.
I HAVE TO STOP THEM.

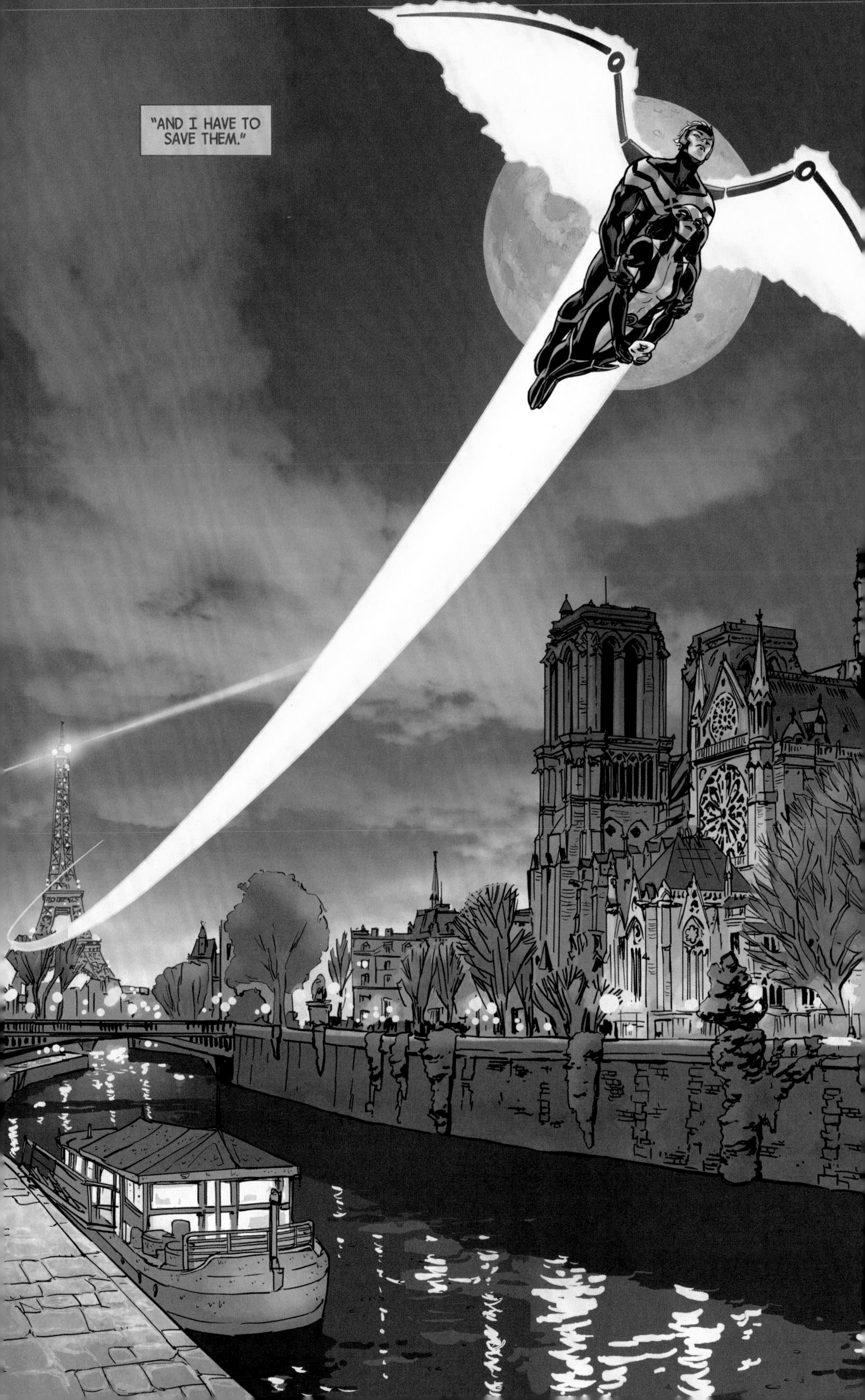
"AND I HAVE TO SAVE THEM."

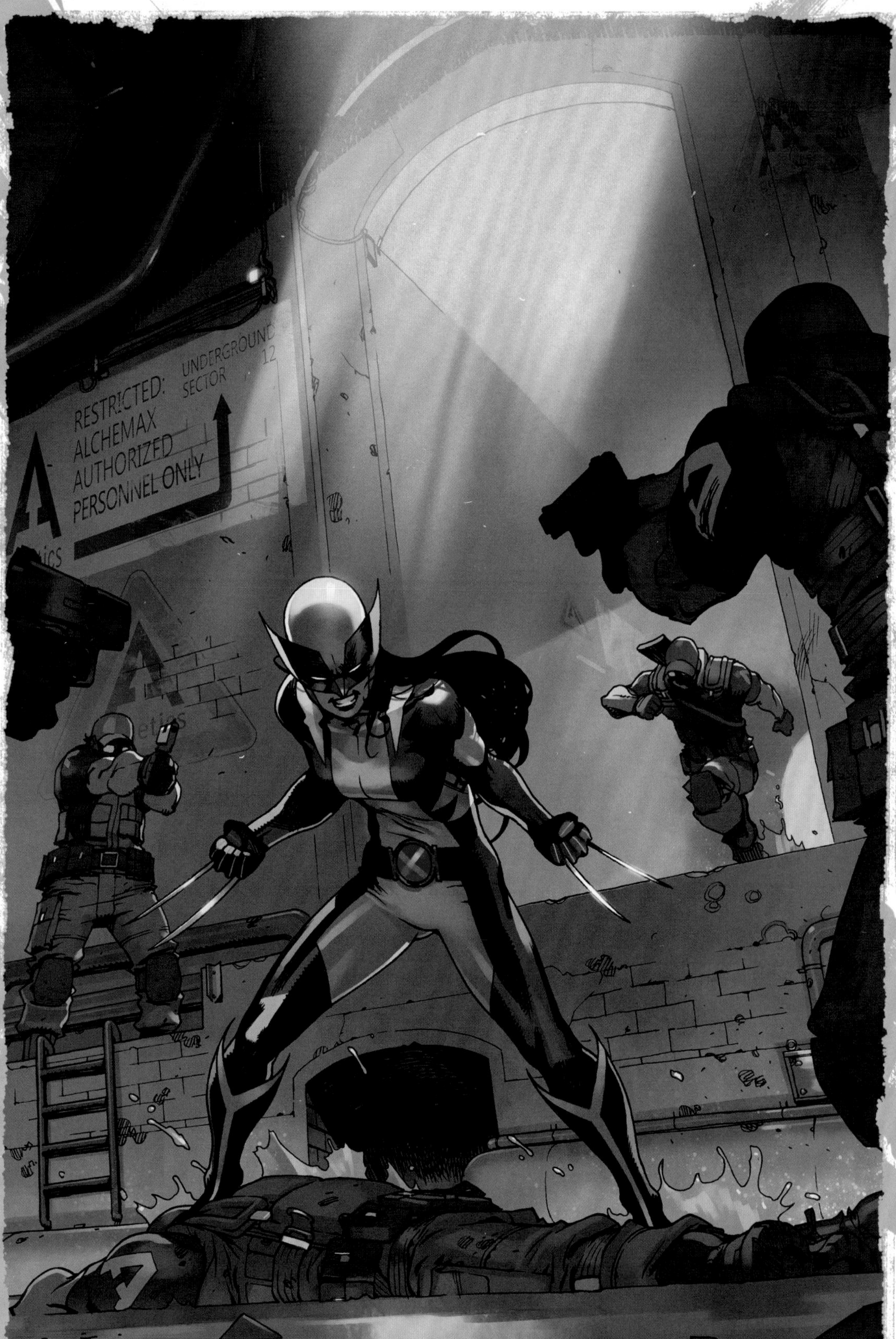
RESTRICTED:
ALCHEMAX
AUTHORIZED
PERSONNEL ONLY
UNDERGROUND
SECTOR 12

2

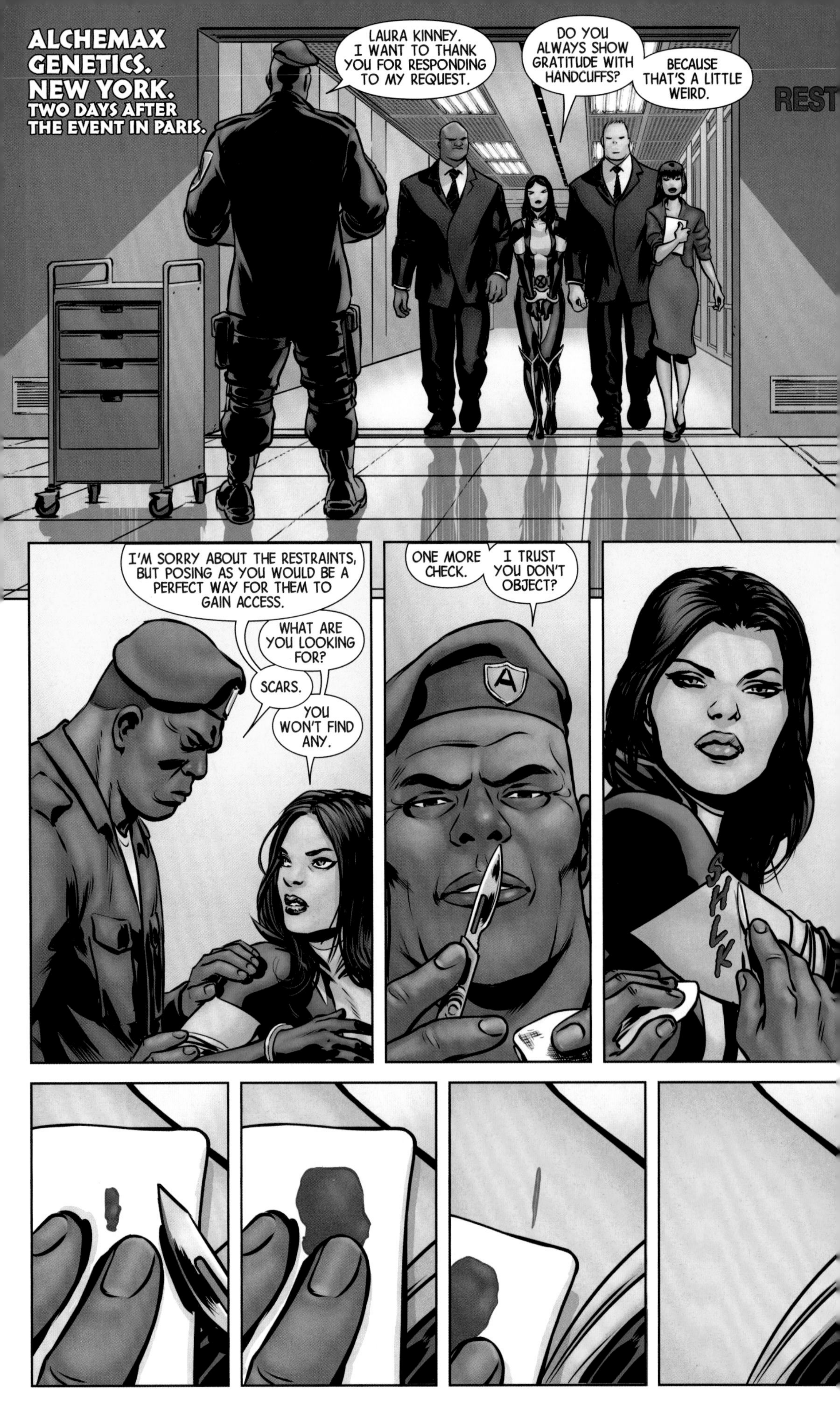
ALCHEMAX GENETICS. NEW YORK. TWO DAYS AFTER THE EVENT IN PARIS.
LAURA KINNEY. I WANT TO THANK YOU FOR RESPONDING TO MY REQUEST.
DO YOU ALWAYS SHOW GRATITUDE WITH HANDCUFFS?
BECAUSE THAT'S A LITTLE WEIRD.
REST
I'M SORRY ABOUT THE RESTRAINTS, BUT POSING AS YOU WOULD BE A PERFECT WAY FOR THEM TO GAIN ACCESS.
WHAT ARE YOU LOOKING FOR?
SCARS.
YOU WON'T FIND ANY.
ONE MORE CHECK.
I TRUST YOU DON'T OBJECT?
SHLK

SATISFIED?

YES. AGAIN, I'M SORRY FOR THE RESTRAINTS.

WHAT RESTRAINTS?

SNIKT

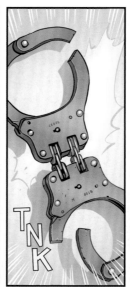

TNK

IF YOU'LL TURN YOUR ATTENTION TO THE SCREEN...

RESTRICTED

LAST WEEK, FOUR OF OUR EXPERIMENTS--

FOUR PEOPLE.

I'M SORRY?

YOUR EXPERIMENTS ARE PEOPLE.

I WOULDN'T CALL THEM THAT.

START CALLING THEM THAT IF YOU WANT MY HELP.

IT'S ALL RIGHT, CAPTAIN MOONEY--

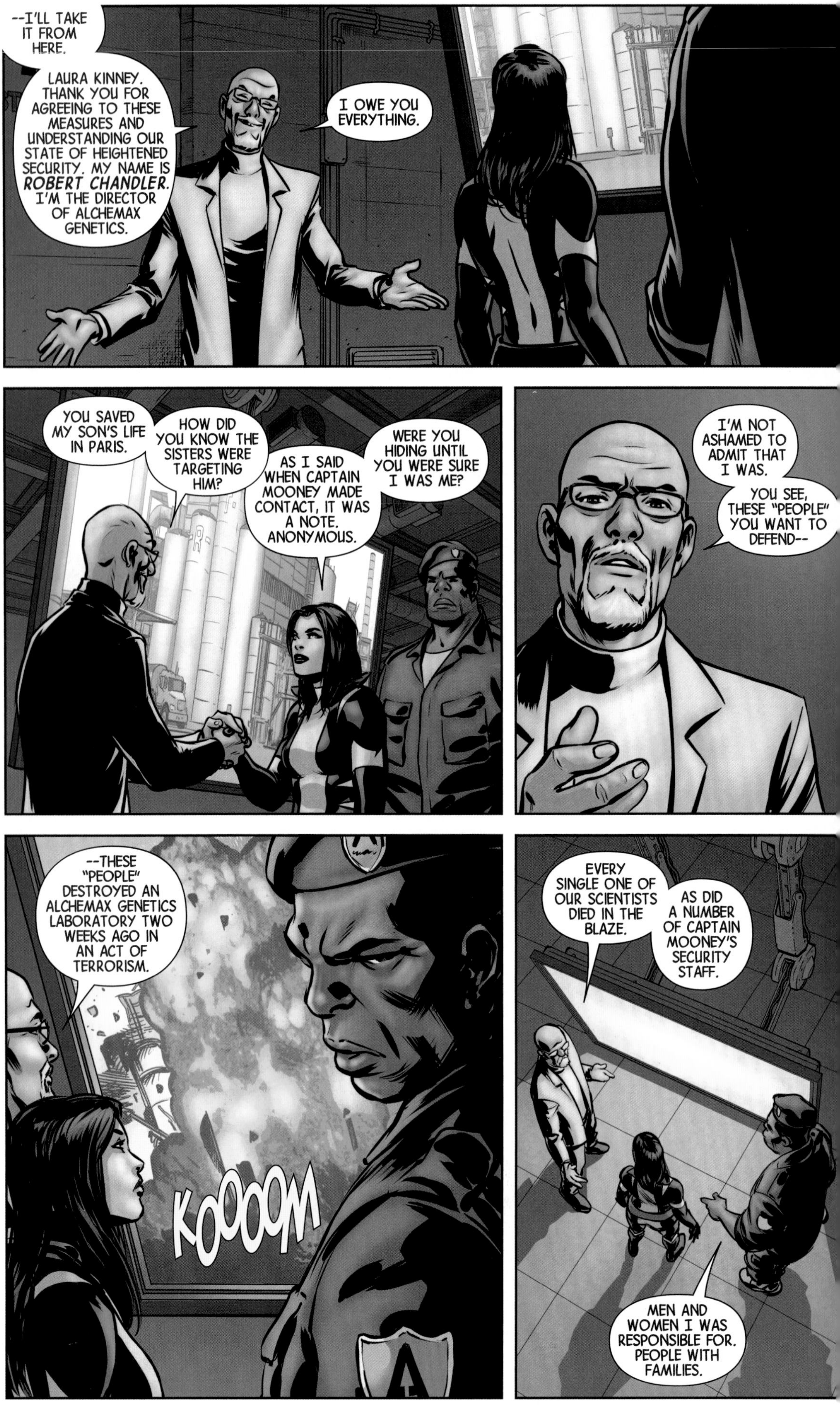
--I'LL TAKE IT FROM HERE.
LAURA KINNEY. THANK YOU FOR AGREEING TO THESE MEASURES AND UNDERSTANDING OUR STATE OF HEIGHTENED SECURITY. MY NAME IS ROBERT CHANDLER. I'M THE DIRECTOR OF ALCHEMAX GENETICS.
I OWE YOU EVERYTHING.
YOU SAVED MY SON'S LIFE IN PARIS.
HOW DID YOU KNOW THE SISTERS WERE TARGETING HIM?
AS I SAID WHEN CAPTAIN MOONEY MADE CONTACT, IT WAS A NOTE. ANONYMOUS.
WERE YOU HIDING UNTIL YOU WERE SURE I WAS ME?
I'M NOT ASHAMED TO ADMIT THAT I WAS.
YOU SEE, THESE "PEOPLE" YOU WANT TO DEFEND--
--THESE "PEOPLE" DESTROYED AN ALCHEMAX GENETICS LABORATORY TWO WEEKS AGO IN AN ACT OF TERRORISM.
KOOOOM
EVERY SINGLE ONE OF OUR SCIENTISTS DIED IN THE BLAZE.
AS DID A NUMBER OF CAPTAIN MOONEY'S SECURITY STAFF.
MEN AND WOMEN I WAS RESPONSIBLE FOR. PEOPLE WITH FAMILIES.

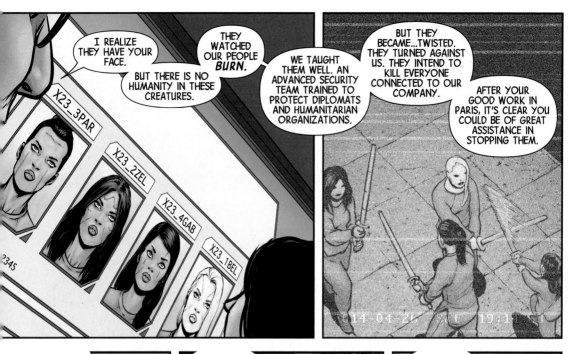

I REALIZE THEY HAVE YOUR FACE.

BUT THERE IS NO HUMANITY IN THESE CREATURES.

THEY WATCHED OUR PEOPLE *BURN*.

WE TAUGHT THEM WELL. AN ADVANCED SECURITY TEAM TRAINED TO PROTECT DIPLOMATS AND HUMANITARIAN ORGANIZATIONS.

BUT THEY BECAME...TWISTED. THEY TURNED AGAINST US. THEY INTEND TO KILL EVERYONE CONNECTED TO OUR COMPANY.

AFTER YOUR GOOD WORK IN PARIS, IT'S CLEAR YOU COULD BE OF GREAT ASSISTANCE IN STOPPING THEM.

X23_3PAR
X23_2ZEL
X23_4GAB
X23_1BEL

14-04-26   19:1

HAVE QUESTIONS... 'M ASSUMING I'M OING TO HATE THE ANSWERS.

WHAT YOU SUSPECT IS TRUE. THEY'RE YOUR CLONES.

MY PREDECESSOR ACQUIRED YOUR DNA. ALCHEMAX TRIED TO MAKE MORE OF YOU. THEY FAILED. WHILE OUR CLONES LOOKED LIKE YOU, NONE OF THEM DEVELOPED YOUR HEALING FACTOR OR CLAWS.

NOR DID THEY DEVELOP YOUR CONSCIENCE.

FOR THE RECORD, I REALIZE THIS IS A DISASTER OF OUR OWN MAKING. IF IT WERE UP TO ME, WE WOULD HANDLE THIS OURSELVES.

BUT THE LONGER THEY'RE OUT THERE, THE MORE PEOPLE COULD DIE.

THEN I SHOULDN'T BE HERE TALKING TO YOU.

I WILL FIND THEM. I WILL STOP THEM FROM KILLING INNOCENTS. I WILL DO WHAT'S RIGHT.

THAT'S ALL I COULD ASK FOR. THANK YOU.

FOLLOW HER.

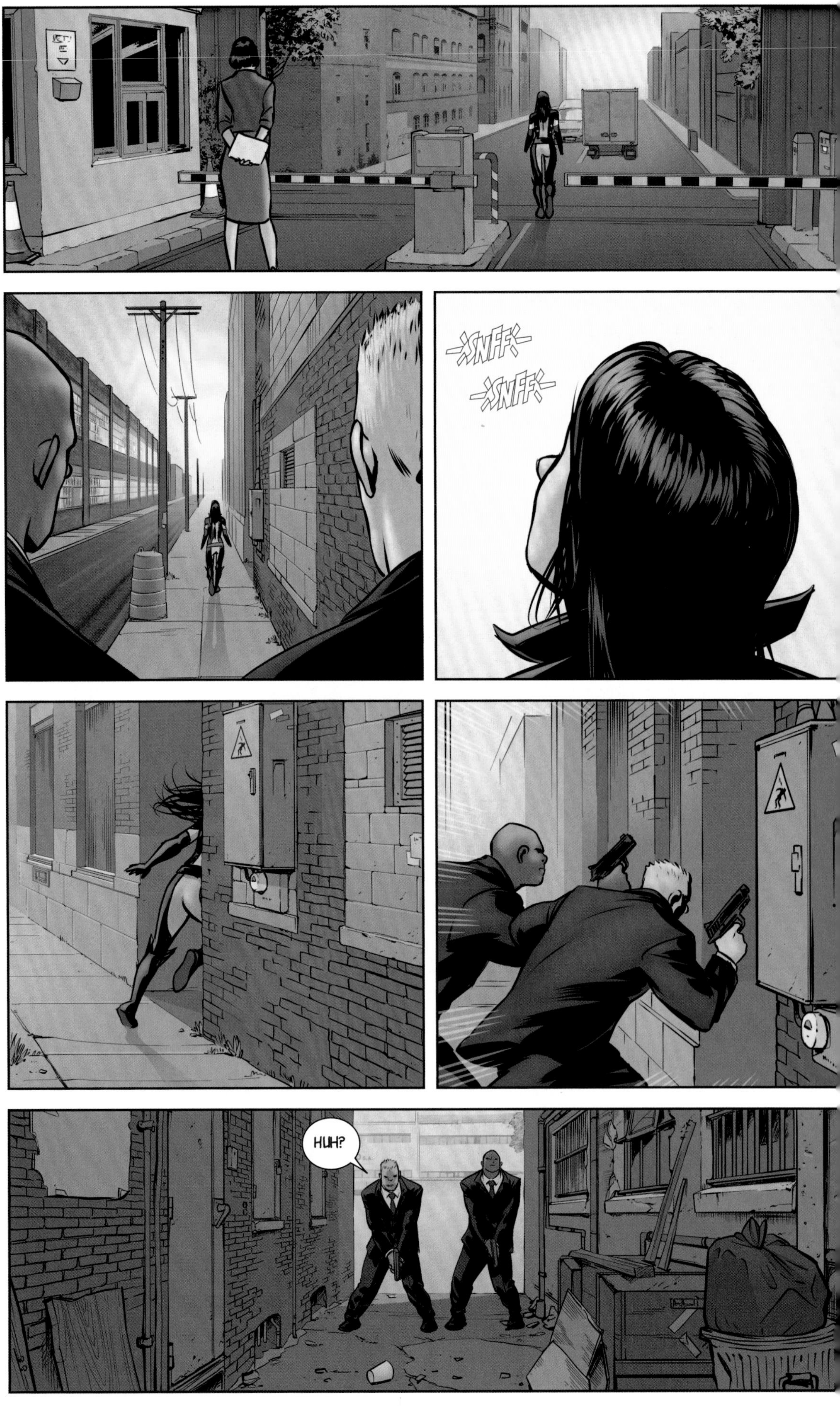
SNFF
SNFF
HUH?

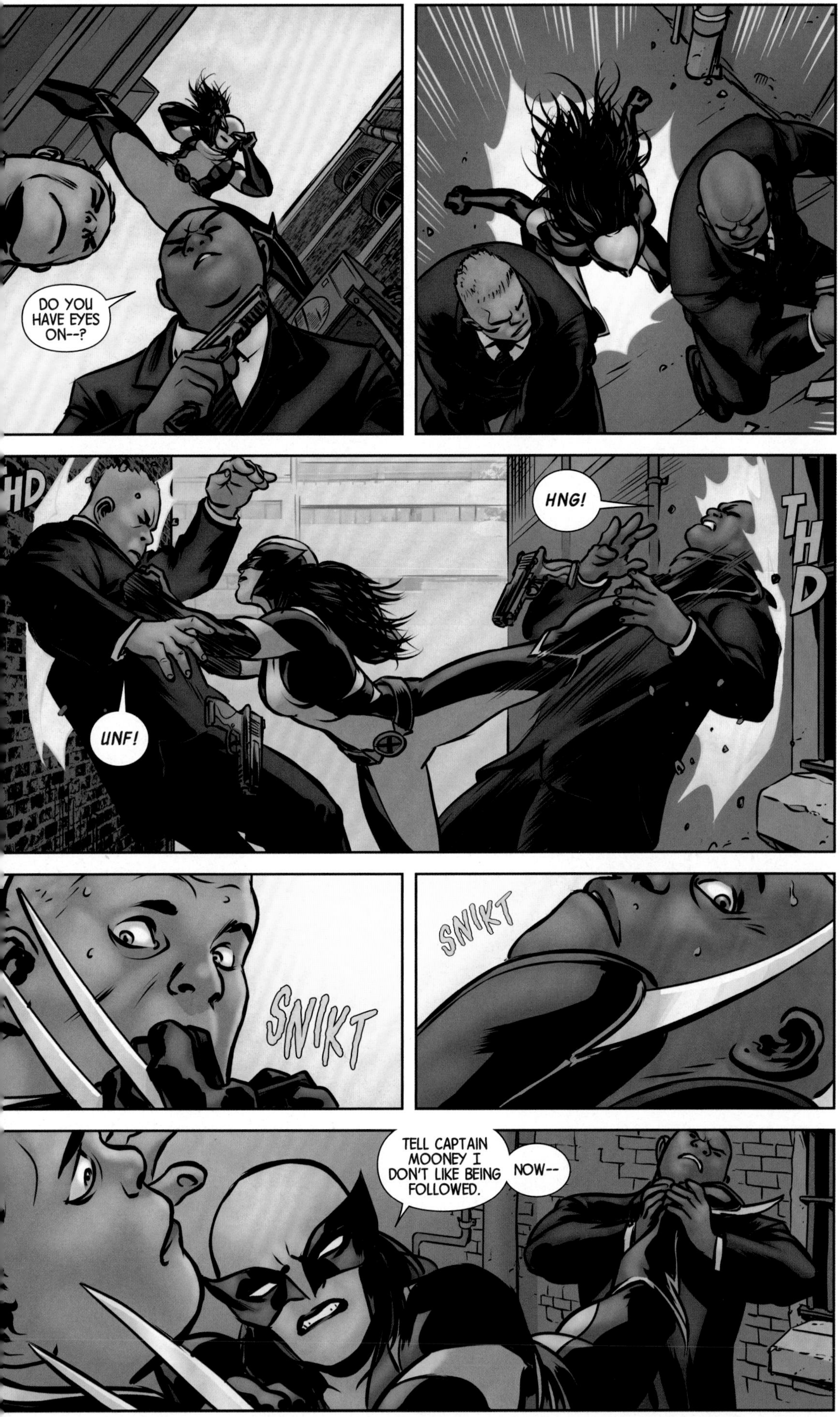
DO YOU HAVE EYES ON--?
THD
HNG!
THD
UNF!
SNIKT
SNIKT
TELL CAPTAIN MOONEY I DON'T LIKE BEING FOLLOWED.
NOW--

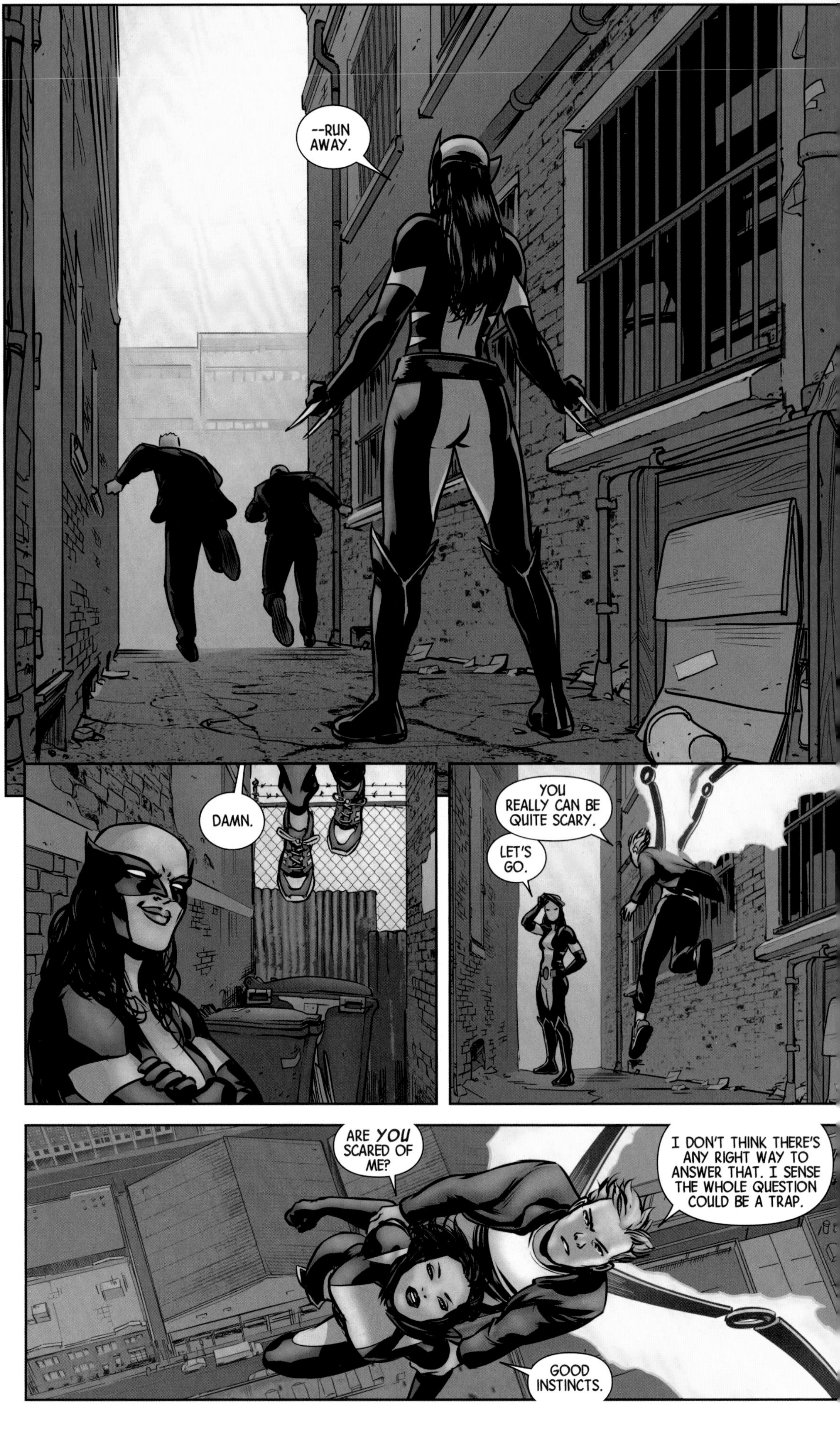
--RUN AWAY.
DAMN.
YOU REALLY CAN BE QUITE SCARY.
LET'S GO.
ARE *YOU* SCARED OF ME?
I DON'T THINK THERE'S ANY RIGHT WAY TO ANSWER THAT. I SENSE THE WHOLE QUESTION COULD BE A TRAP.
GOOD INSTINCTS.

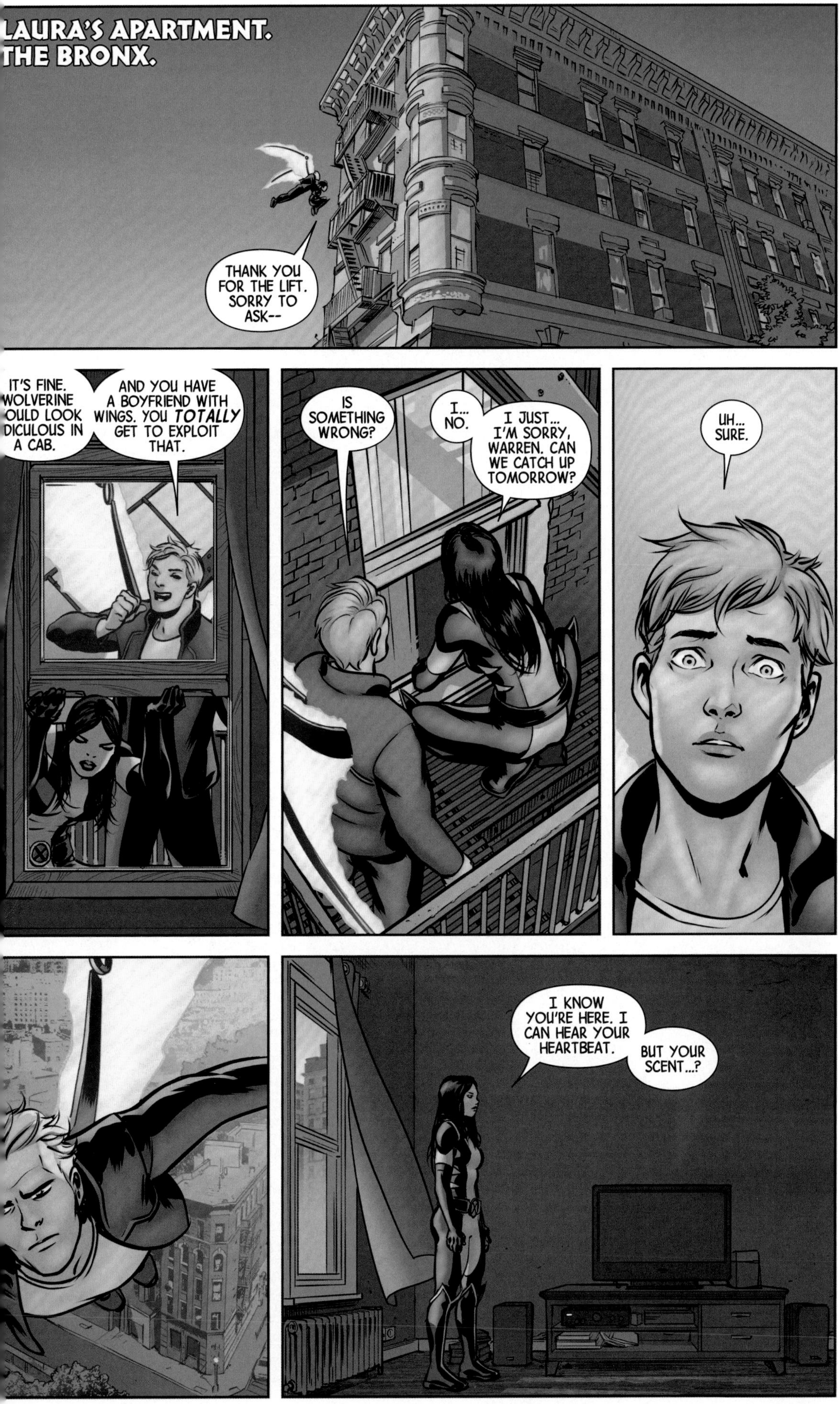

LAURA'S APARTMENT. THE BRONX.
THANK YOU FOR THE LIFT. SORRY TO ASK--
IT'S FINE. WOLVERINE OULD LOOK DICULOUS IN A CAB.
AND YOU HAVE A BOYFRIEND WITH WINGS. YOU *TOTALLY* GET TO EXPLOIT THAT.
IS SOMETHING WRONG?
I... NO.
I JUST... I'M SORRY, WARREN. CAN WE CATCH UP TOMORROW?
UH... SURE.
I KNOW YOU'RE HERE. I CAN HEAR YOUR HEARTBEAT.
BUT YOUR SCENT...?

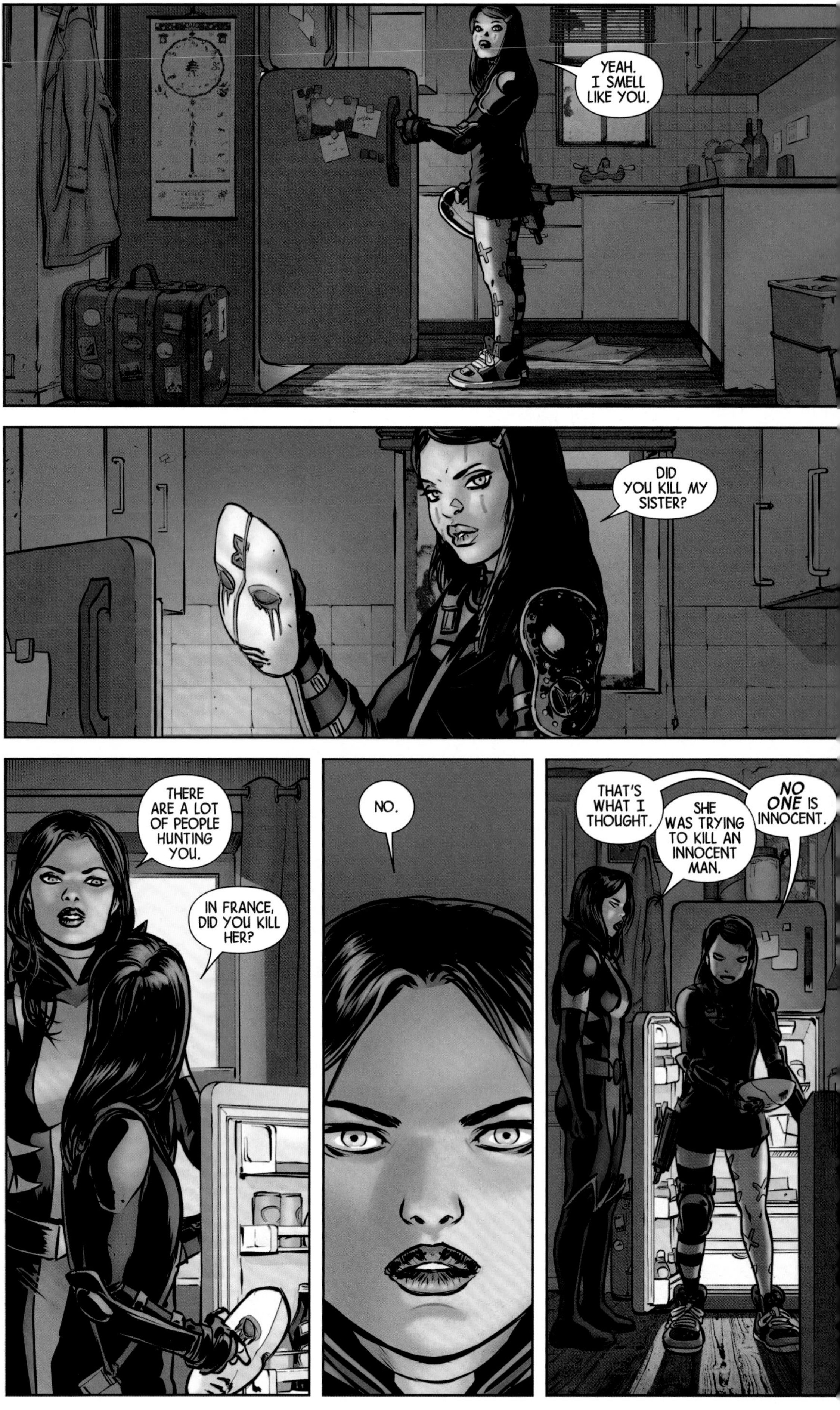
YEAH. I SMELL LIKE YOU.
DID YOU KILL MY SISTER?
THERE ARE A LOT OF PEOPLE HUNTING YOU.
IN FRANCE, DID YOU KILL HER?
NO.
THAT'S WHAT I THOUGHT.
SHE WAS TRYING TO KILL AN INNOCENT MAN.
NO ONE IS INNOCENT.

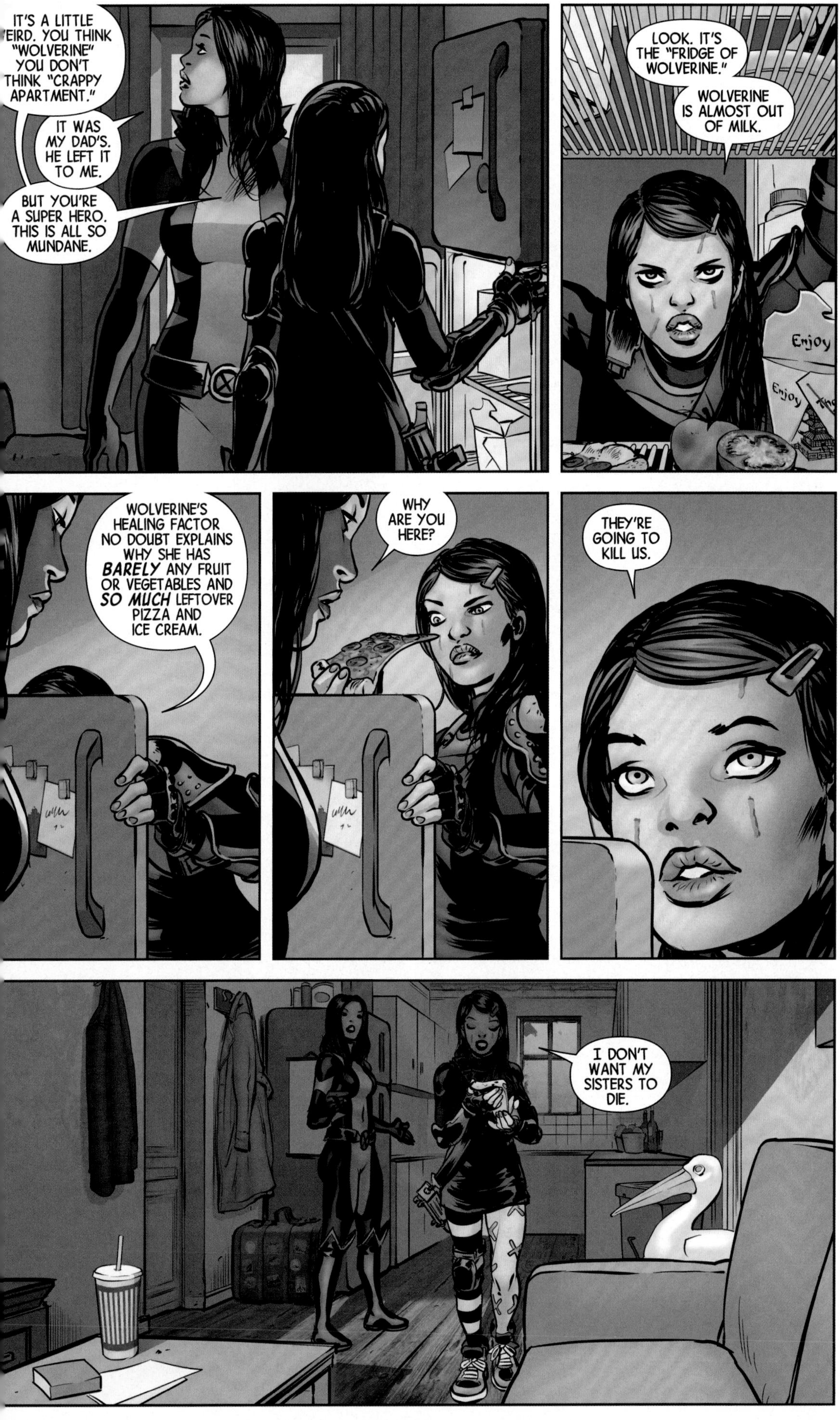
IT'S A LITTLE 'EIRD. YOU THINK "WOLVERINE" YOU DON'T THINK "CRAPPY APARTMENT."
IT WAS MY DAD'S. HE LEFT IT TO ME.
BUT YOU'RE A SUPER HERO. THIS IS ALL SO MUNDANE.
LOOK. IT'S THE "FRIDGE OF WOLVERINE."
WOLVERINE IS ALMOST OUT OF MILK.
Enjoy
Enjoy
WOLVERINE'S HEALING FACTOR NO DOUBT EXPLAINS WHY SHE HAS BARELY ANY FRUIT OR VEGETABLES AND SO MUCH LEFTOVER PIZZA AND ICE CREAM.
WHY ARE YOU HERE?
THEY'RE GOING TO KILL US.
I DON'T WANT MY SISTERS TO DIE.

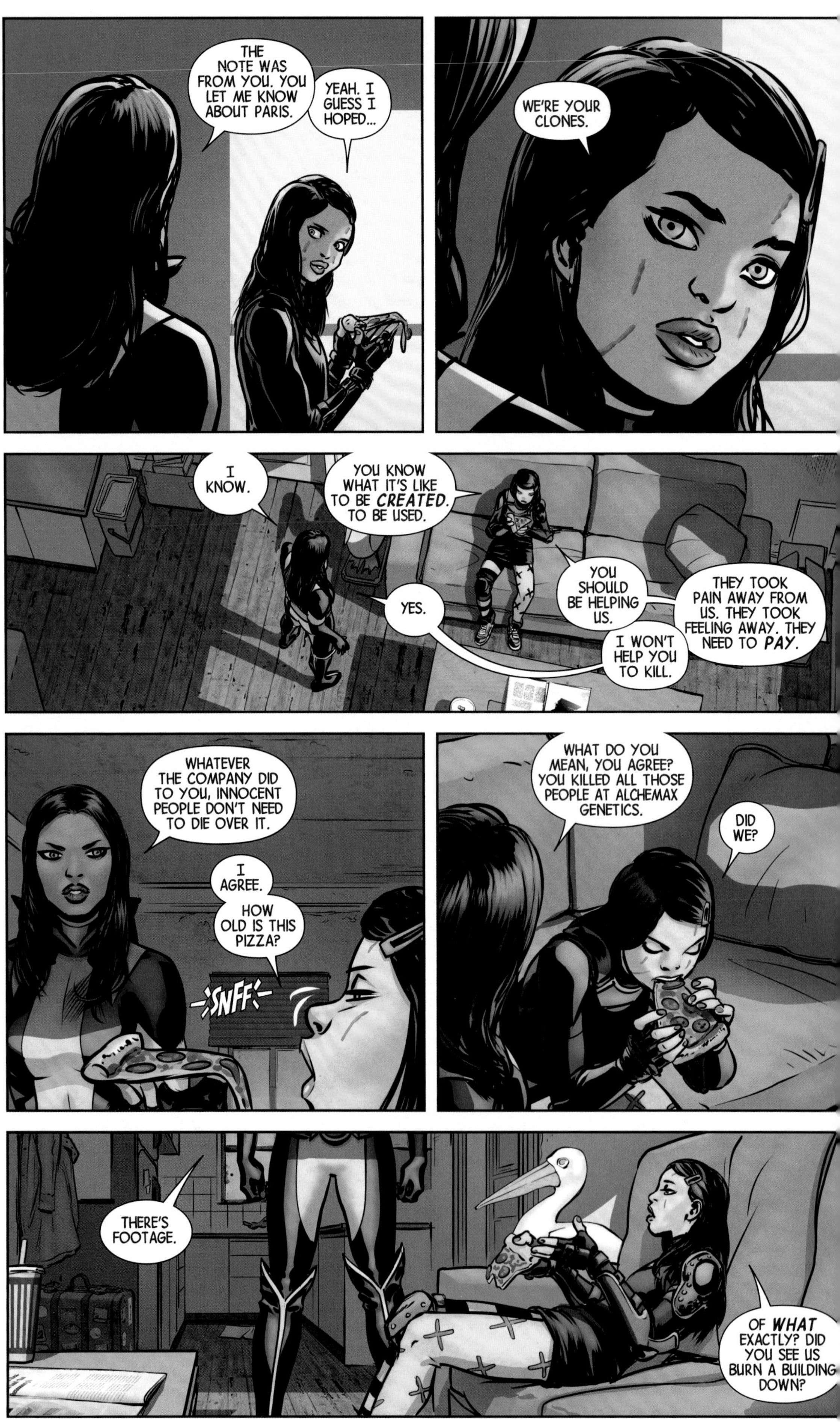
THE NOTE WAS FROM YOU. YOU LET ME KNOW ABOUT PARIS.
YEAH. I GUESS I HOPED...
WE'RE YOUR CLONES.
I KNOW.
YOU KNOW WHAT IT'S LIKE TO BE *CREATED*. TO BE USED.
YES.
YOU SHOULD BE HELPING US.
THEY TOOK PAIN AWAY FROM US. THEY TOOK FEELING AWAY. THEY NEED TO *PAY*.
I WON'T HELP YOU TO KILL.
WHATEVER THE COMPANY DID TO YOU, INNOCENT PEOPLE DON'T NEED TO DIE OVER IT.
I AGREE.
HOW OLD IS THIS PIZZA?
SNFF
WHAT DO YOU MEAN, YOU AGREE? YOU KILLED ALL THOSE PEOPLE AT ALCHEMAX GENETICS.
DID WE?
THERE'S FOOTAGE.
OF *WHAT* EXACTLY? DID YOU SEE US BURN A BUILDING DOWN?

THERE ARE PEOPLE WHO NEED TO DIE FOR WHAT THEY DID TO US. TWO OF MY SISTERS THINK THEY SHOULD *SUFFER* FIRST.

YOU DON'T?

DON'T HUNT US. *HELP* US.

-SNFF-

YEAH. THAT'S SMOKE YOU SMELL. I SET YOUR BEDROOM ON FIRE.

WHAT?!

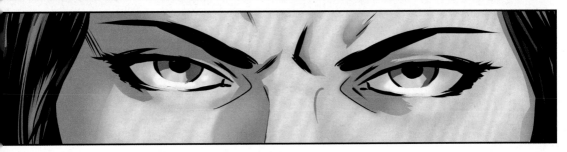

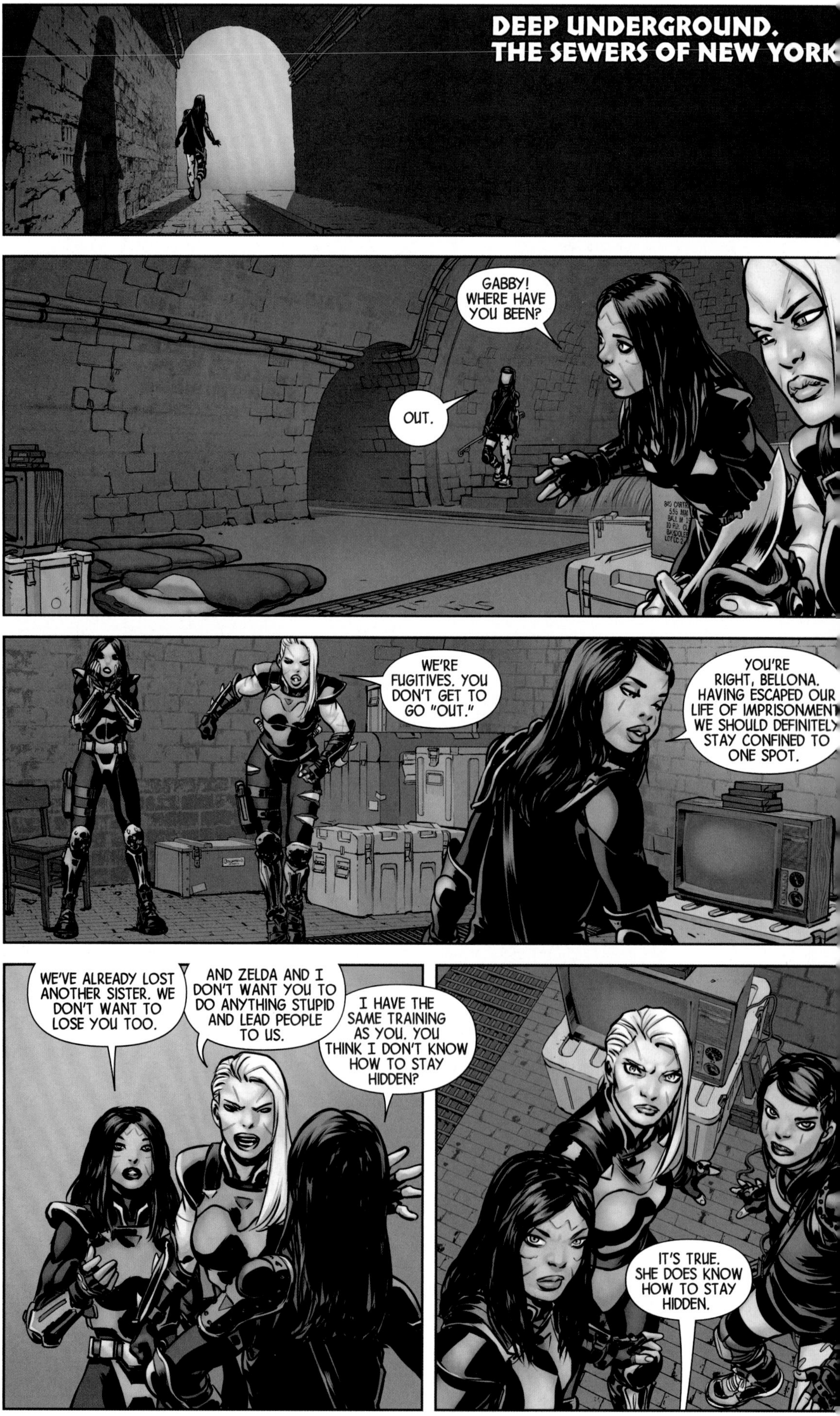
DEEP UNDERGROUND. THE SEWERS OF NEW YORK
GABBY! WHERE HAVE YOU BEEN?
OUT.
WE'RE FUGITIVES. YOU DON'T GET TO GO "OUT."
YOU'RE RIGHT, BELLONA. HAVING ESCAPED OUR LIFE OF IMPRISONMENT WE SHOULD DEFINITELY STAY CONFINED TO ONE SPOT.
WE'VE ALREADY LOST ANOTHER SISTER. WE DON'T WANT TO LOSE YOU TOO.
AND ZELDA AND I DON'T WANT YOU TO DO ANYTHING STUPID AND LEAD PEOPLE TO US.
I HAVE THE SAME TRAINING AS YOU. YOU THINK I DON'T KNOW HOW TO STAY HIDDEN?
IT'S TRUE. SHE DOES KNOW HOW TO STAY HIDDEN.

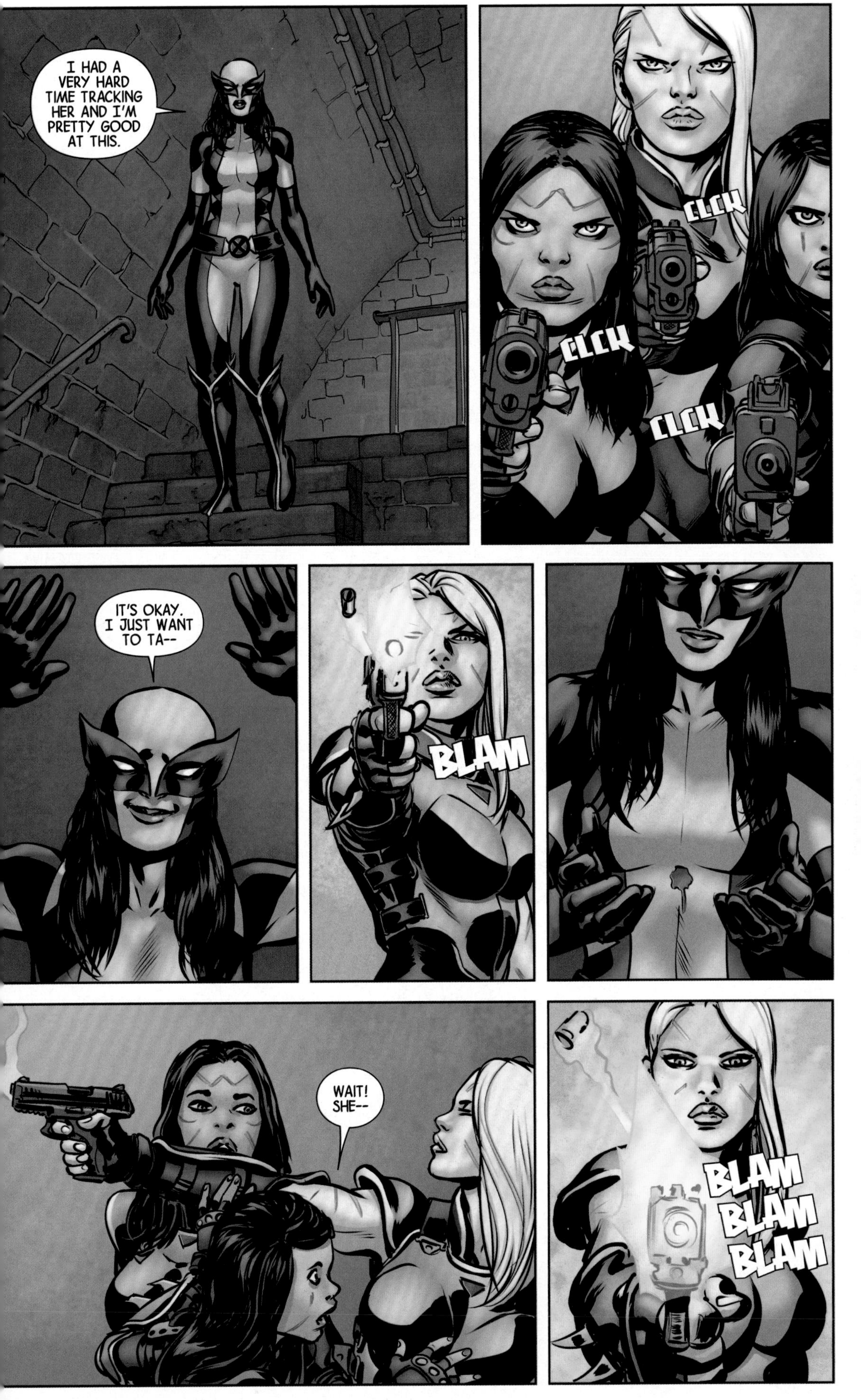
I HAD A VERY HARD TIME TRACKING HER AND I'M PRETTY GOOD AT THIS.
CLCK
CLCK
CLCK
IT'S OKAY. I JUST WANT TO TA--
BLAM
WAIT! SHE--
BLAM
BLAM
BLAM

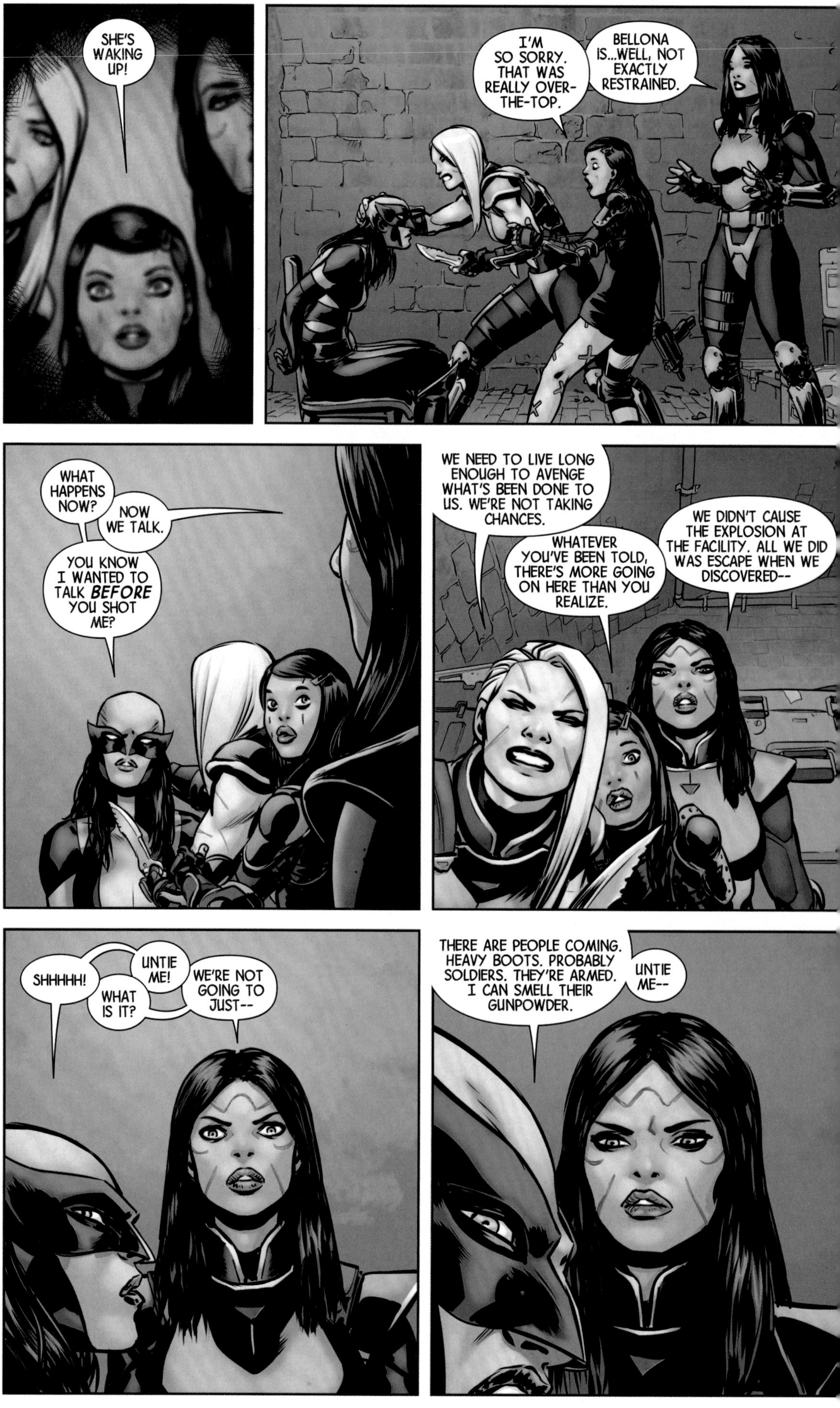
SHE'S WAKING UP!
I'M SO SORRY. THAT WAS REALLY OVER-THE-TOP.
BELLONA IS...WELL, NOT EXACTLY RESTRAINED.
WHAT HAPPENS NOW?
NOW WE TALK.
YOU KNOW I WANTED TO TALK *BEFORE* YOU SHOT ME?
WE NEED TO LIVE LONG ENOUGH TO AVENGE WHAT'S BEEN DONE TO US. WE'RE NOT TAKING CHANCES.
WHATEVER YOU'VE BEEN TOLD, THERE'S MORE GOING ON HERE THAN YOU REALIZE.
WE DIDN'T CAUSE THE EXPLOSION AT THE FACILITY. ALL WE DID WAS ESCAPE WHEN WE DISCOVERED--
SHHHHH!
UNTIE ME!
WHAT IS IT?
WE'RE NOT GOING TO JUST--
THERE ARE PEOPLE COMING. HEAVY BOOTS. PROBABLY SOLDIERS. THEY'RE ARMED. I CAN SMELL THEIR GUNPOWDER.
UNTIE ME--

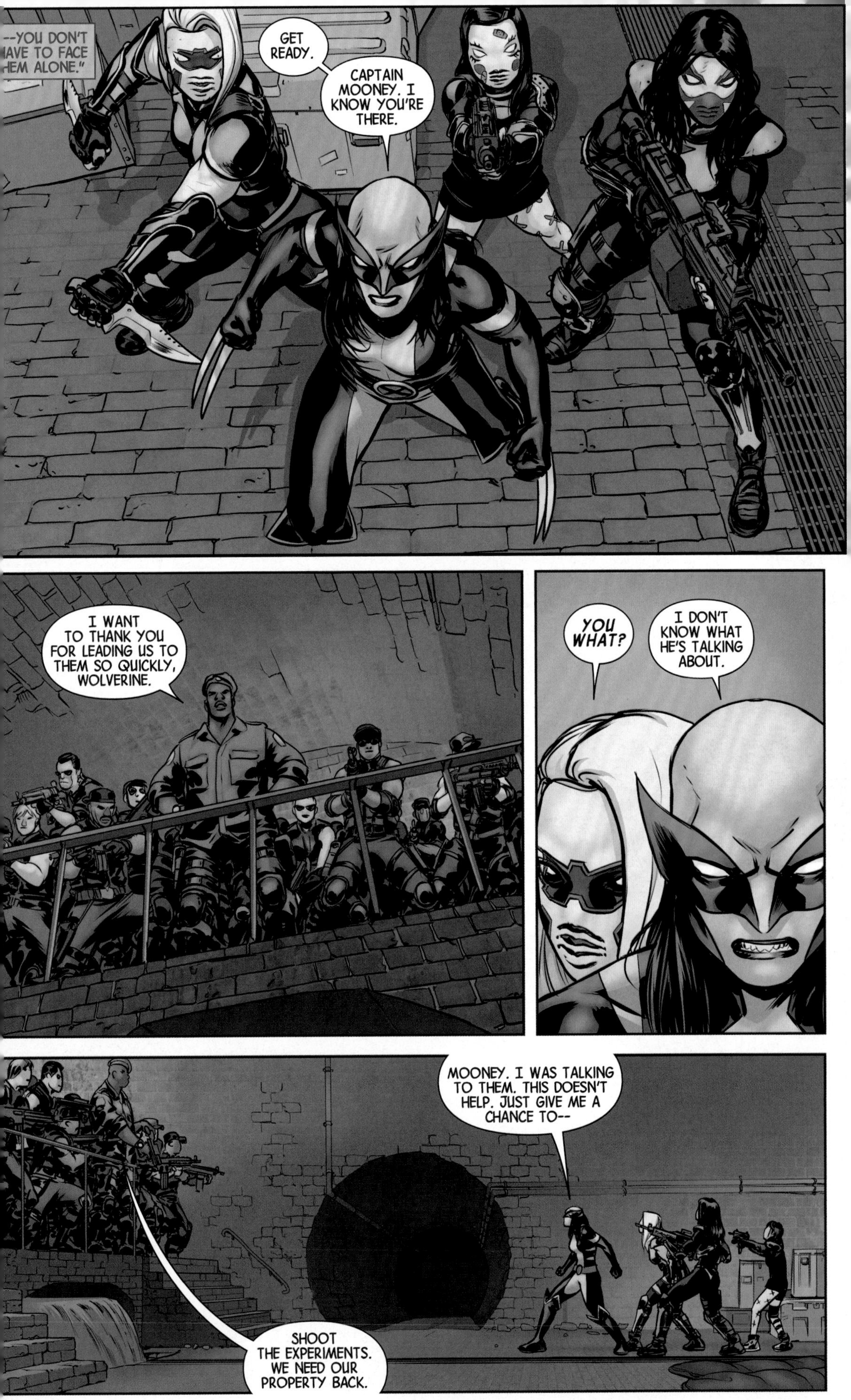
--YOU DON'T
HAVE TO FACE
THEM ALONE."
GET READY.
CAPTAIN MOONEY. I KNOW YOU'RE THERE.
I WANT TO THANK YOU FOR LEADING US TO THEM SO QUICKLY, WOLVERINE.
YOU WHAT?
I DON'T KNOW WHAT HE'S TALKING ABOUT.
MOONEY. I WAS TALKING TO THEM. THIS DOESN'T HELP. JUST GIVE ME A CHANCE TO--
SHOOT THE EXPERIMENTS. WE NEED OUR PROPERTY BACK.

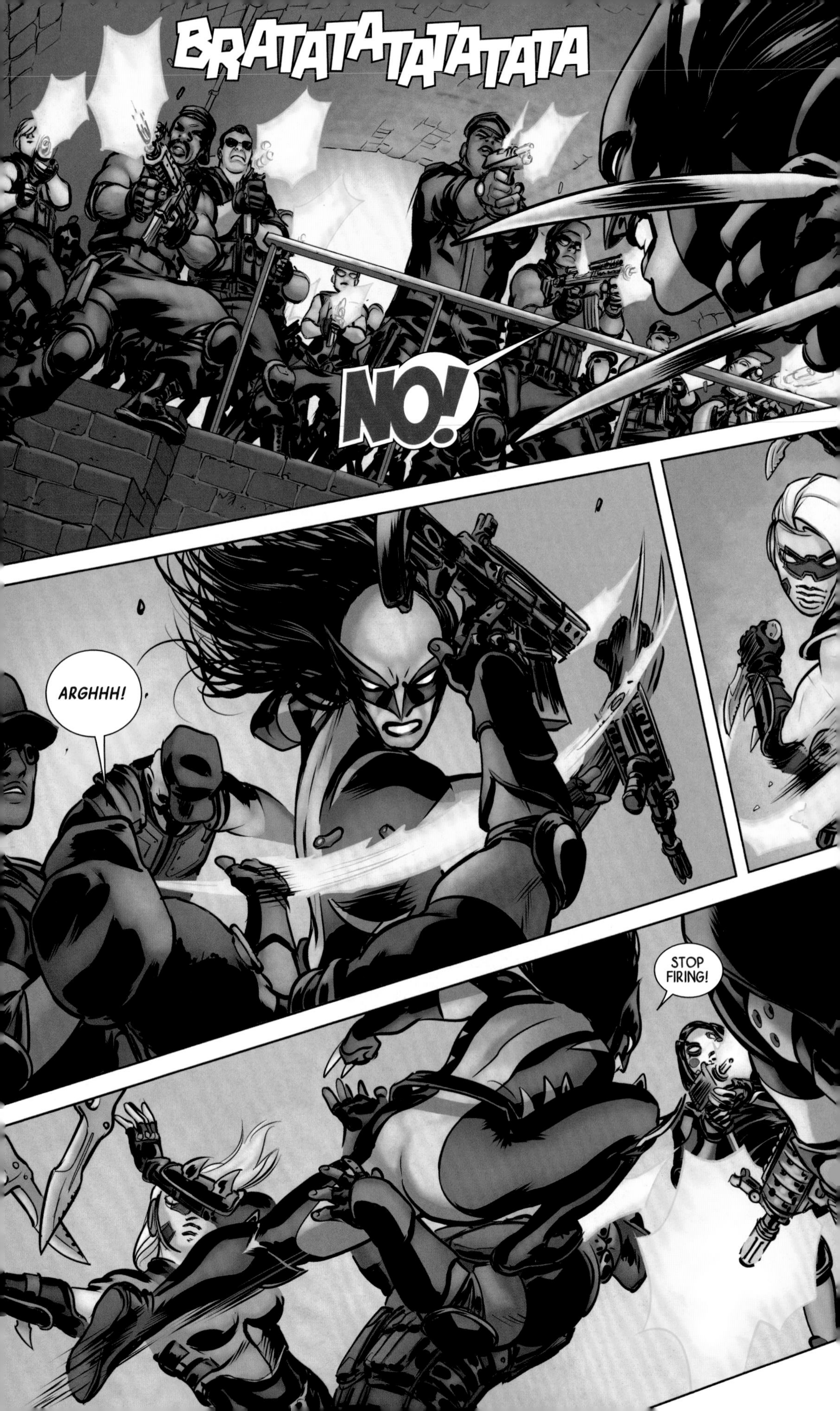
BRATATATATATATA
NO!
ARGHHH!
STOP FIRING!

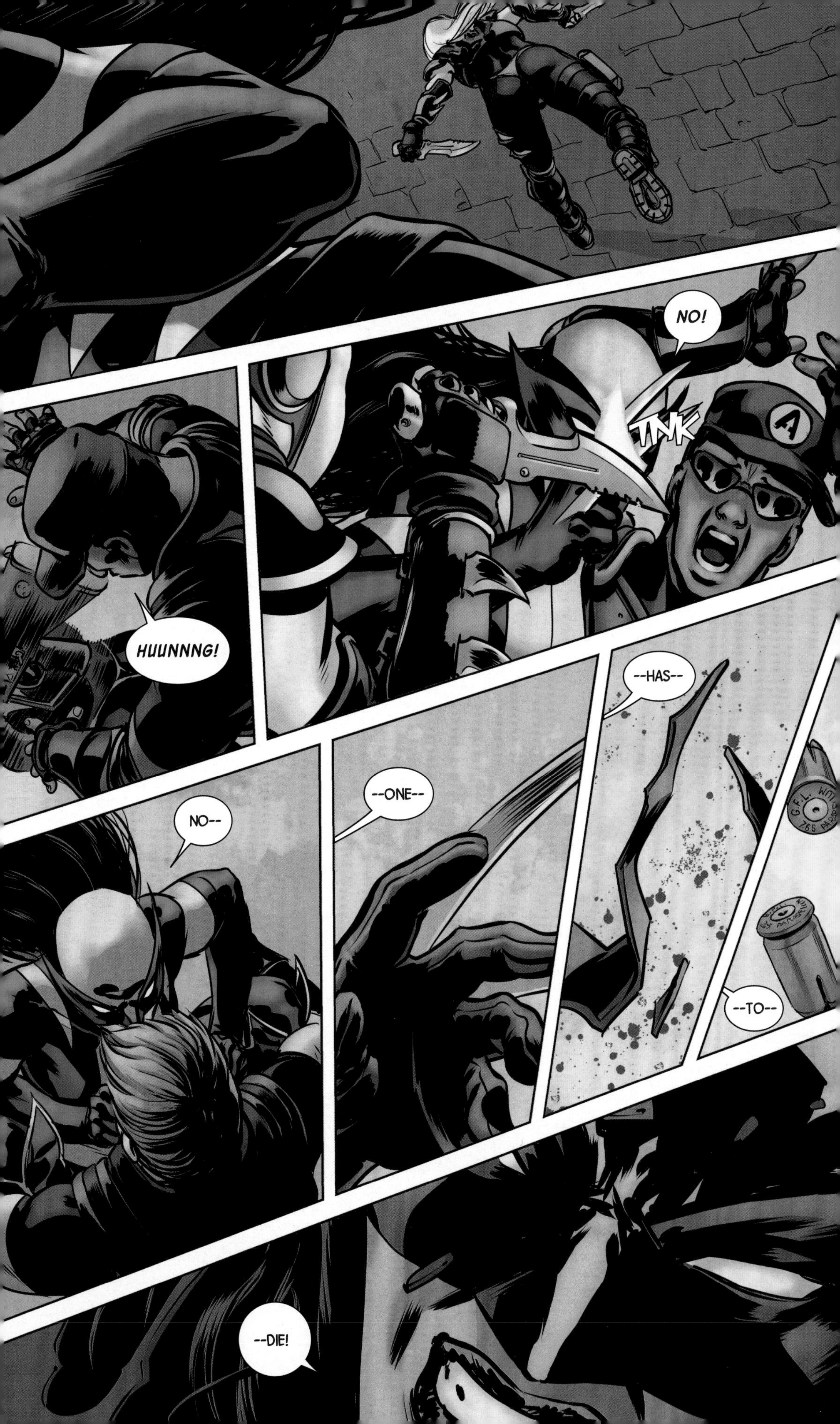
NO!
TNK
HUUNNNG!
NO--
--ONE--
--HAS--
--TO--
--DIE!

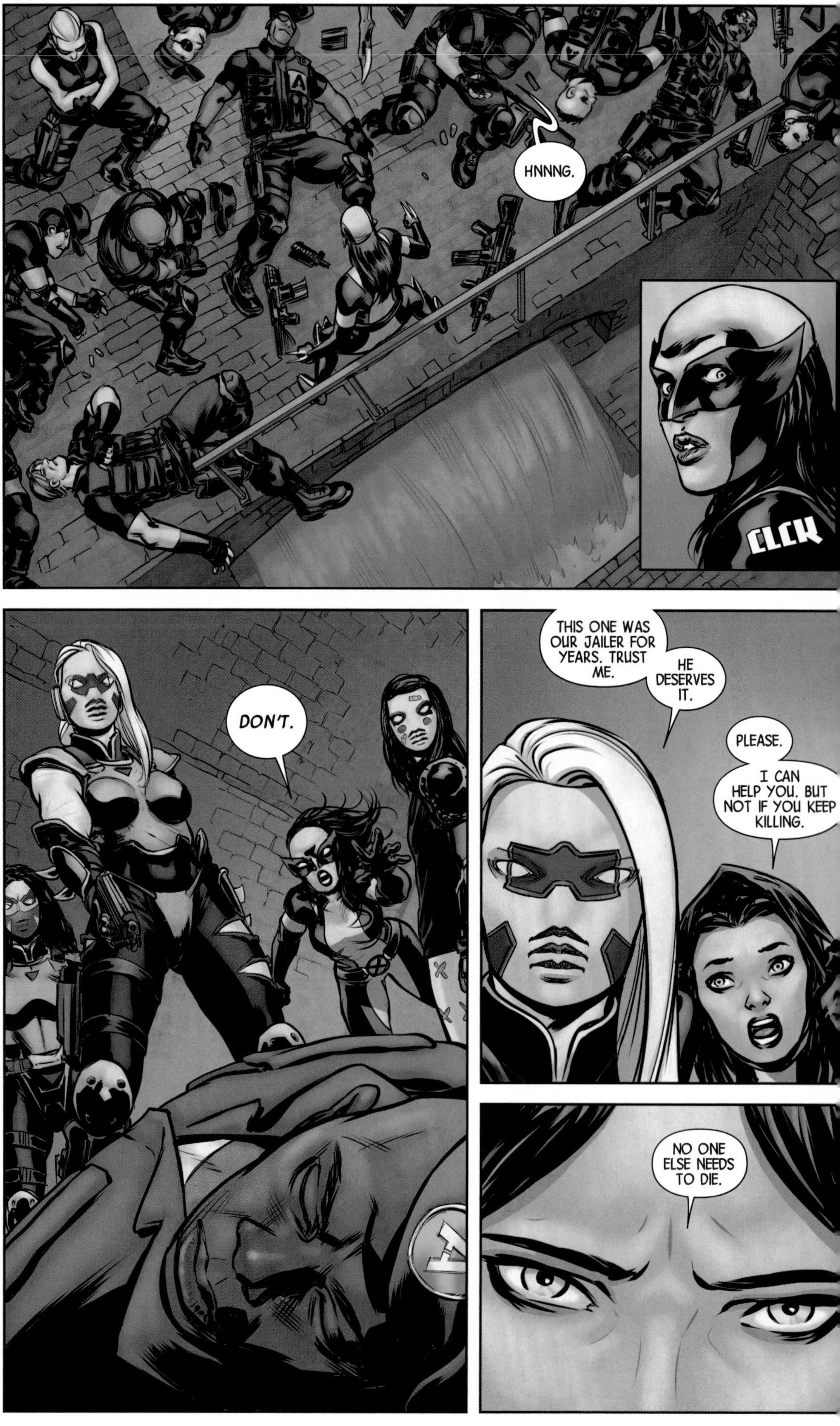
HNNNG.
CLCK
DON'T.
THIS ONE WAS OUR JAILER FOR YEARS. TRUST ME.
HE DESERVES IT.
PLEASE.
I CAN HELP YOU. BUT NOT IF YOU KEEP KILLING.
NO ONE ELSE NEEDS TO DIE.

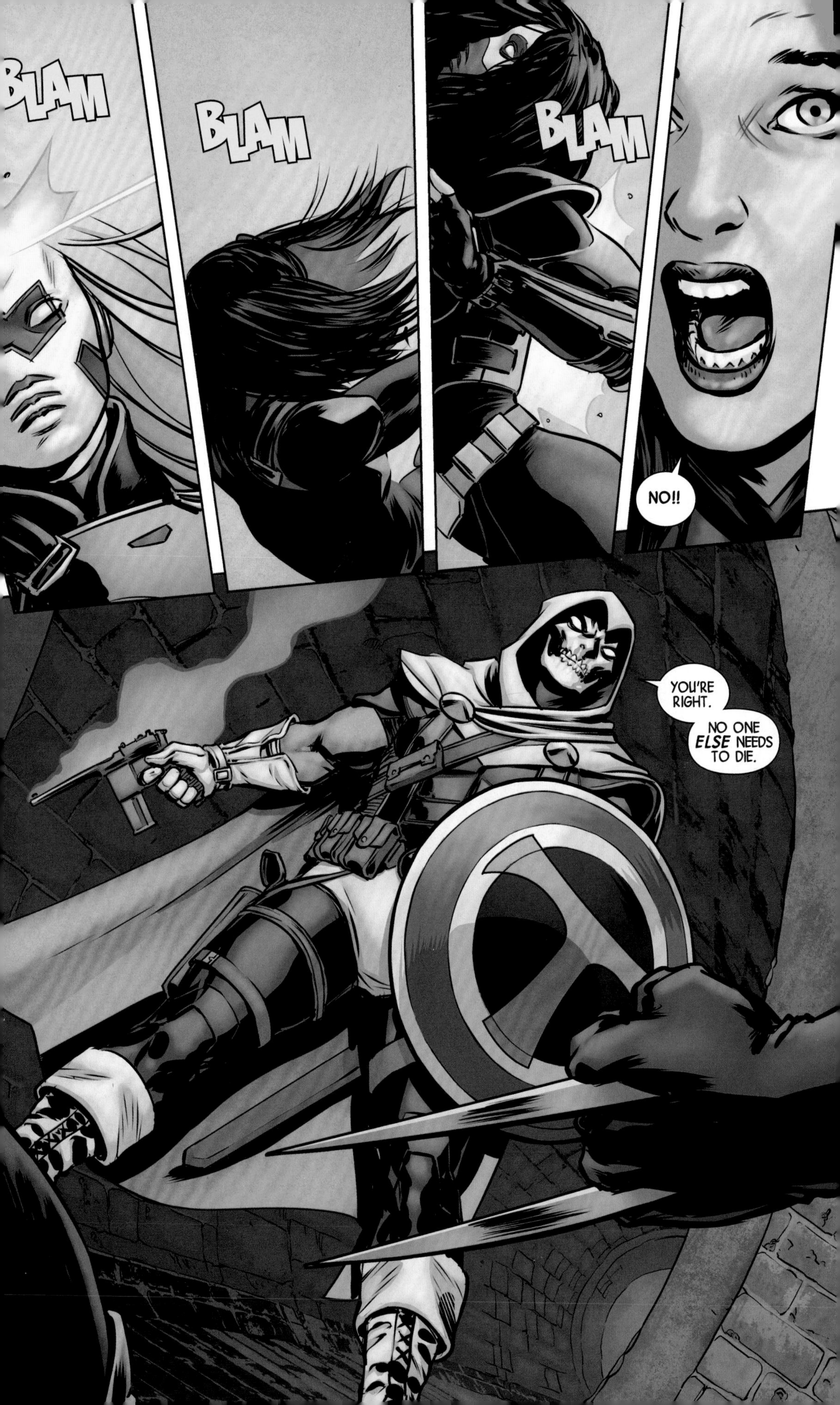
BLAM
BLAM
BLAM
NO!!
YOU'RE RIGHT.
NO ONE *ELSE* NEEDS TO DIE.

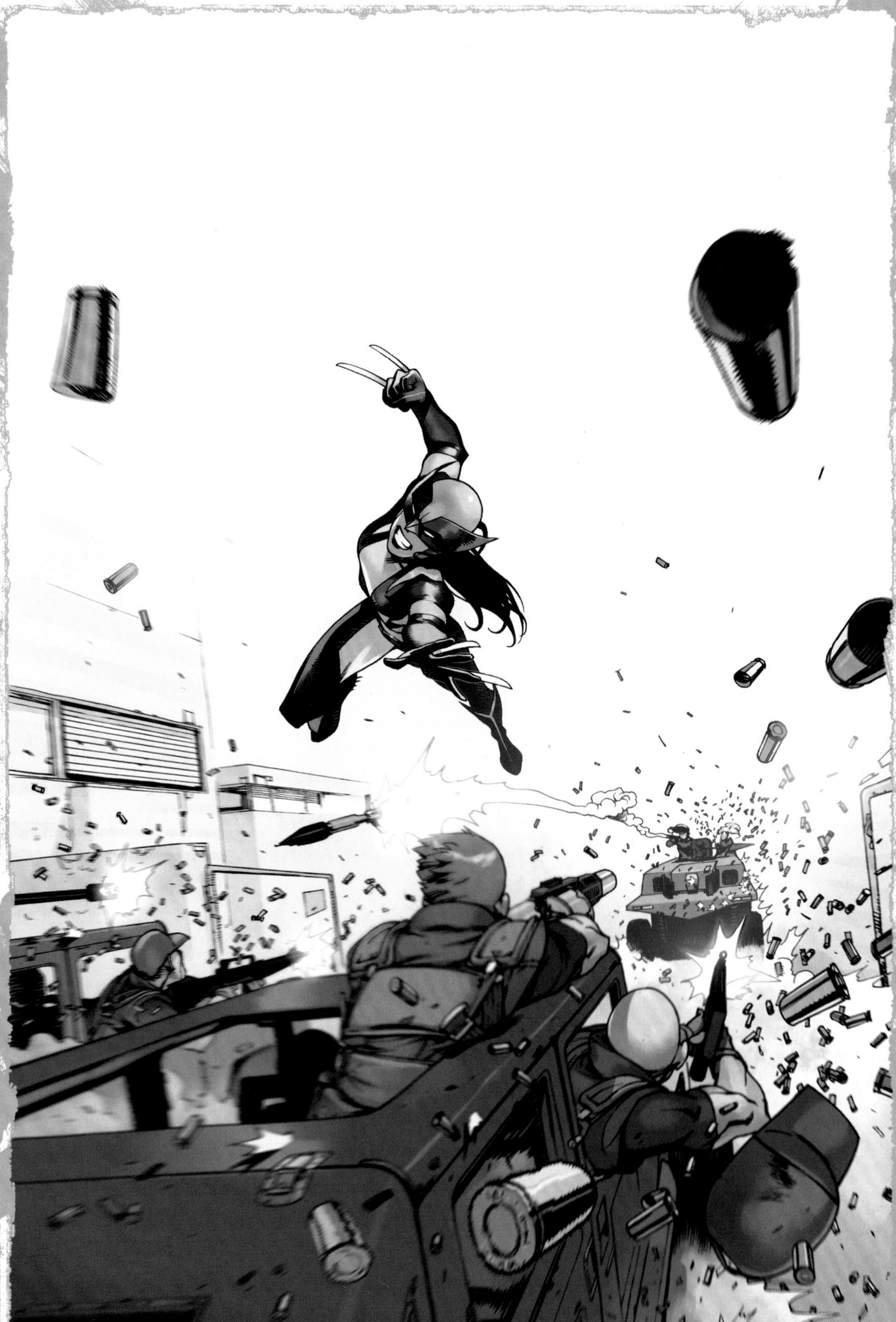

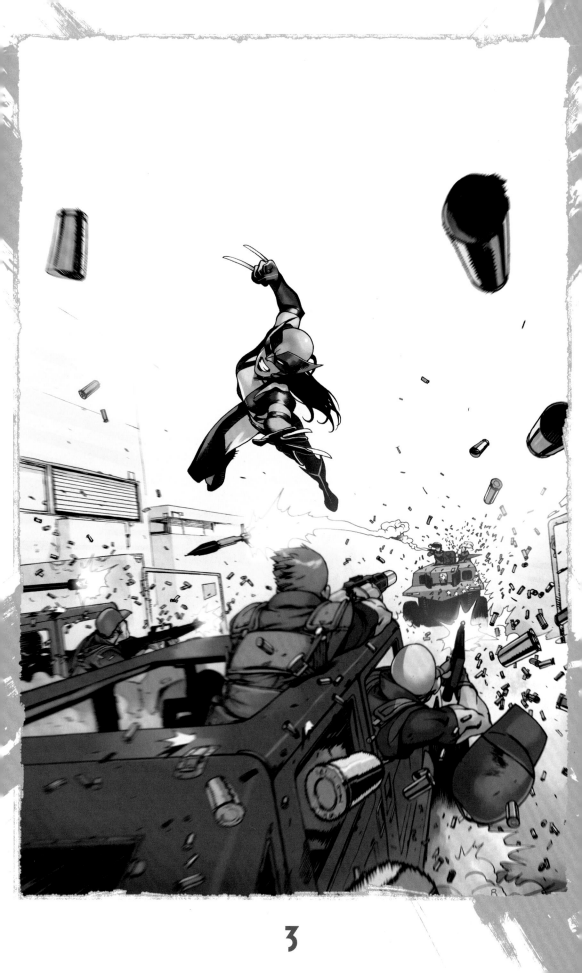

DEEP UNDERGROUND. THE SEWERS OF NEW YORK.

TASKMASTER TO ALCHEMAX ONE. YOU CAN SEND IN YOUR RETRIEVAL CREW.

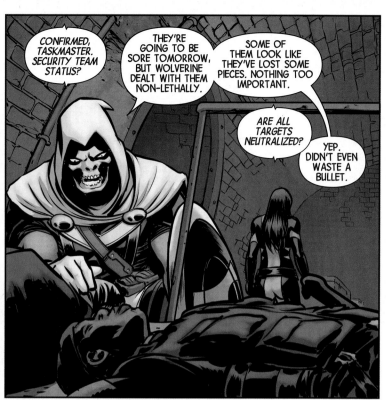

CONFIRMED, TASKMASTER. SECURITY TEAM STATUS?

THEY'RE GOING TO BE SORE TOMORROW, BUT WOLVERINE DEALT WITH THEM NON-LETHALLY.

SOME OF THEM LOOK LIKE THEY'VE LOST SOME PIECES. NOTHING TOO IMPORTANT.

ARE ALL TARGETS NEUTRALIZED?

YEP. DIDN'T EVEN WASTE A BULLET.

THREE SISTERS. ALL TERMINATED.

AND WOLVERINE?

SHE--

SNIKT

UM...

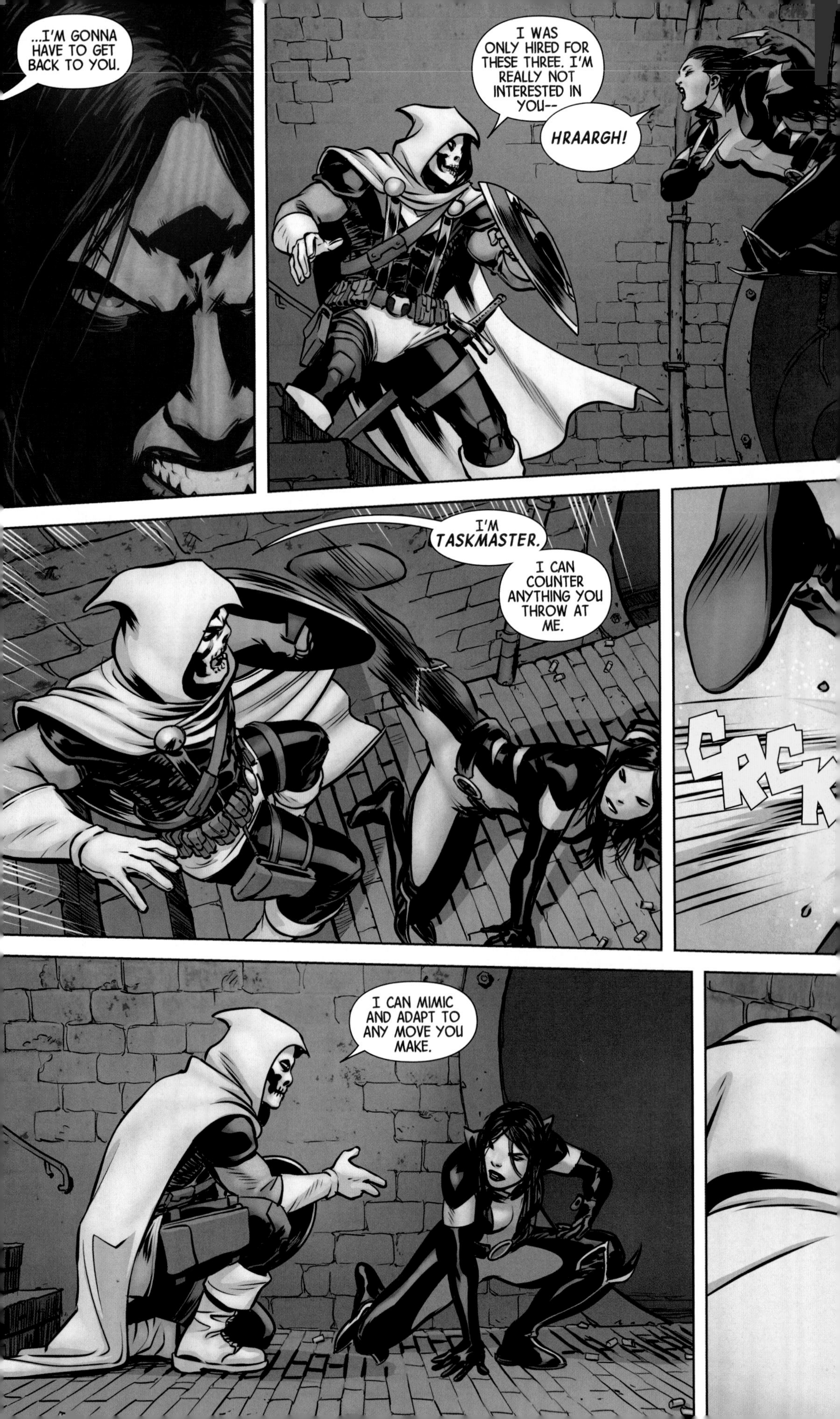

...I'M GONNA HAVE TO GET BACK TO YOU.
I WAS ONLY HIRED FOR THESE THREE. I'M REALLY NOT INTERESTED IN YOU--
HRAARGH!
I'M TASKMASTER.
I CAN COUNTER ANYTHING YOU THROW AT ME.
CRACK
I CAN MIMIC AND ADAPT TO ANY MOVE YOU MAKE.

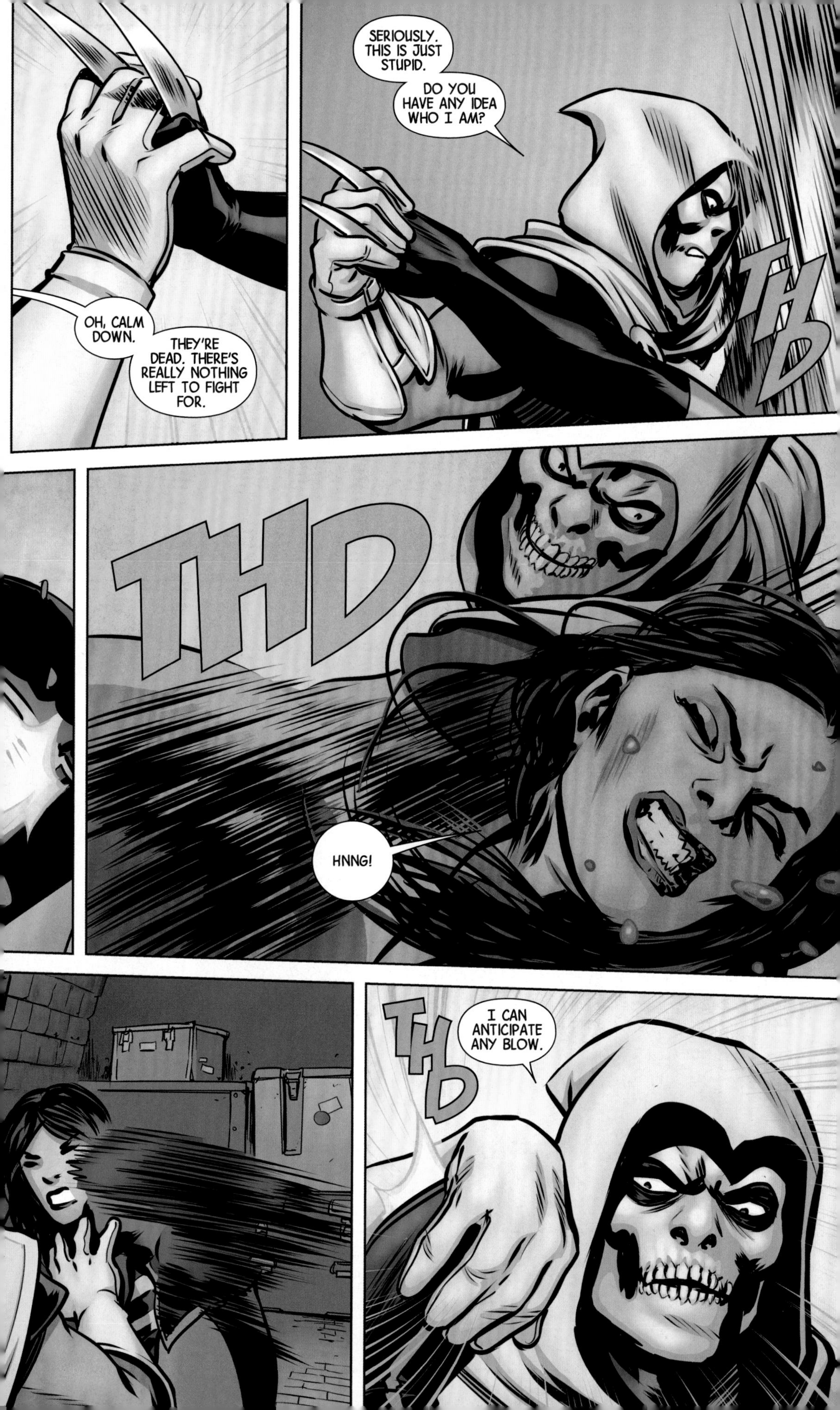

OH, CALM DOWN.
THEY'RE DEAD. THERE'S REALLY NOTHING LEFT TO FIGHT FOR.
SERIOUSLY. THIS IS JUST STUPID.
DO YOU HAVE ANY IDEA WHO I AM?
THD
THD
HNNG!
THD
I CAN ANTICIPATE ANY BLOW.

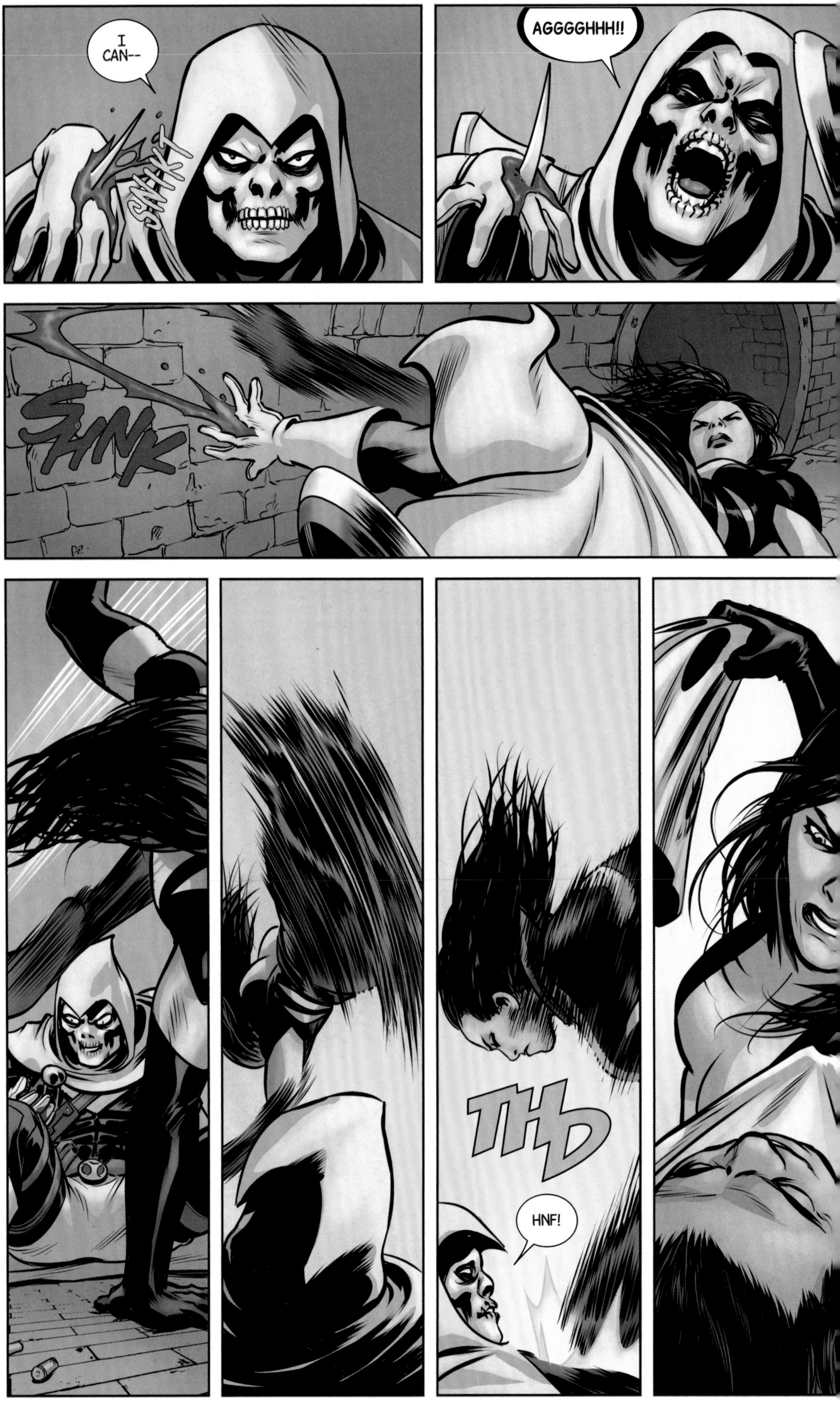
I CAN--
SNIKT
AGGGGHHH!!
SHNK
THD
HNF!

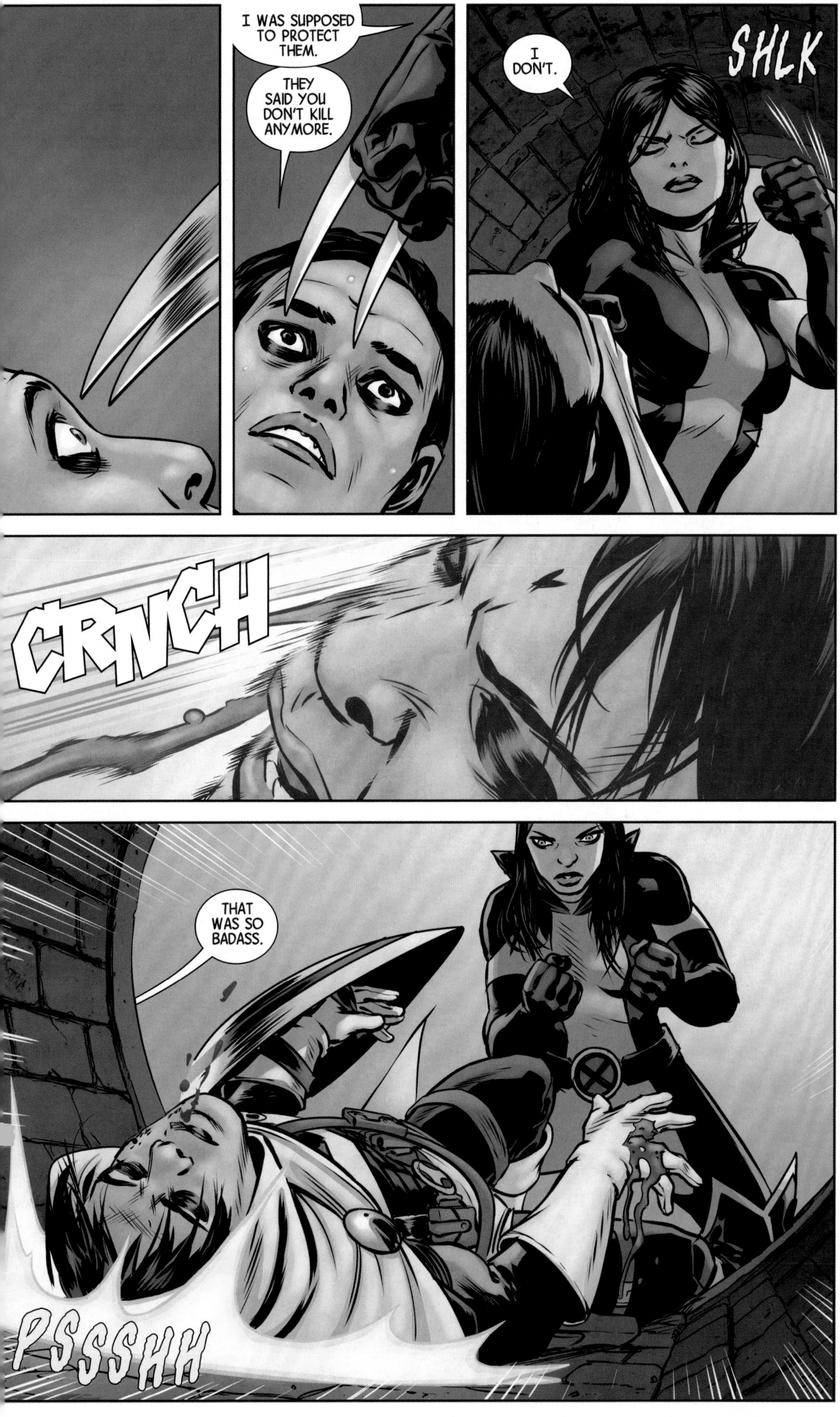

I WAS SUPPOSED TO PROTECT THEM.
THEY SAID YOU DON'T KILL ANYMORE.
I DON'T.
SHLK
CRNCH
THAT WAS SO BADASS.
PSSSHH

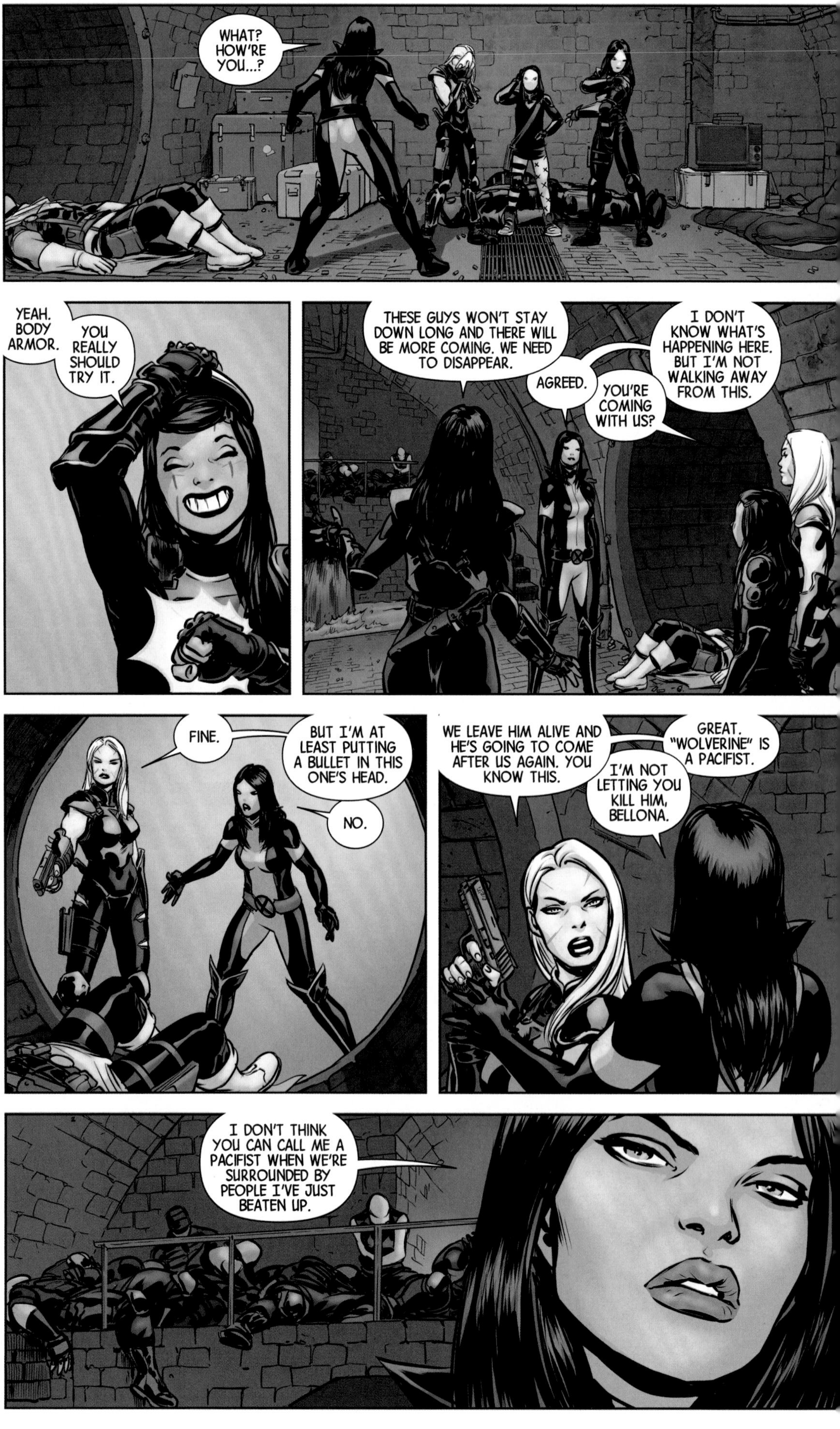
WHAT? HOW'RE YOU...?
YEAH. BODY ARMOR.
YOU REALLY SHOULD TRY IT.
THESE GUYS WON'T STAY DOWN LONG AND THERE WILL BE MORE COMING. WE NEED TO DISAPPEAR.
AGREED.
I DON'T KNOW WHAT'S HAPPENING HERE. BUT I'M NOT WALKING AWAY FROM THIS.
YOU'RE COMING WITH US?
FINE.
BUT I'M AT LEAST PUTTING A BULLET IN THIS ONE'S HEAD.
NO.
WE LEAVE HIM ALIVE AND HE'S GOING TO COME AFTER US AGAIN. YOU KNOW THIS.
GREAT. "WOLVERINE" IS A PACIFIST.
I'M NOT LETTING YOU KILL HIM, BELLONA.
I DON'T THINK YOU CAN CALL ME A PACIFIST WHEN WE'RE SURROUNDED BY PEOPLE I'VE JUST BEATEN UP.

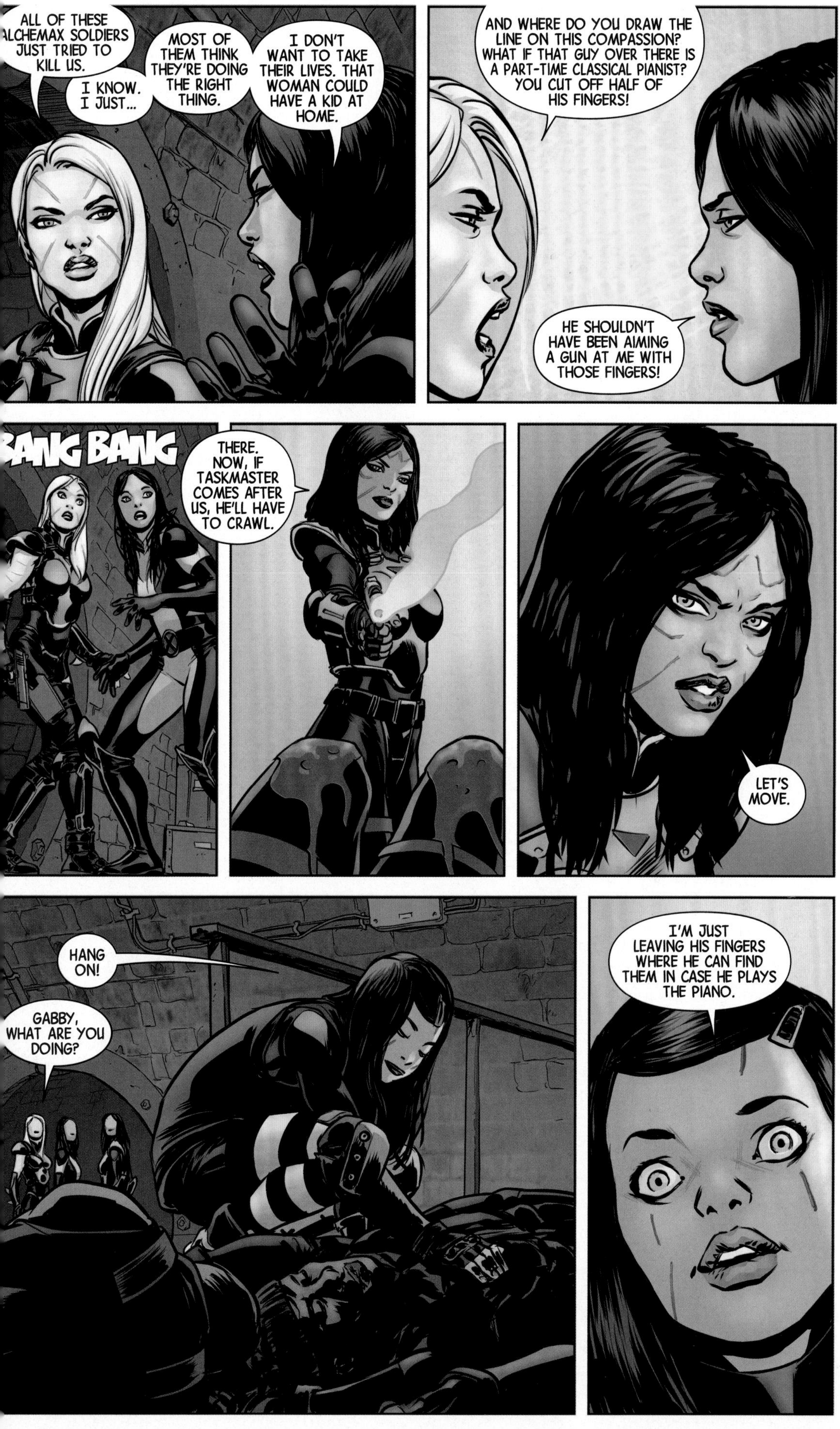
ALL OF THESE ALCHEMAX SOLDIERS JUST TRIED TO KILL US.
I KNOW. I JUST...
MOST OF THEM THINK THEY'RE DOING THE RIGHT THING.
I DON'T WANT TO TAKE THEIR LIVES. THAT WOMAN COULD HAVE A KID AT HOME.
AND WHERE DO YOU DRAW THE LINE ON THIS COMPASSION? WHAT IF THAT GUY OVER THERE IS A PART-TIME CLASSICAL PIANIST? YOU CUT OFF HALF OF HIS FINGERS!
HE SHOULDN'T HAVE BEEN AIMING A GUN AT ME WITH THOSE FINGERS!
BANG BANG
THERE. NOW, IF TASKMASTER COMES AFTER US, HE'LL HAVE TO CRAWL.
LET'S MOVE.
HANG ON!
GABBY, WHAT ARE YOU DOING?
I'M JUST LEAVING HIS FINGERS WHERE HE CAN FIND THEM IN CASE HE PLAYS THE PIANO.

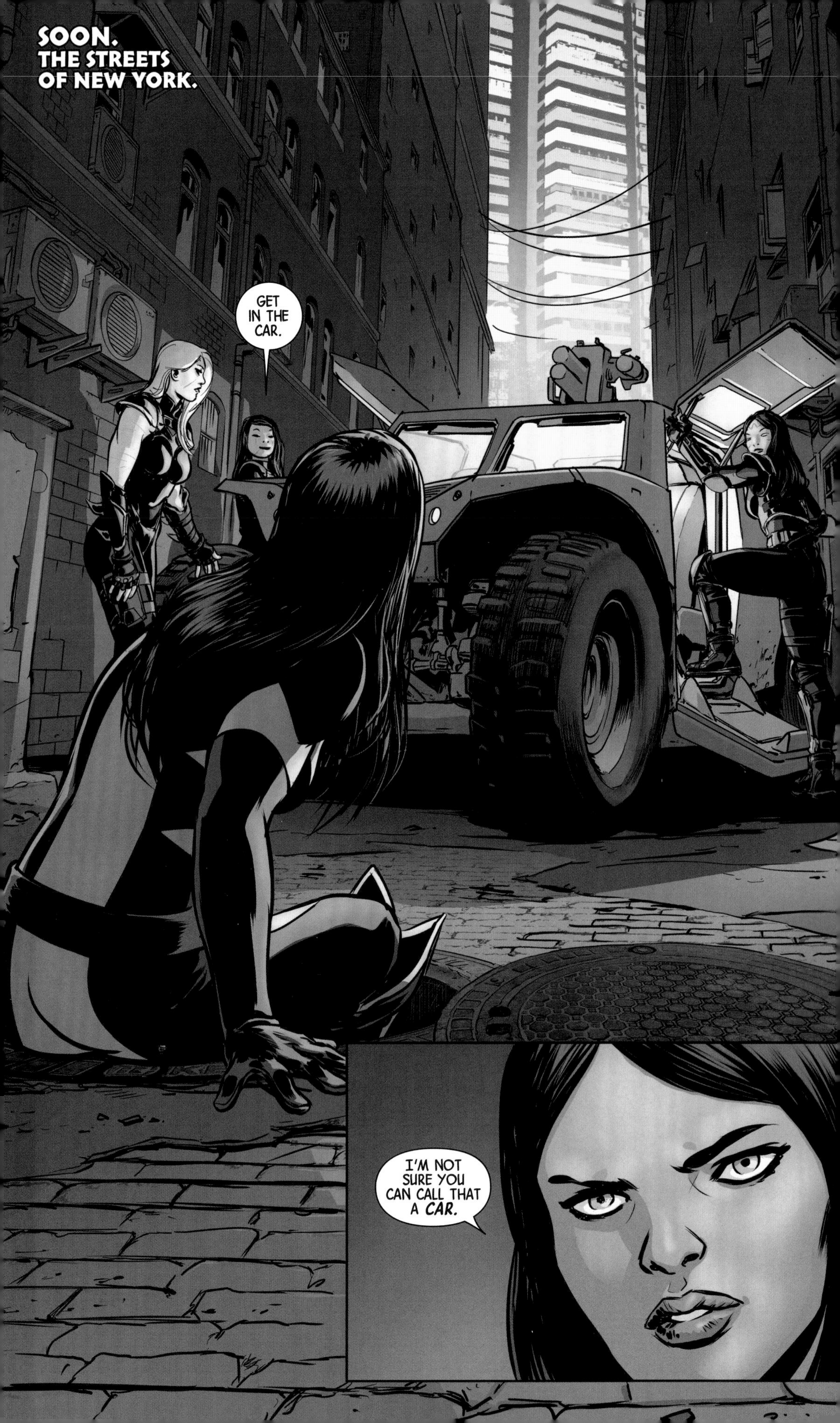
SOON. THE STREETS OF NEW YORK.
GET IN THE CAR.
I'M NOT SURE YOU CAN CALL THAT A *CAR.*

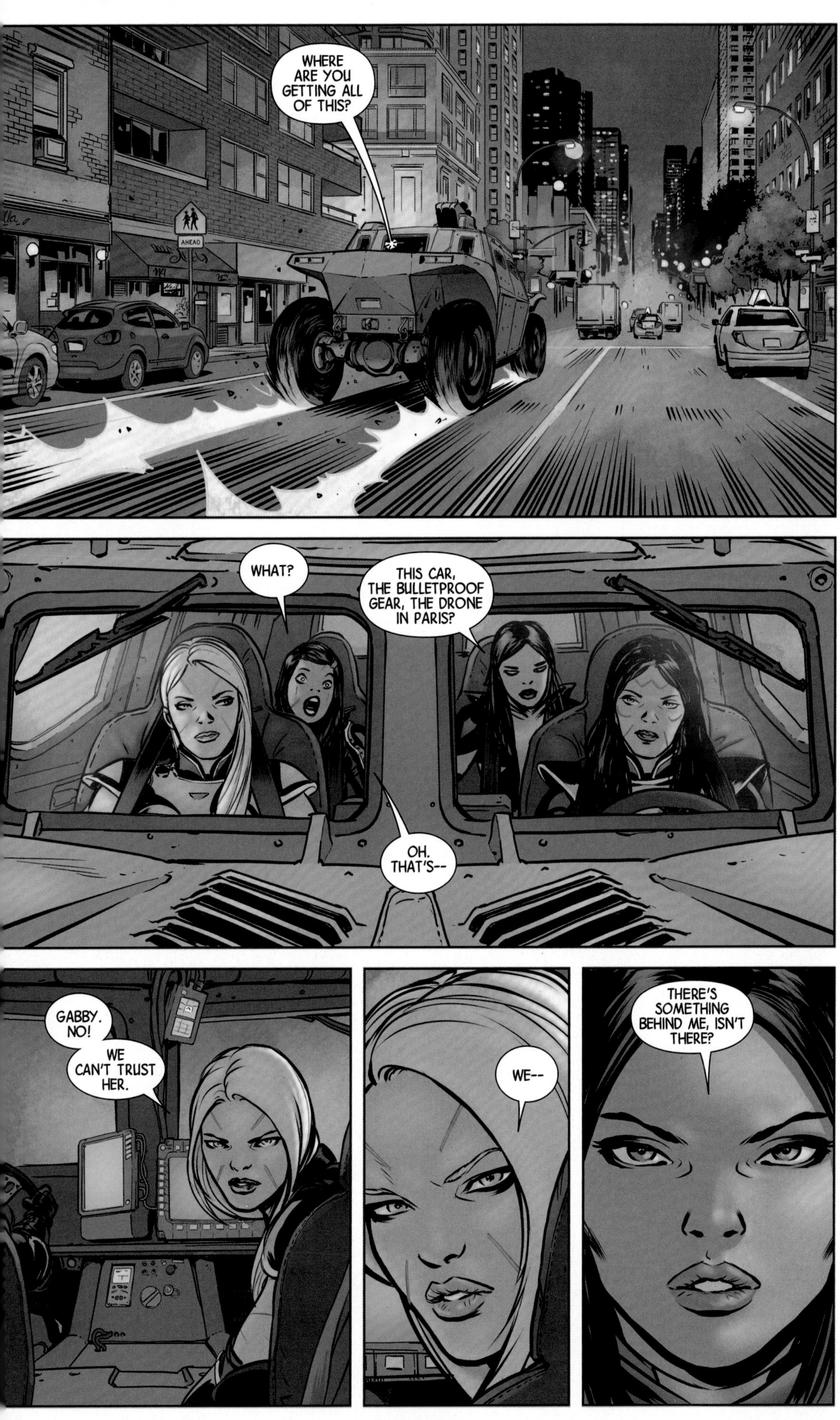
WHERE ARE YOU GETTING ALL OF THIS?
AHEAD
WHAT?
THIS CAR, THE BULLETPROOF GEAR, THE DRONE IN PARIS?
OH. THAT'S--
GABBY. NO!
WE CAN'T TRUST HER.
WE--
THERE'S SOMETHING BEHIND ME, ISN'T THERE?

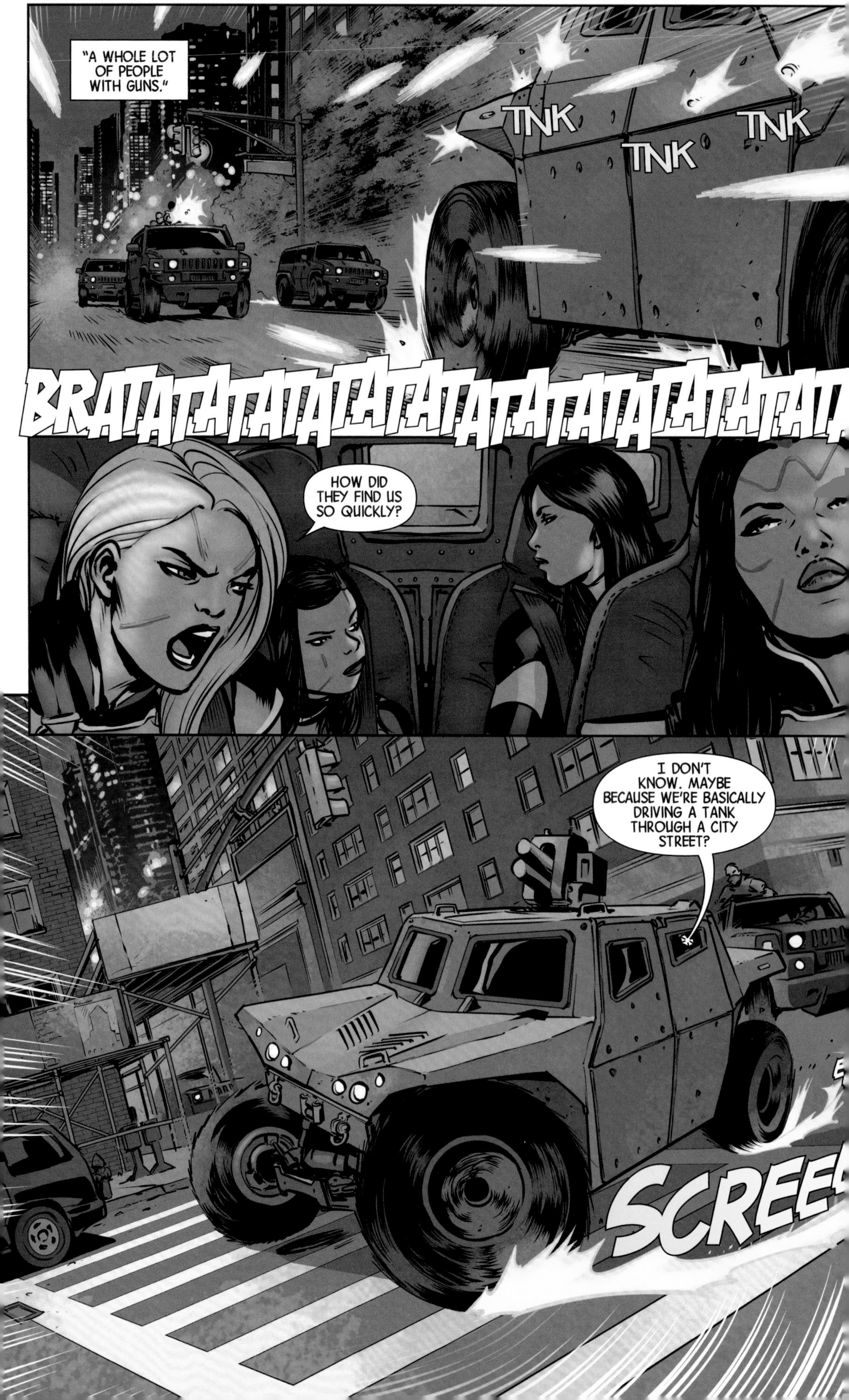
"A WHOLE LOT OF PEOPLE WITH GUNS."
TNK
TNK
TNK
BRATATATATATATATATATATATATATATA
HOW DID THEY FIND US SO QUICKLY?
I DON'T KNOW. MAYBE BECAUSE WE'RE BASICALLY DRIVING A TANK THROUGH A CITY STREET?
SCREE

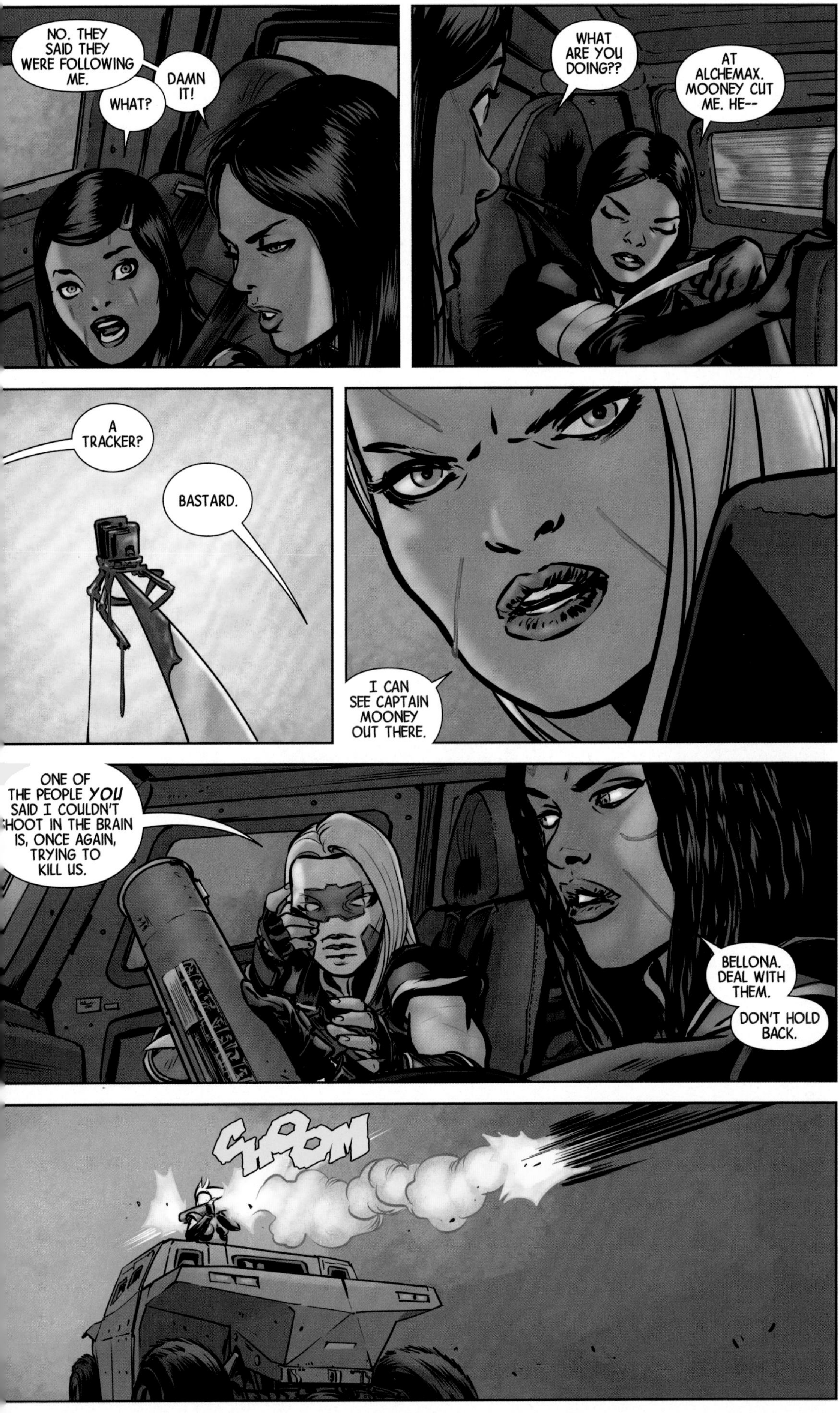
NO. THEY SAID THEY WERE FOLLOWING ME.
WHAT?
DAMN IT!
WHAT ARE YOU DOING??
AT ALCHEMAX. MOONEY CUT ME. HE--
A TRACKER?
BASTARD.
I CAN SEE CAPTAIN MOONEY OUT THERE.
ONE OF THE PEOPLE YOU SAID I COULDN'T SHOOT IN THE BRAIN IS, ONCE AGAIN, TRYING TO KILL US.
BELLONA. DEAL WITH THEM.
DON'T HOLD BACK.
CHOOM

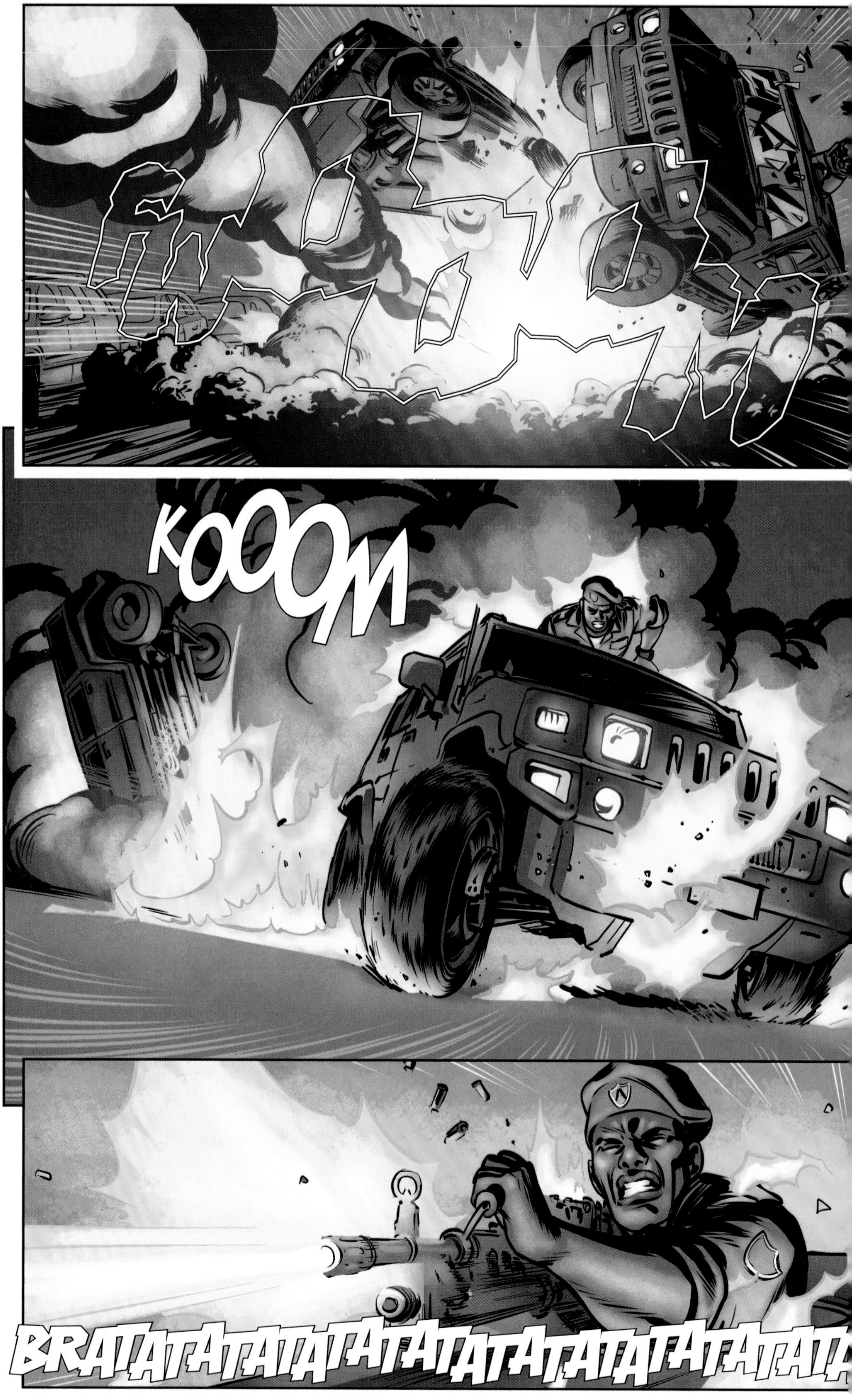
KOOOM
BRATATATATATATATATATATATATATA

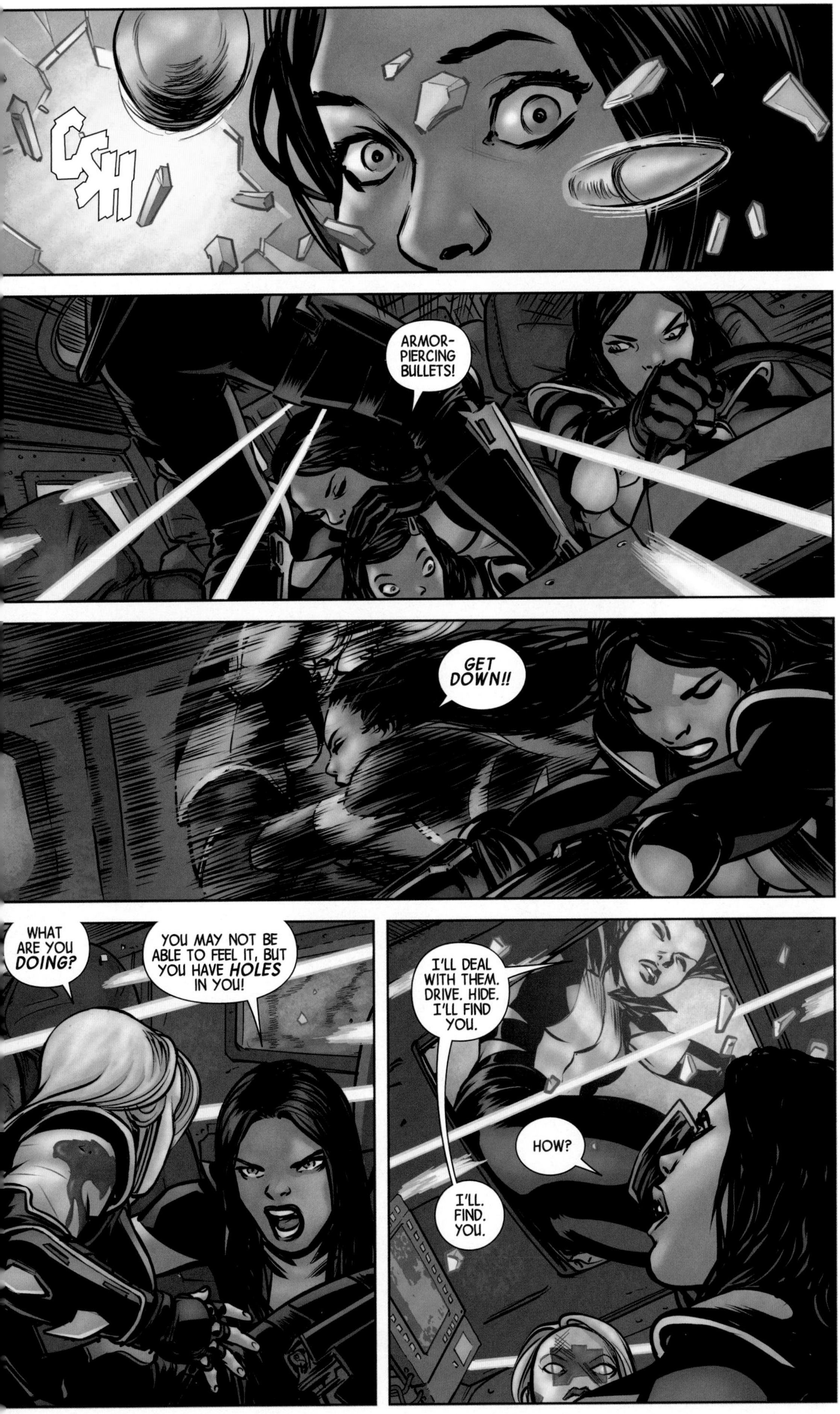
CSH
ARMOR-PIERCING BULLETS!
GET DOWN!!
WHAT ARE YOU DOING?
YOU MAY NOT BE ABLE TO FEEL IT, BUT YOU HAVE HOLES IN YOU!
I'LL DEAL WITH THEM. DRIVE. HIDE. I'LL FIND YOU.
HOW?
I'LL. FIND. YOU.

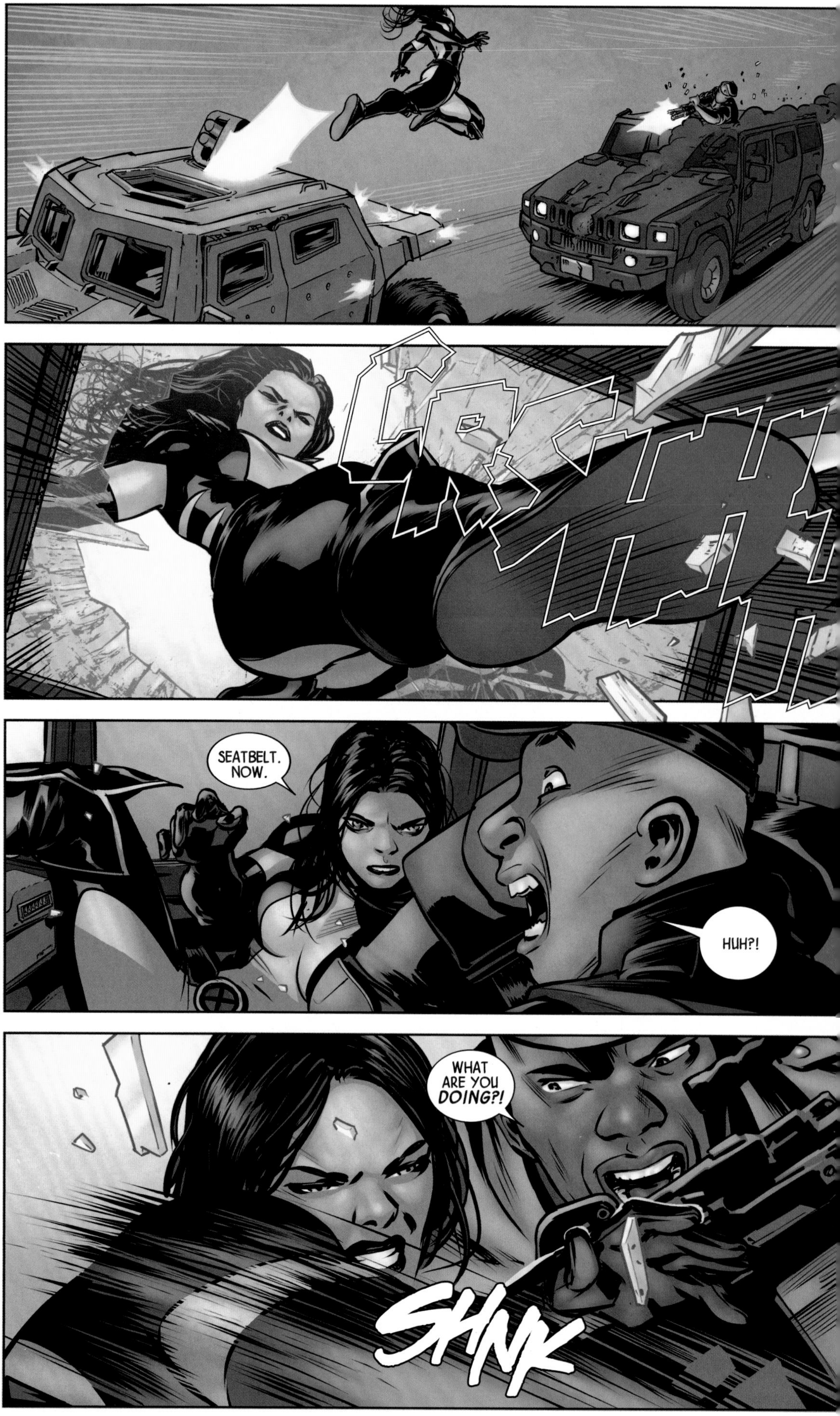
CRASH
SEATBELT. NOW.
HUH?!
WHAT ARE YOU DOING?!
SHNK

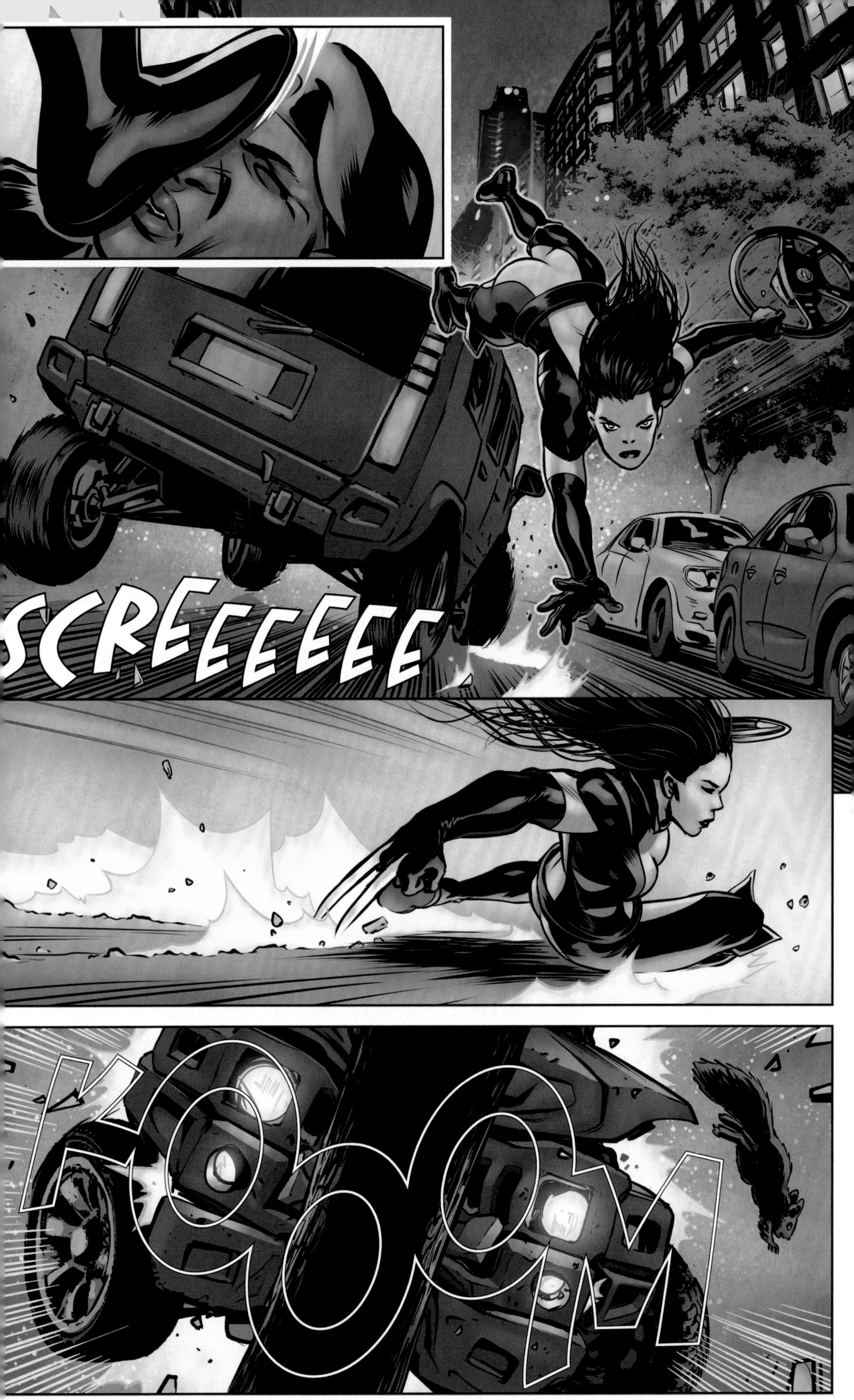
SCREEEEEEE
KOOOOM

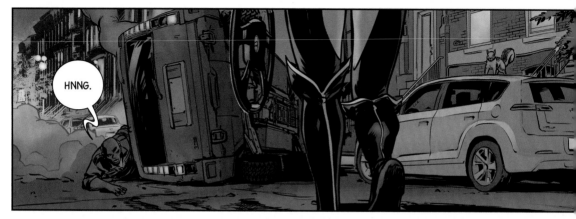

HNNG.

UNTIL I COMPLETELY UNDERSTAND WHAT'S GOING ON, THE SISTERS ARE UNDER MY PROTECTION.

THD

HEH. THEY'RE NOT SISTERS.

THEY'RE NOT EVEN HUMAN. THEY'RE LIKE YOU. EXPERIMENTS PRETENDING.

CAPTAIN MOONEY. IF ALCHEMAX GENETICS COMES AFTER THEM AGAIN, I WON'T HOLD BACK.

I'VE ALREADY BEATEN YOU UNCONSCIOUS ONCE TODAY, AND NOW I'/ LEAVING YOU IN THE WRECKAGE OF A CAR CRASH, ALONE AND BLEEDING. THAT'S ME HOLDING BACK.

WE KNOW WHERE YOU LIVE. WE KNOW YOUR FRIENDS. WE KNOW YOUR X-MEN. WE KNOW ABOUT THAT BOY WHO FLIES YOU AROUND.

YOU CAN'T STEAL OUR PROPERTY. WE OWN THEM. YOU CAN'T HIDE FROM US!

I WON'T BE HIDING.

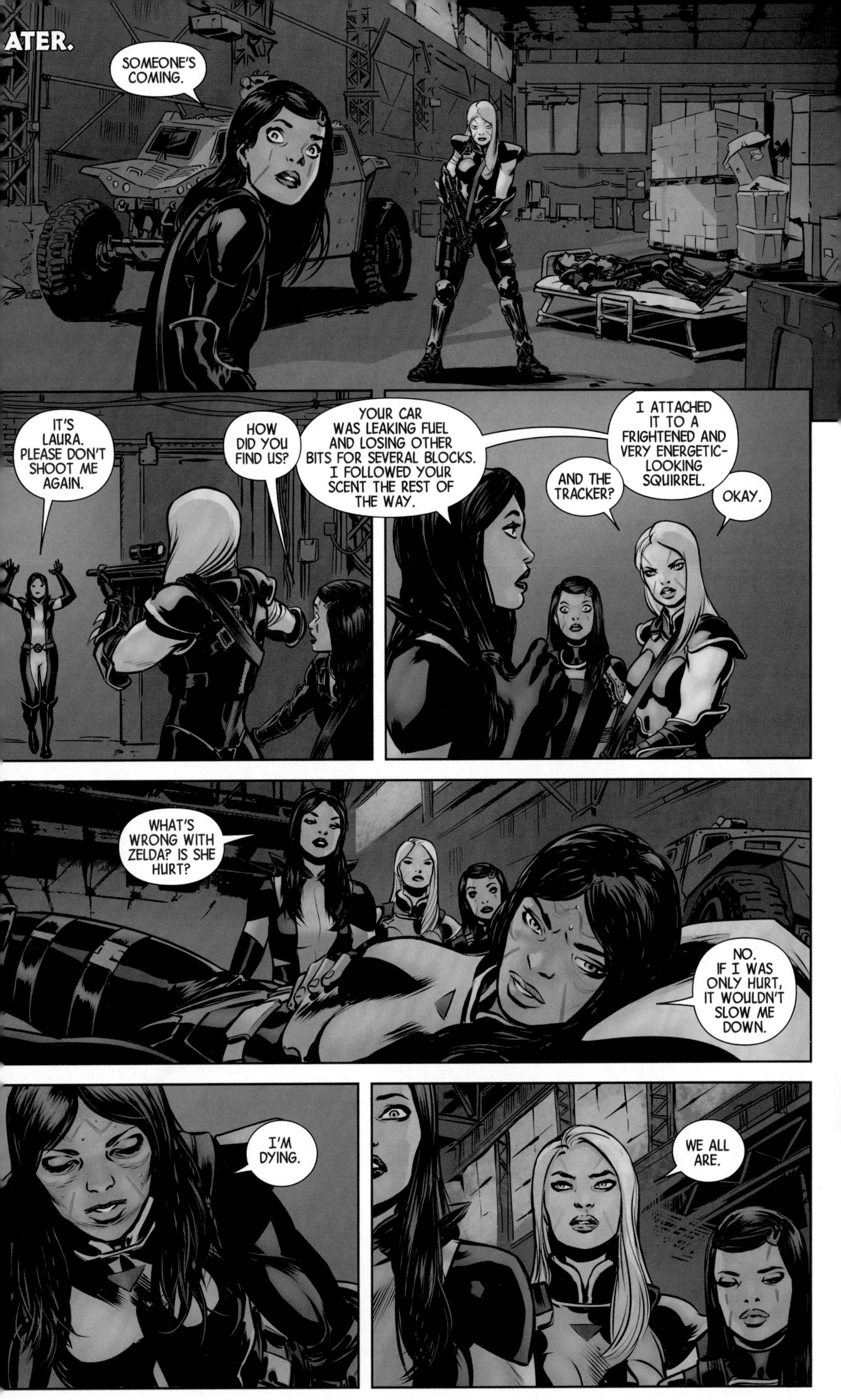
ATER.
SOMEONE'S COMING.
IT'S LAURA. PLEASE DON'T SHOOT ME AGAIN.
HOW DID YOU FIND US?
YOUR CAR WAS LEAKING FUEL AND LOSING OTHER BITS FOR SEVERAL BLOCKS. I FOLLOWED YOUR SCENT THE REST OF THE WAY.
AND THE TRACKER?
I ATTACHED IT TO A FRIGHTENED AND VERY ENERGETIC-LOOKING SQUIRREL.
OKAY.
WHAT'S WRONG WITH ZELDA? IS SHE HURT?
NO. IF I WAS ONLY HURT, IT WOULDN'T SLOW ME DOWN.
I'M DYING.
WE ALL ARE.

WHATEVER THOSE BASTARDS DID TO OUR MINDS TO TAKE AWAY OUR PAIN, IT TOOK SOMETHING ELSE TOO. IT TOOK YEARS FROM US.

AS SOON AS WE UNDERSTOOD HOW LITTLE TIME WE HAD, WE DID EVERYTHING WE HAD TO DO TO ESCAPE.

BUT WE DIDN'T BLOW UP THE FACILITY.

I WOULD HAVE HAPPILY BLOWN IT UP.

WE WERE TOO BUSY RUNNING.

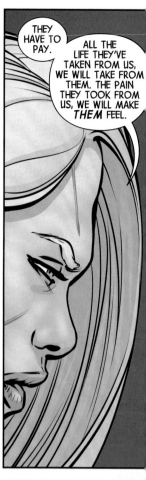

THEY HAVE TO PAY.

ALL THE LIFE THEY'VE TAKEN FROM US, WE WILL TAKE FROM THEM. THE PAIN THEY TOOK FROM US, WE WILL MAKE *THEM* FEEL.

REVENGE DOESN'T SOUND LIKE THE BEST USE OF YOUR TIME.

YOU CAN'T BE KILLED, AND YOU THINK YOU CAN LECTURE US ON WHAT TO DO WITH OUR LIVES?!

NO. I KNOW SOME VERY INTELLIGENT PEOPLE WHO MAY BE ABLE TO *SAVE* YOUR LIVES.

I CAN'T GO TO ANY OF THE PEOPLE I USUALLY WOULD. ALCHEMAX GENETICS COULD BE WATCHING THEM.

BUT THERE'S SOMEONE HERE IN NEW YORK. HE...I *THINK* HE'D HELP US.

BUT I'M WARNING YOU--

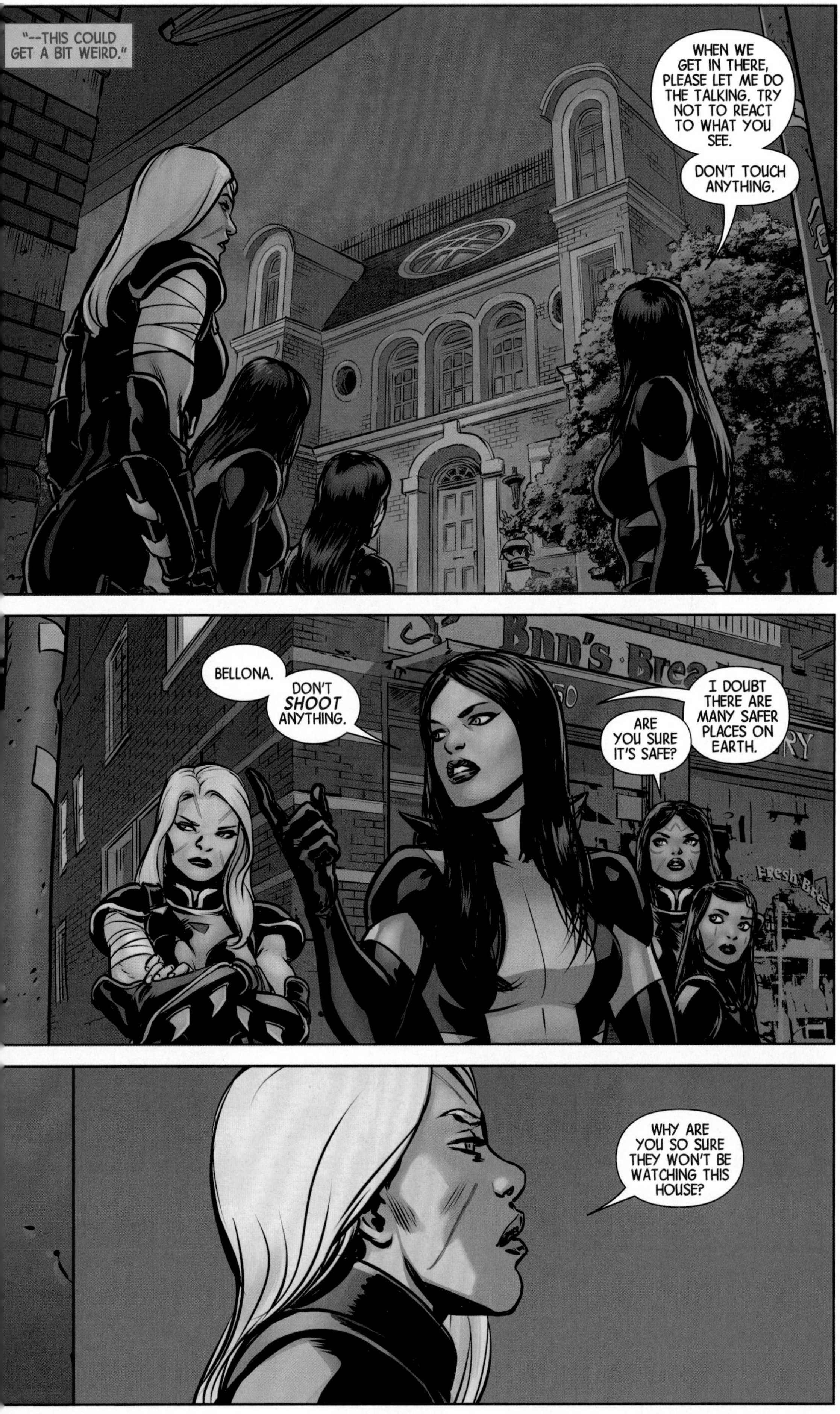
"--THIS COULD GET A BIT WEIRD."
WHEN WE GET IN THERE, PLEASE LET ME DO THE TALKING. TRY NOT TO REACT TO WHAT YOU SEE.
DON'T TOUCH ANYTHING.
BELLONA.
DON'T *SHOOT* ANYTHING.
ARE YOU SURE IT'S SAFE?
I DOUBT THERE ARE MANY SAFER PLACES ON EARTH.
WHY ARE YOU SO SURE THEY WON'T BE WATCHING THIS HOUSE?

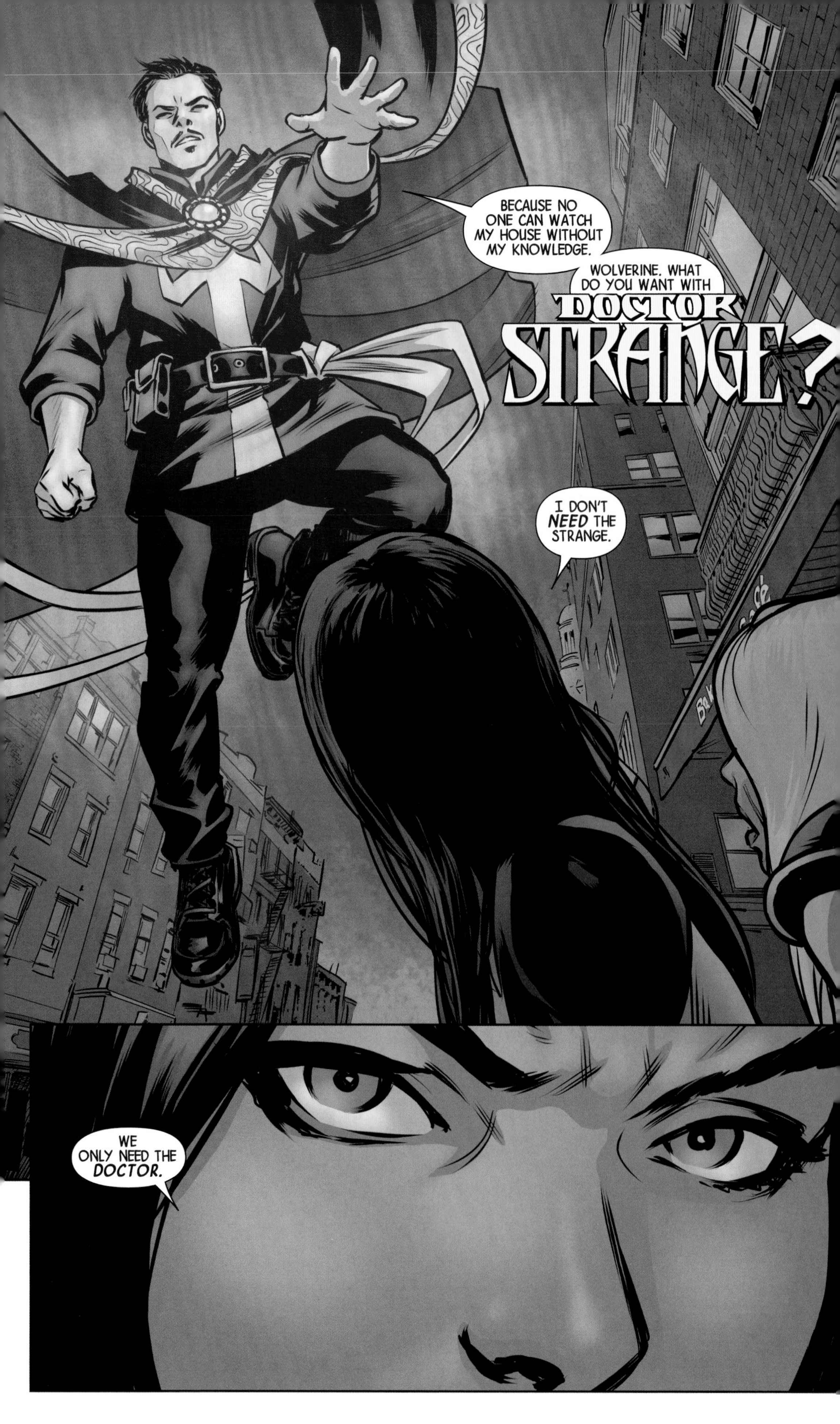
BECAUSE NO ONE CAN WATCH MY HOUSE WITHOUT MY KNOWLEDGE.
WOLVERINE. WHAT DO YOU WANT WITH
DOCTOR STRANGE?
I DON'T *NEED* THE STRANGE.
WE ONLY NEED THE *DOCTOR*.

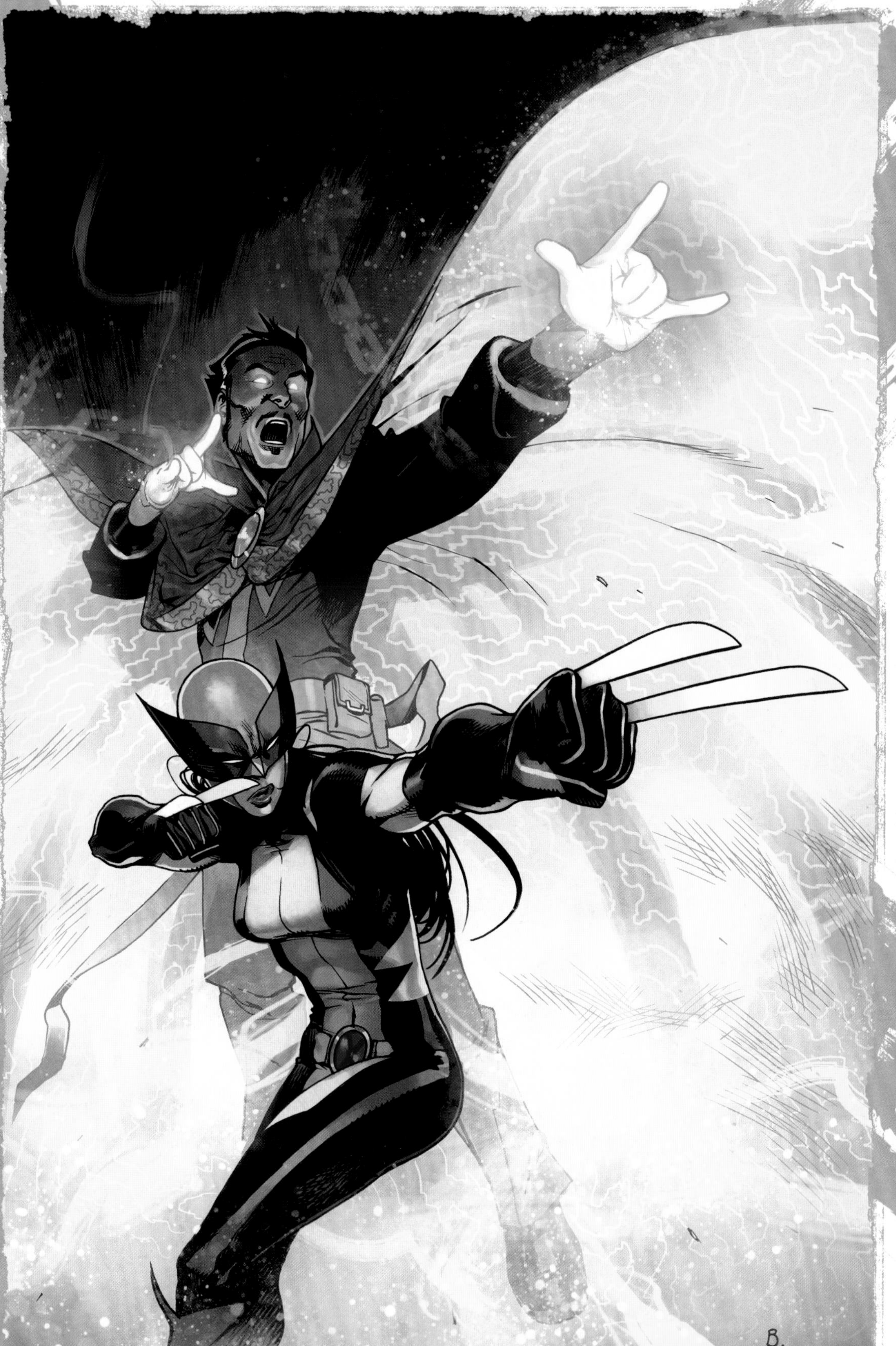
B.

4

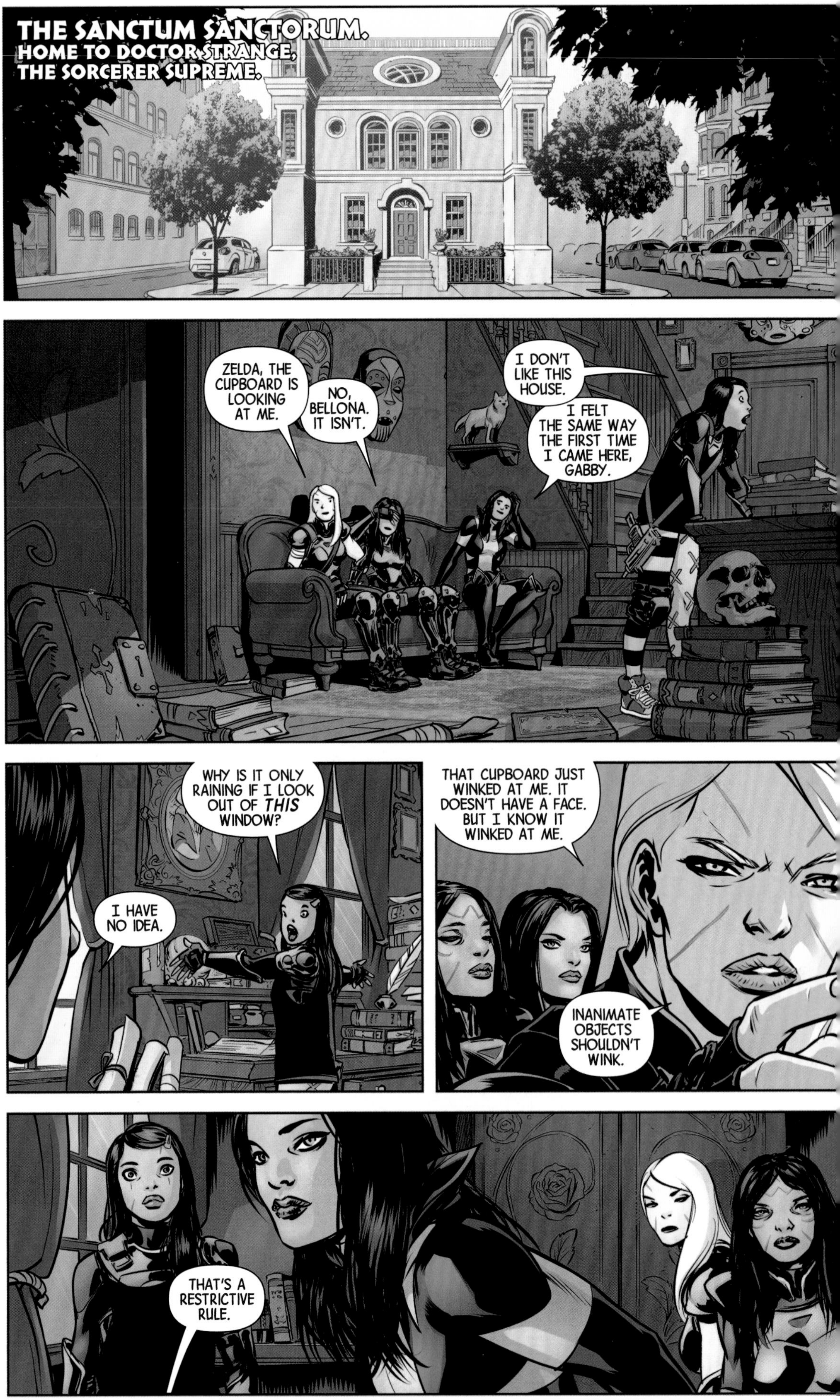
THE SANCTUM SANCTORUM.
HOME TO DOCTOR STRANGE, THE SORCERER SUPREME.
ZELDA, THE CUPBOARD IS LOOKING AT ME.
NO, BELLONA. IT ISN'T.
I DON'T LIKE THIS HOUSE.
I FELT THE SAME WAY THE FIRST TIME I CAME HERE, GABBY.
WHY IS IT ONLY RAINING IF I LOOK OUT OF *THIS* WINDOW?
I HAVE NO IDEA.
THAT CUPBOARD JUST WINKED AT ME. IT DOESN'T HAVE A FACE. BUT I KNOW IT WINKED AT ME.
INANIMATE OBJECTS SHOULDN'T WINK.
THAT'S A RESTRICTIVE RULE.

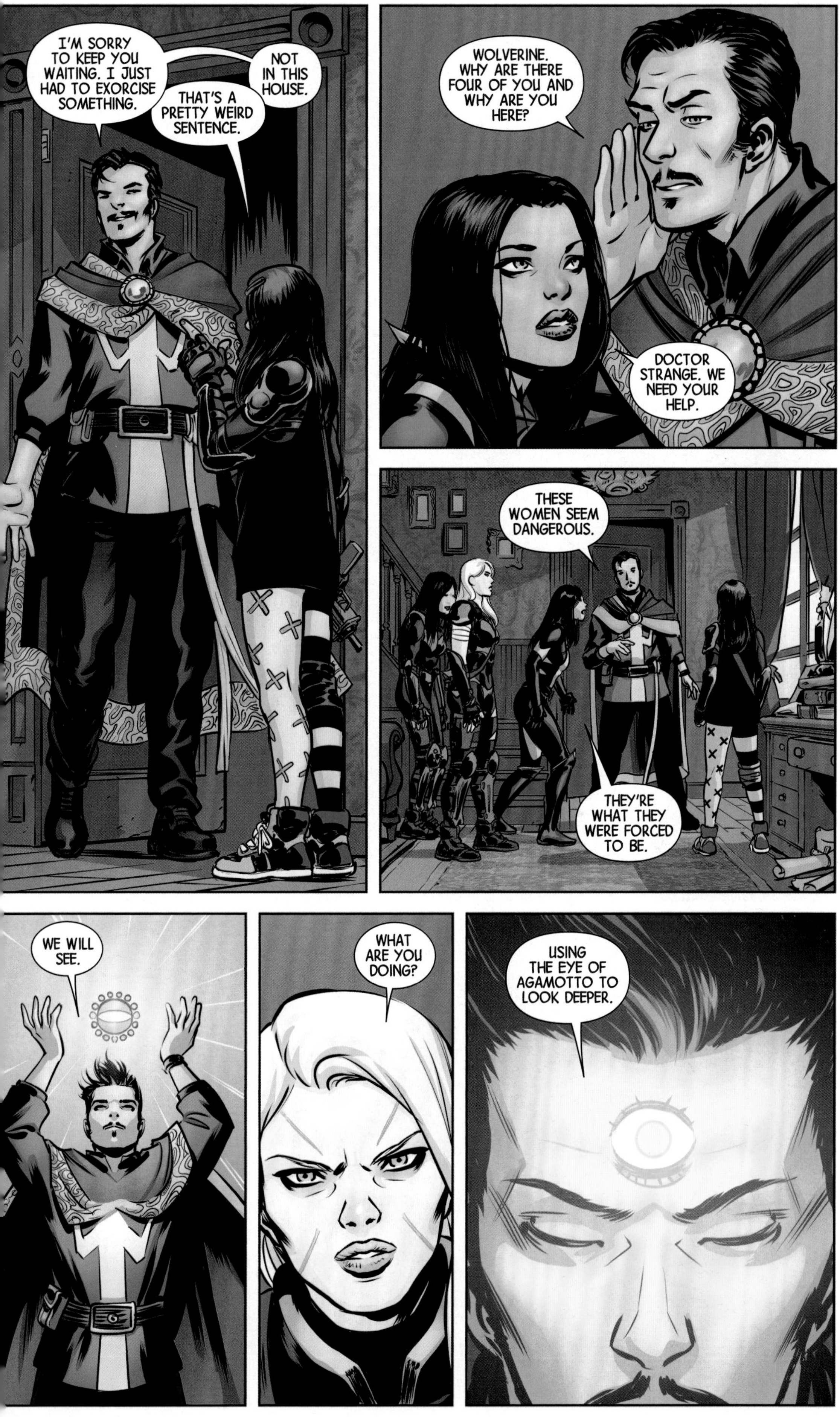
I'M SORRY TO KEEP YOU WAITING. I JUST HAD TO EXORCISE SOMETHING.
THAT'S A PRETTY WEIRD SENTENCE.
NOT IN THIS HOUSE.
WOLVERINE. WHY ARE THERE FOUR OF YOU AND WHY ARE YOU HERE?
DOCTOR STRANGE. WE NEED YOUR HELP.
THESE WOMEN SEEM DANGEROUS.
THEY'RE WHAT THEY WERE FORCED TO BE.
WE WILL SEE.
WHAT ARE YOU DOING?
USING THE EYE OF AGAMOTTO TO LOOK DEEPER.

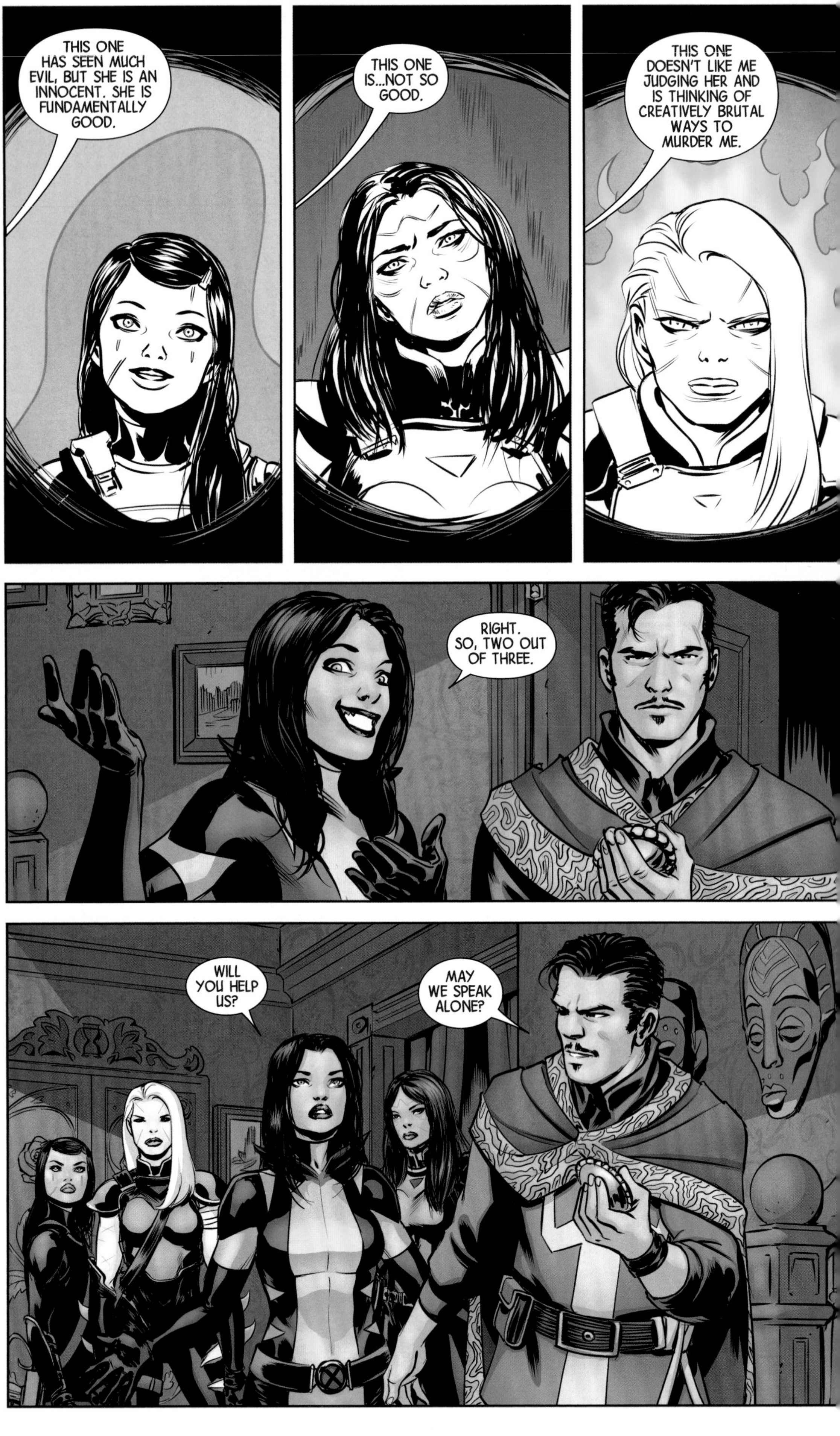
THIS ONE HAS SEEN MUCH EVIL, BUT SHE IS AN INNOCENT. SHE IS FUNDAMENTALLY GOOD.
THIS ONE IS...NOT SO GOOD.
THIS ONE DOESN'T LIKE ME JUDGING HER AND IS THINKING OF CREATIVELY BRUTAL WAYS TO MURDER ME.
RIGHT. SO, TWO OUT OF THREE.
WILL YOU HELP US?
MAY WE SPEAK ALONE?

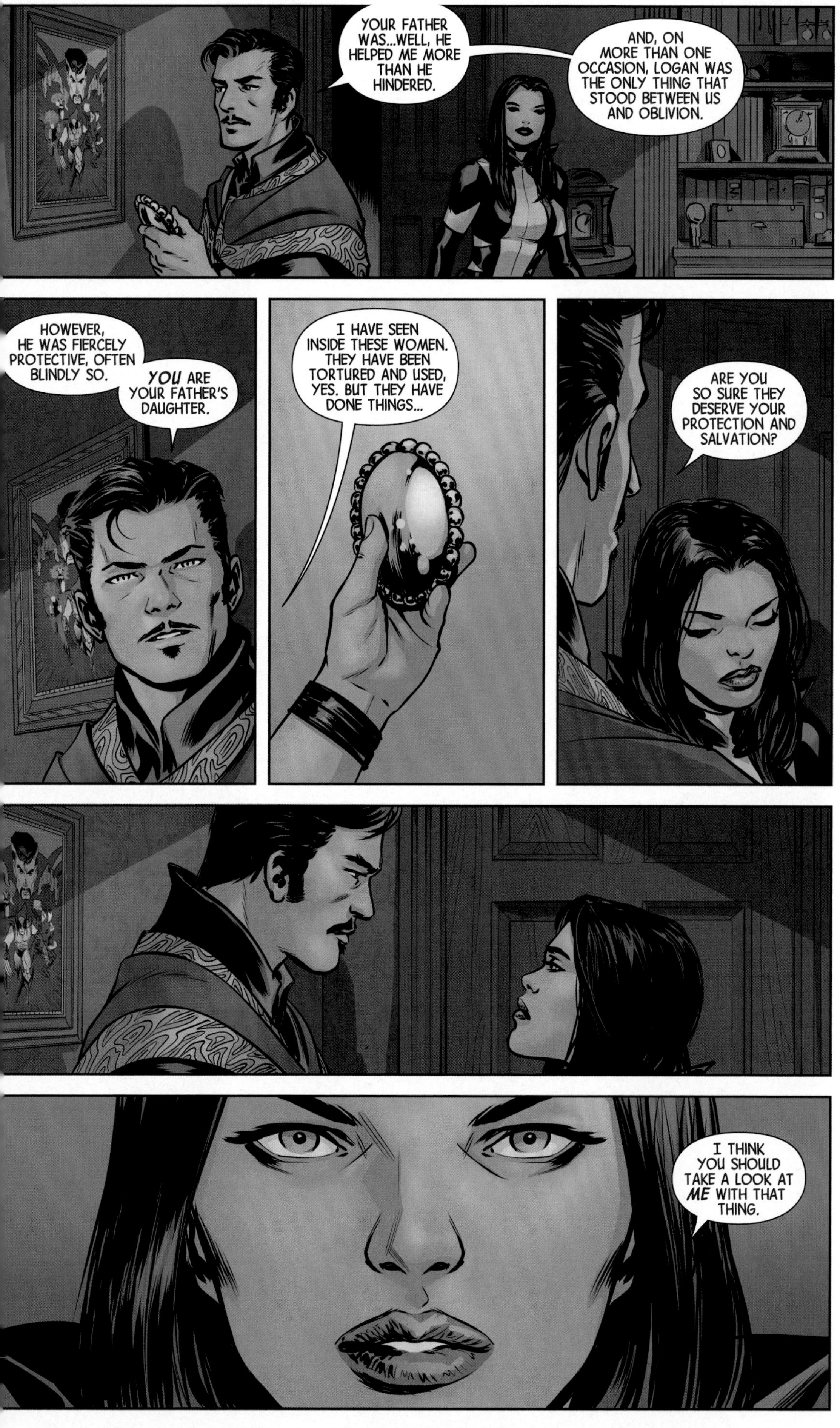
YOUR FATHER WAS...WELL, HE HELPED ME MORE THAN HE HINDERED.
AND, ON MORE THAN ONE OCCASION, LOGAN WAS THE ONLY THING THAT STOOD BETWEEN US AND OBLIVION.
HOWEVER, HE WAS FIERCELY PROTECTIVE, OFTEN BLINDLY SO.
YOU ARE YOUR FATHER'S DAUGHTER.
I HAVE SEEN INSIDE THESE WOMEN. THEY HAVE BEEN TORTURED AND USED, YES. BUT THEY HAVE DONE THINGS...
ARE YOU SO SURE THEY DESERVE YOUR PROTECTION AND SALVATION?
I THINK YOU SHOULD TAKE A LOOK AT *ME* WITH THAT THING.

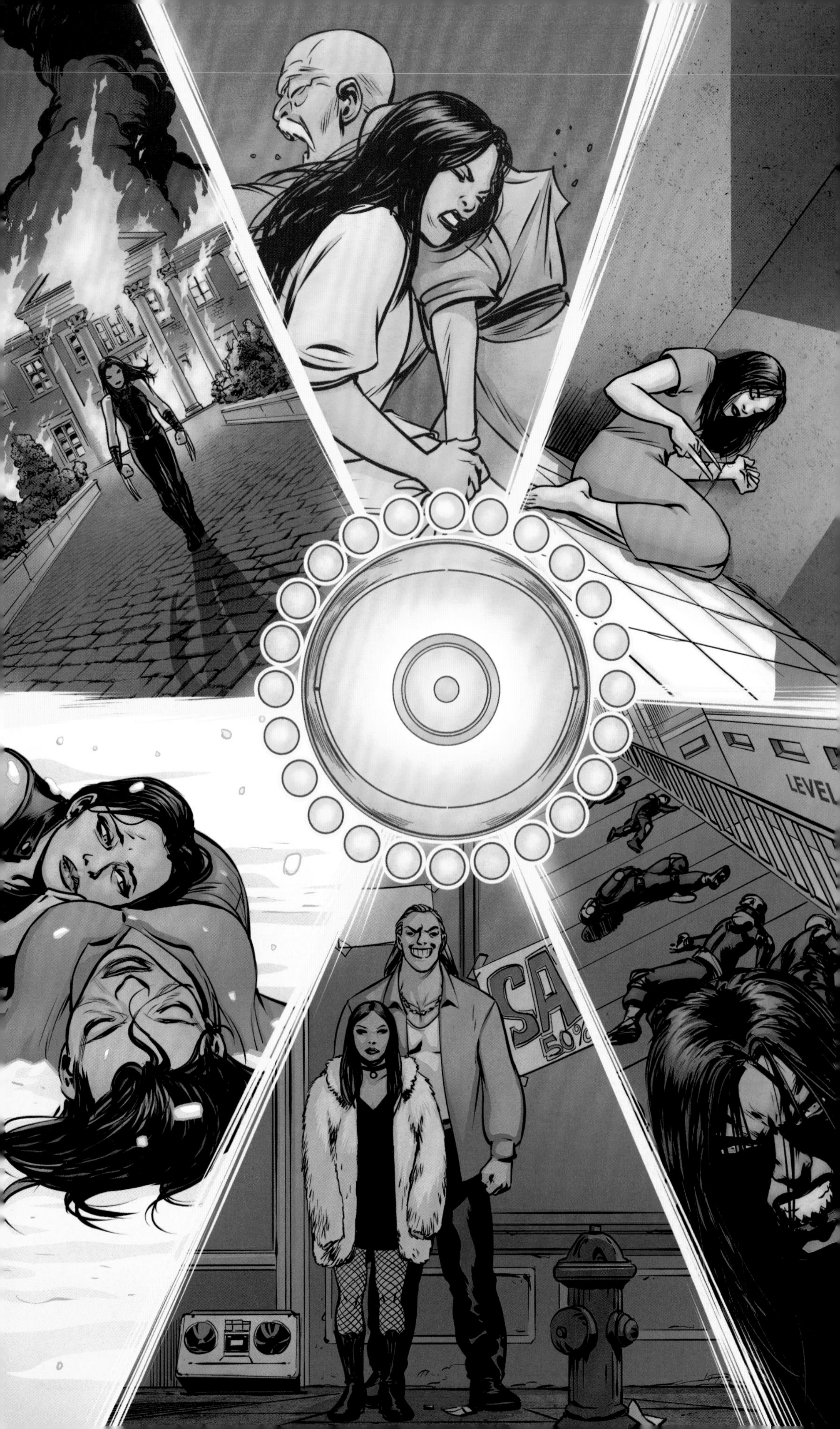
LEVEL
SA
50%

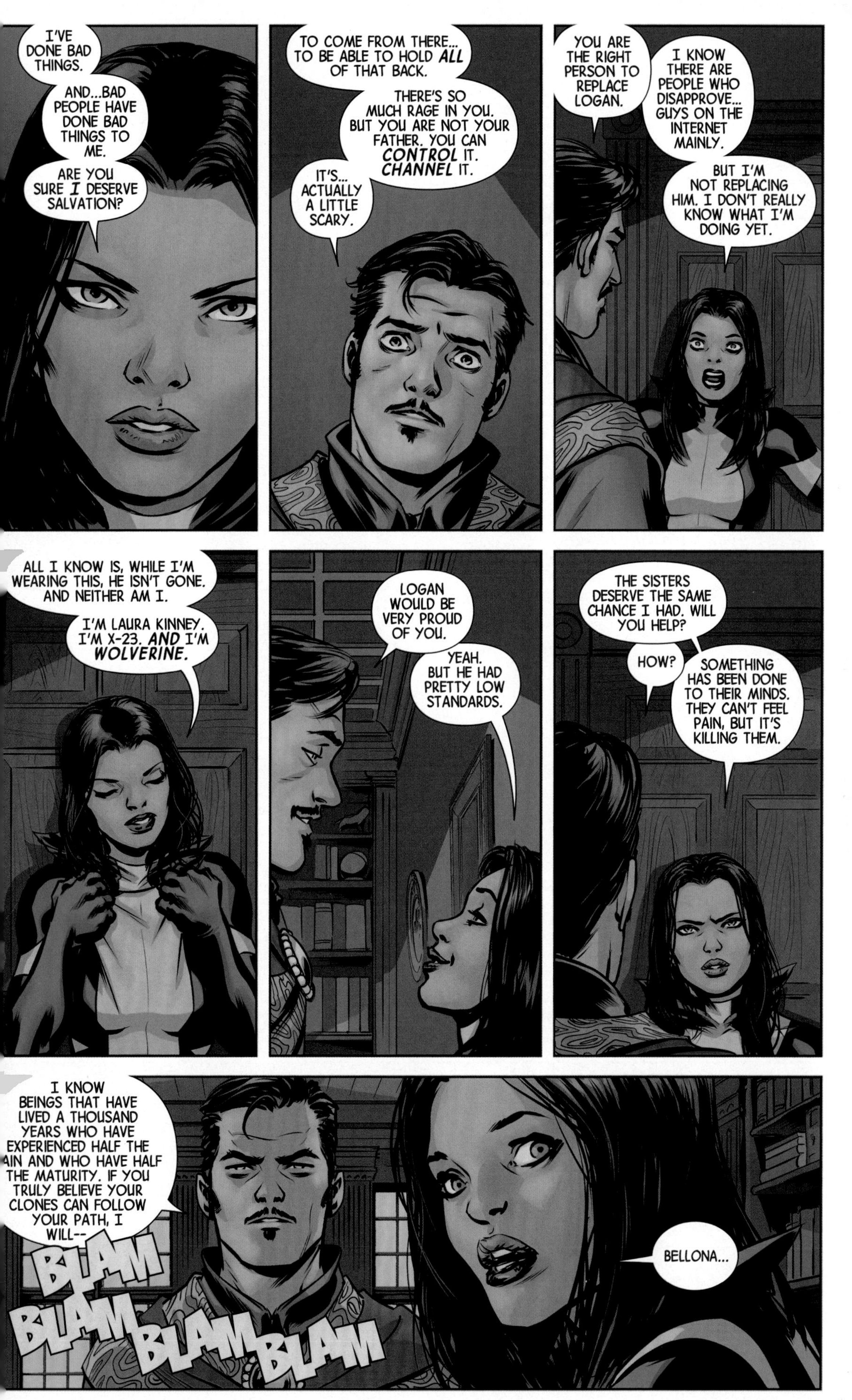

I'VE DONE BAD THINGS.
AND...BAD PEOPLE HAVE DONE BAD THINGS TO ME.
ARE YOU SURE *I* DESERVE SALVATION?
TO COME FROM THERE... TO BE ABLE TO HOLD *ALL* OF THAT BACK.
THERE'S SO MUCH RAGE IN YOU. BUT YOU ARE NOT YOUR FATHER. YOU CAN *CONTROL* IT. *CHANNEL* IT.
IT'S... ACTUALLY A LITTLE SCARY.
YOU ARE THE RIGHT PERSON TO REPLACE LOGAN.
I KNOW THERE ARE PEOPLE WHO DISAPPROVE... GUYS ON THE INTERNET MAINLY.
BUT I'M NOT REPLACING HIM. I DON'T REALLY KNOW WHAT I'M DOING YET.
ALL I KNOW IS, WHILE I'M WEARING THIS, HE ISN'T GONE. AND NEITHER AM I.
I'M LAURA KINNEY. I'M X-23. *AND* I'M *WOLVERINE.*
LOGAN WOULD BE VERY PROUD OF YOU.
YEAH. BUT HE HAD PRETTY LOW STANDARDS.
THE SISTERS DESERVE THE SAME CHANCE I HAD. WILL YOU HELP?
HOW?
SOMETHING HAS BEEN DONE TO THEIR MINDS. THEY CAN'T FEEL PAIN, BUT IT'S KILLING THEM.
I KNOW BEINGS THAT HAVE LIVED A THOUSAND YEARS WHO HAVE EXPERIENCED HALF THE AIN AND WHO HAVE HALF THE MATURITY. IF YOU TRULY BELIEVE YOUR CLONES CAN FOLLOW YOUR PATH, I WILL--
BLAM
BLAM BLAM BLAM
BELLONA...

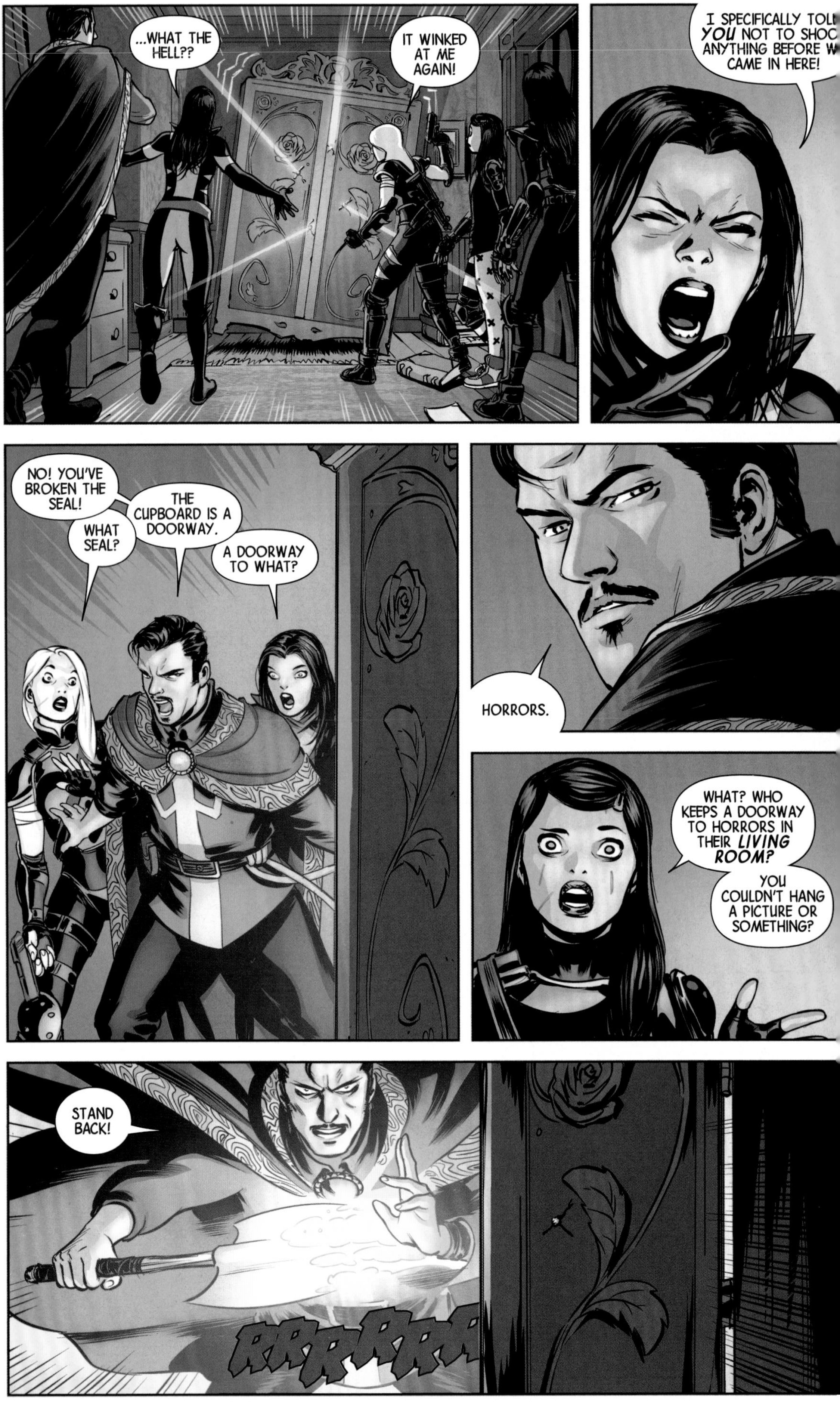

...WHAT THE HELL??
IT WINKED AT ME AGAIN!
I SPECIFICALLY TOL
YOU NOT TO SHOC
ANYTHING BEFORE W
CAME IN HERE!
NO! YOU'VE BROKEN THE SEAL!
WHAT SEAL?
THE CUPBOARD IS A DOORWAY.
A DOORWAY TO WHAT?
HORRORS.
WHAT? WHO KEEPS A DOORWAY TO HORRORS IN THEIR LIVING ROOM?
YOU COULDN'T HANG A PICTURE OR SOMETHING?
STAND BACK!
RRRRRRR

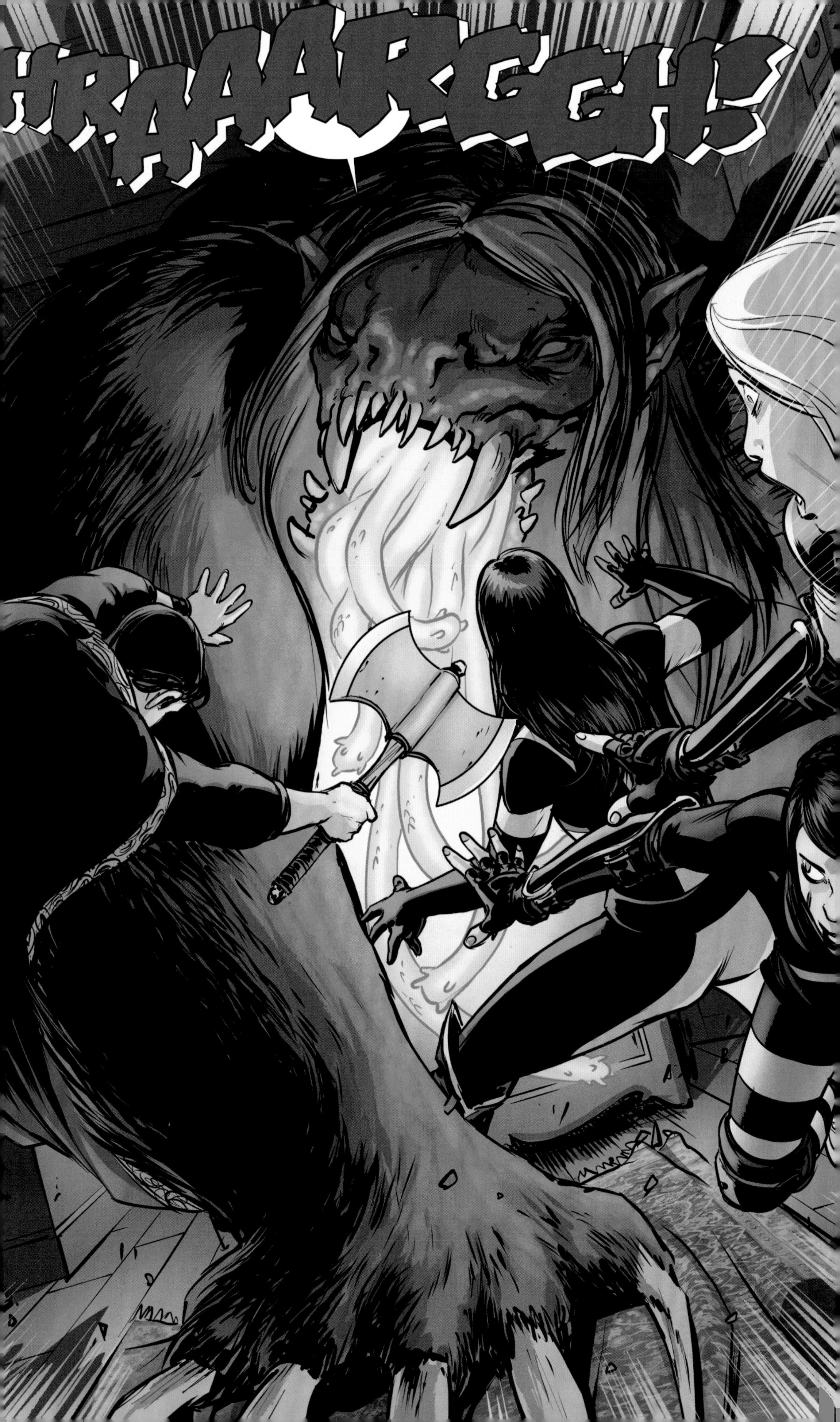
HRAAARGGH!

HNF!

THD

BLAM BLAM

AAAGHHH!

I HAVE TO CLOSE THE GATEWAY!

WHAT ABOUT THE CREATURE?

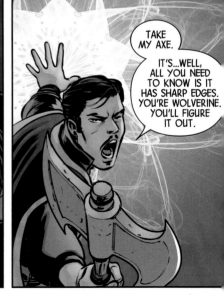

TAKE MY AXE.

IT'S...WELL, ALL YOU NEED TO KNOW IS IT HAS SHARP EDGES. YOU'RE WOLVERINE. YOU'LL FIGURE IT OUT.

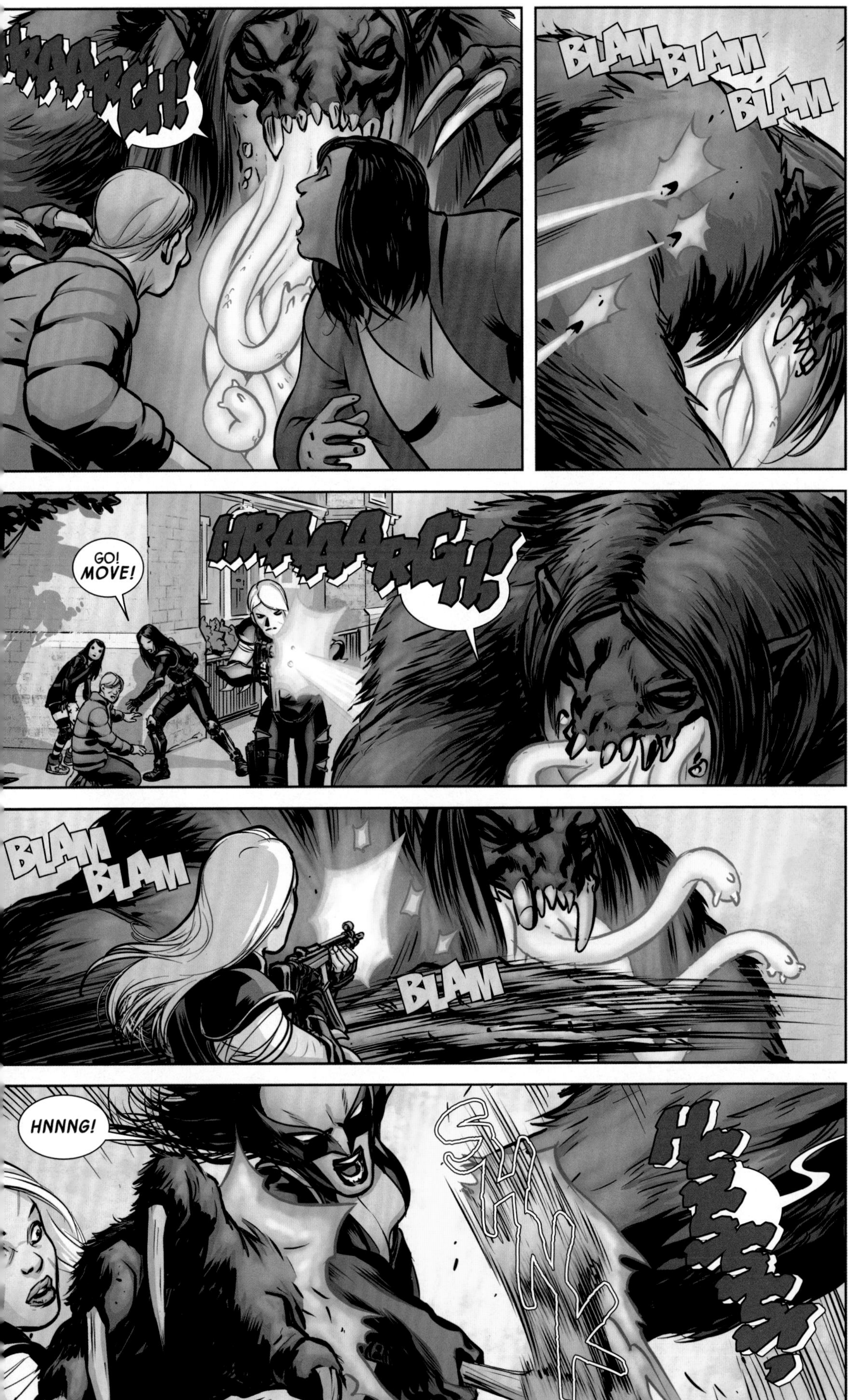
HRAAARGH!
BLAM BLAM BLAM
HRAAAARGH!
GO! MOVE!
BLAM BLAM
BLAM
HNNNG!
SHHNK!

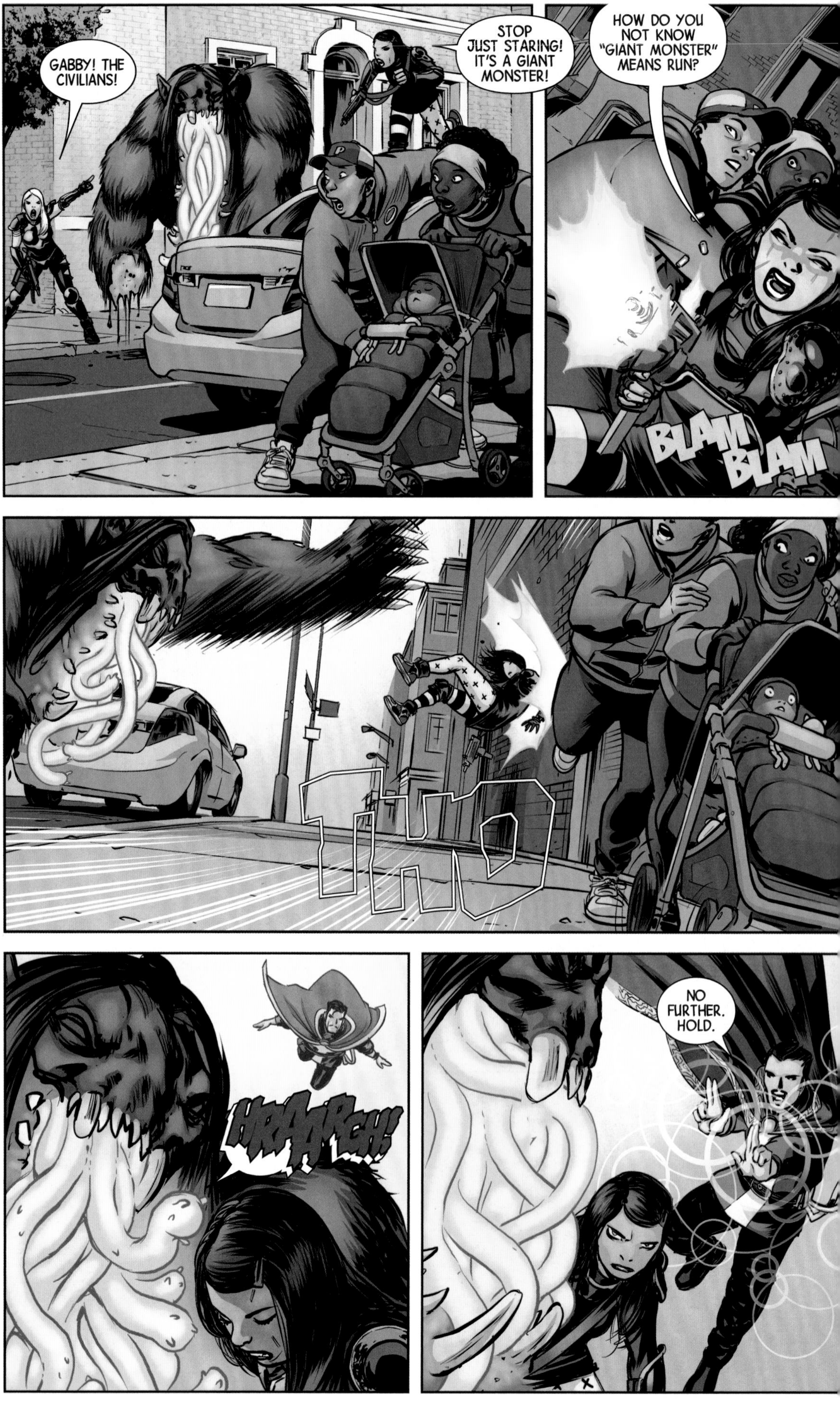
GABBY! THE CIVILIANS!
STOP JUST STARING! IT'S A GIANT MONSTER!
HOW DO YOU NOT KNOW "GIANT MONSTER" MEANS RUN?
BLAM
BLAM
THUD
HRAAARGH!
NO FURTHER. HOLD.

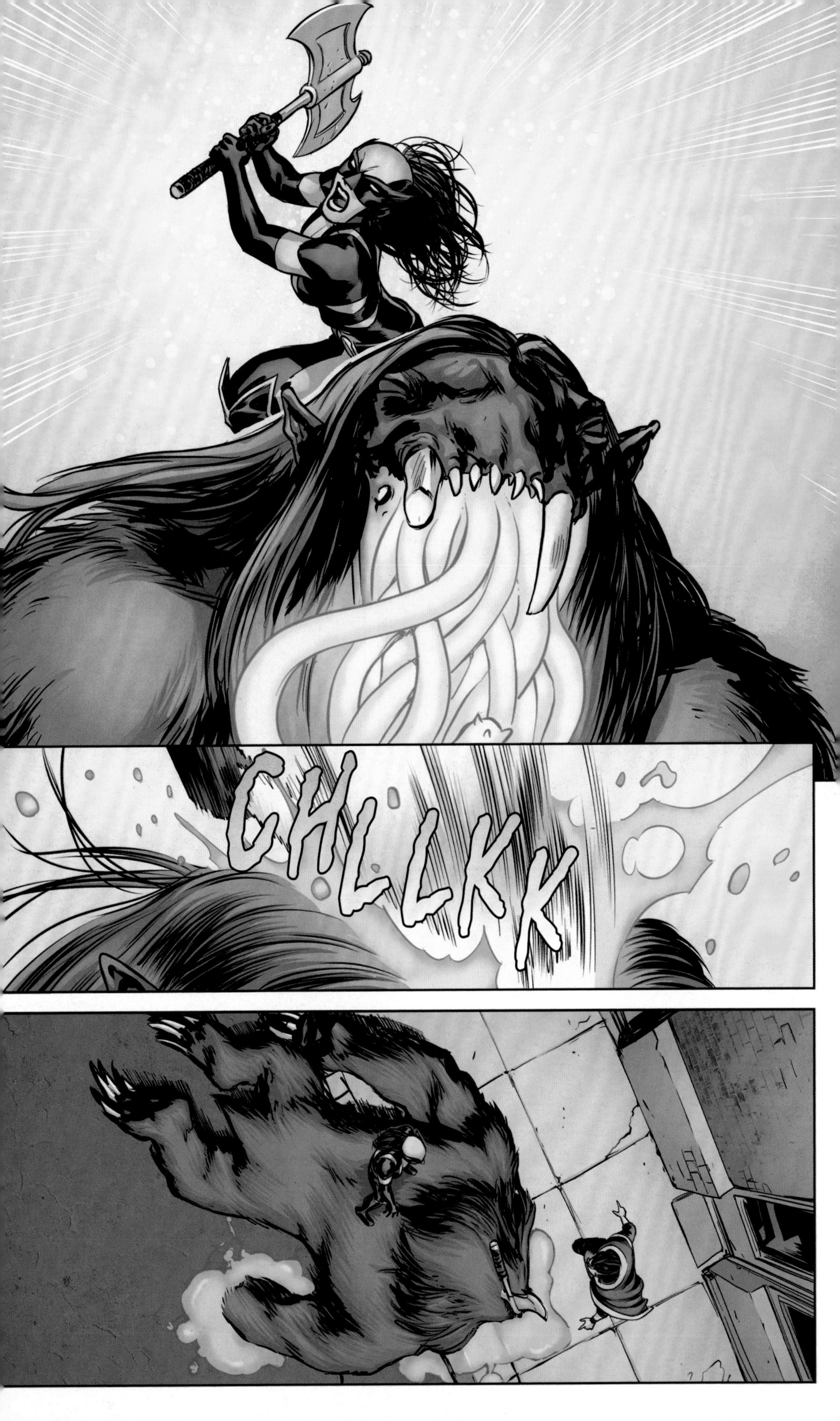
CHLLKK

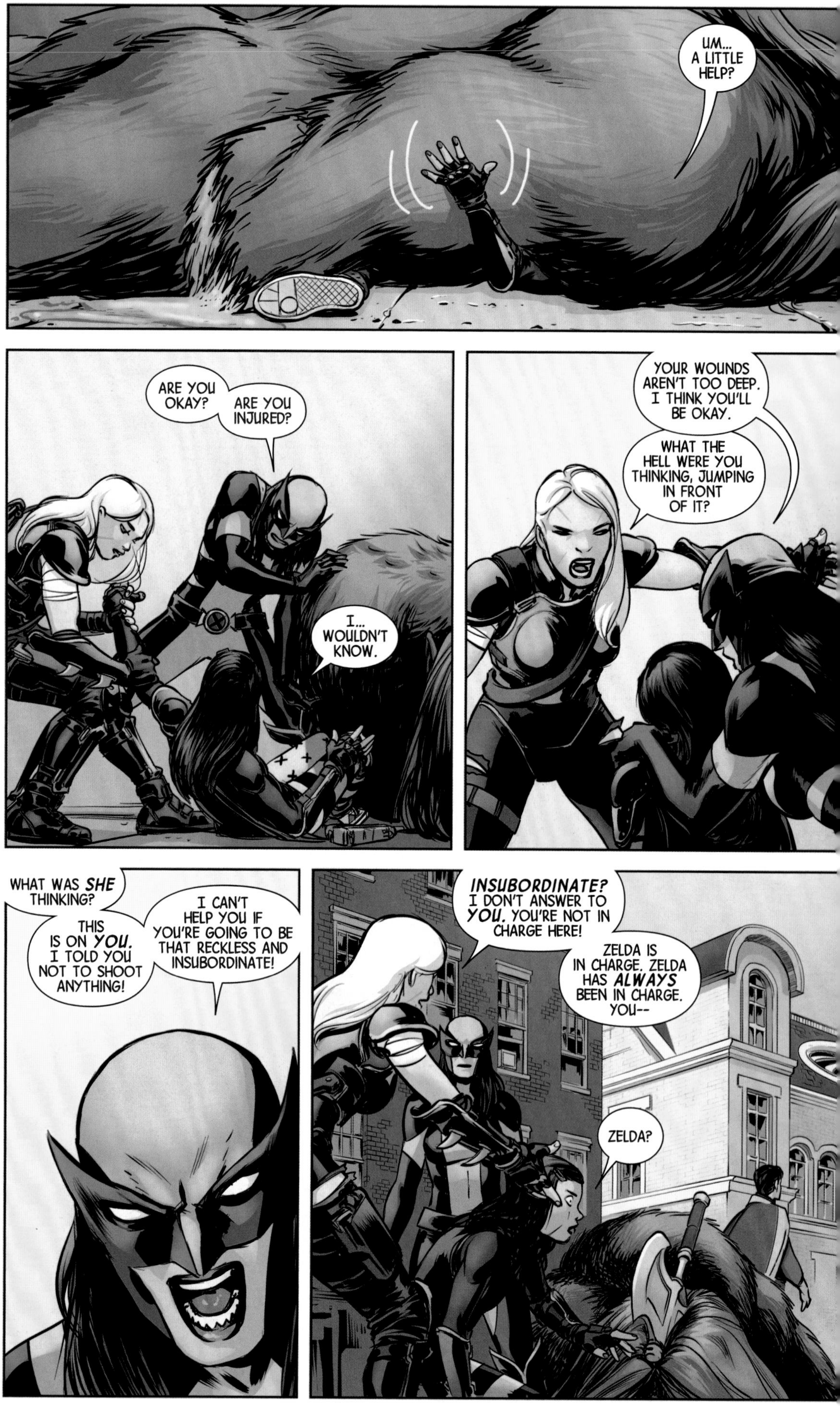
UM... A LITTLE HELP?
ARE YOU OKAY?
ARE YOU INJURED?
I... WOULDN'T KNOW.
YOUR WOUNDS AREN'T TOO DEEP. I THINK YOU'LL BE OKAY.
WHAT THE HELL WERE YOU THINKING, JUMPING IN FRONT OF IT?
WHAT WAS SHE THINKING?
THIS IS ON YOU. I TOLD YOU NOT TO SHOOT ANYTHING!
I CAN'T HELP YOU IF YOU'RE GOING TO BE THAT RECKLESS AND INSUBORDINATE!
INSUBORDINATE? I DON'T ANSWER TO YOU. YOU'RE NOT IN CHARGE HERE!
ZELDA IS IN CHARGE. ZELDA HAS ALWAYS BEEN IN CHARGE. YOU--
ZELDA?

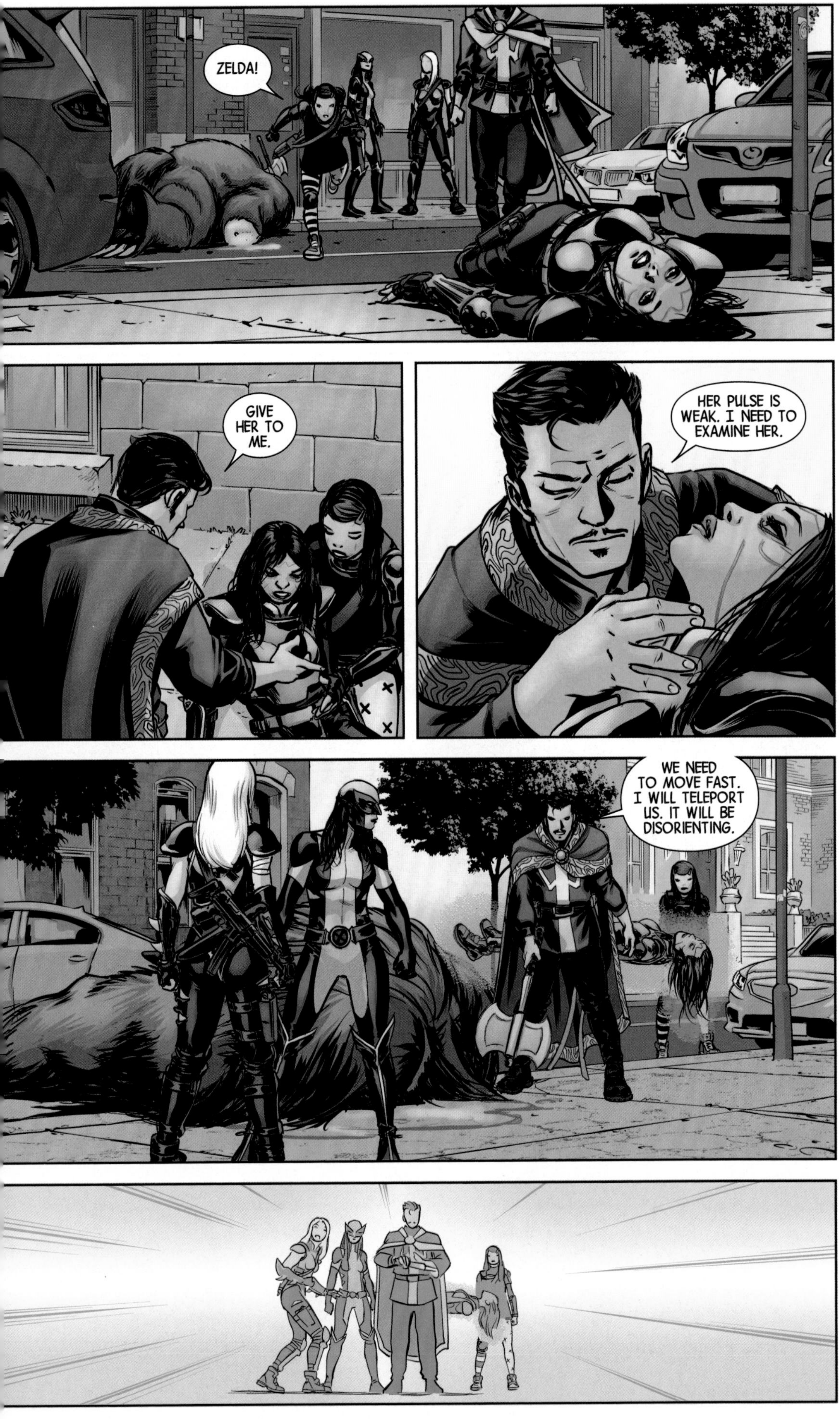
ZELDA!
GIVE HER TO ME.
HER PULSE IS WEAK. I NEED TO EXAMINE HER.
WE NEED TO MOVE FAST. I WILL TELEPORT US. IT WILL BE DISORIENTING.

WHERE ARE WE?

NEW YORK HOSPITAL. I USED TO WORK HERE.

PUT HER ON THE STRETCHER.

I NEED TO LOOK INSIDE HER HEAD *NOW*.

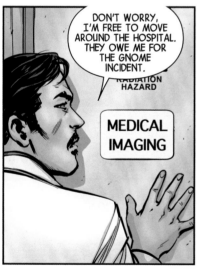

DON'T WORRY, I'M FREE TO MOVE AROUND THE HOSPITAL. THEY OWE ME FOR THE GNOME INCIDENT.

MEDICAL IMAGING

BUT YOU STAY OUT HERE.

I--

WOLVERINE BELIEVES IN YOU, AND I SAW YOU PROTECT PEOPLE. BUT YOU *ALSO* SHOT UP MY FURNITURE, SO THERE'S *NO WAY* I'M LETTING YOU IN A ROOM WITH THIS VERY EXPENSIVE EQUIPMENT.

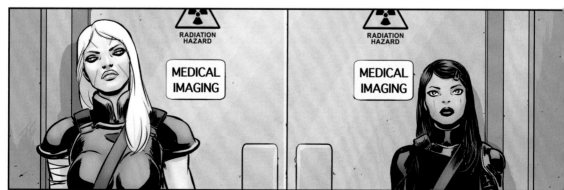

RADIATION HAZARD

MEDICAL IMAGING

RADIATION HAZARD

MEDICAL IMAGING

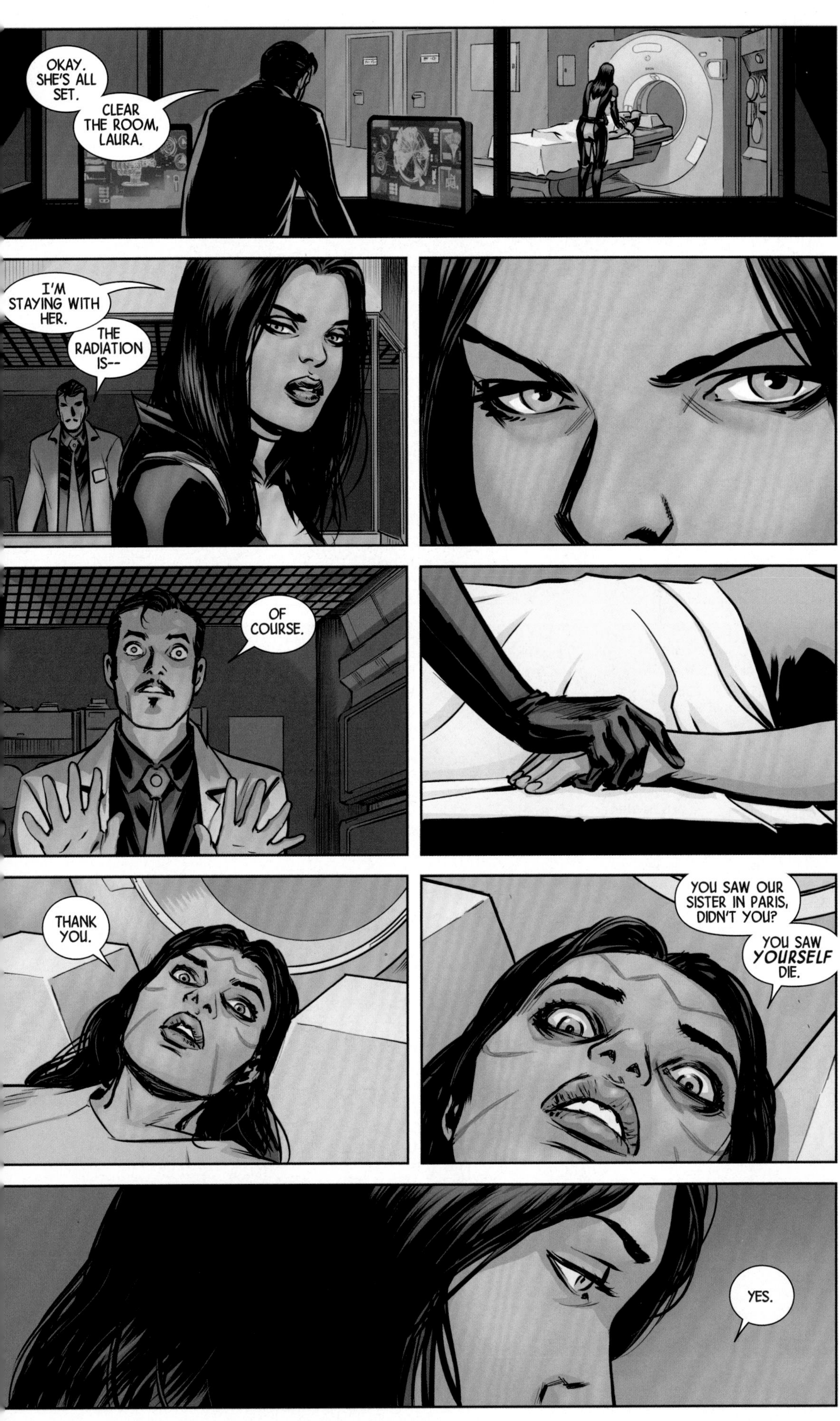
OKAY. SHE'S ALL SET.
CLEAR THE ROOM, LAURA.
I'M STAYING WITH HER.
THE RADIATION IS--
OF COURSE.
THANK YOU.
YOU SAW OUR SISTER IN PARIS, DIDN'T YOU?
YOU SAW *YOURSELF* DIE.
YES.

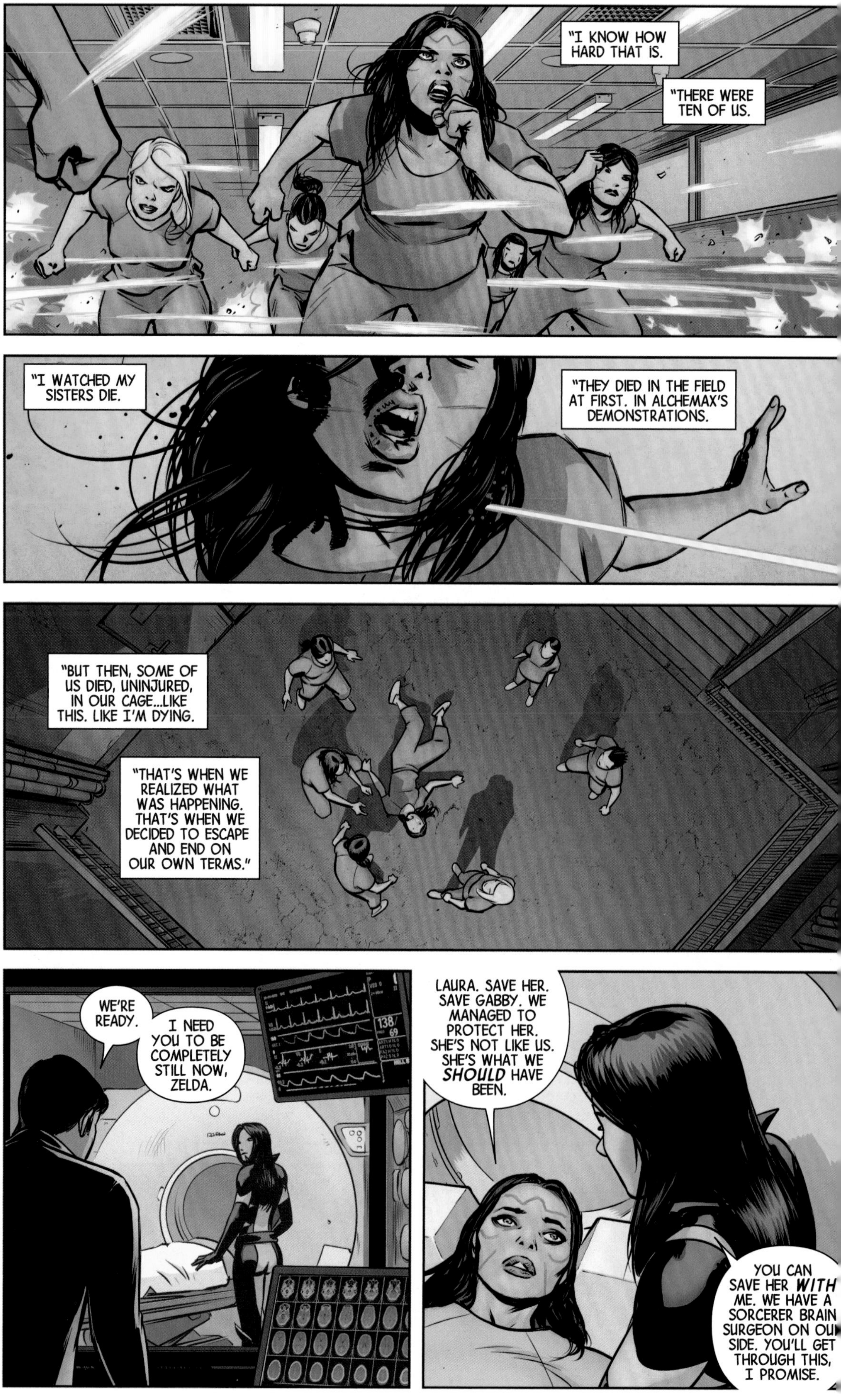
"I KNOW HOW HARD THAT IS.
"THERE WERE TEN OF US.
"I WATCHED MY SISTERS DIE.
"THEY DIED IN THE FIELD AT FIRST. IN ALCHEMAX'S DEMONSTRATIONS.
"BUT THEN, SOME OF US DIED, UNINJURED, IN OUR CAGE...LIKE THIS. LIKE I'M DYING.
"THAT'S WHEN WE REALIZED WHAT WAS HAPPENING. THAT'S WHEN WE DECIDED TO ESCAPE AND END ON OUR OWN TERMS."
WE'RE READY.
I NEED YOU TO BE COMPLETELY STILL NOW, ZELDA.
LAURA. SAVE HER. SAVE GABBY. WE MANAGED TO PROTECT HER. SHE'S NOT LIKE US. SHE'S WHAT WE SHOULD HAVE BEEN.
YOU CAN SAVE HER WITH ME. WE HAVE A SORCERER BRAIN SURGEON ON OU SIDE. YOU'LL GET THROUGH THIS, I PROMISE.

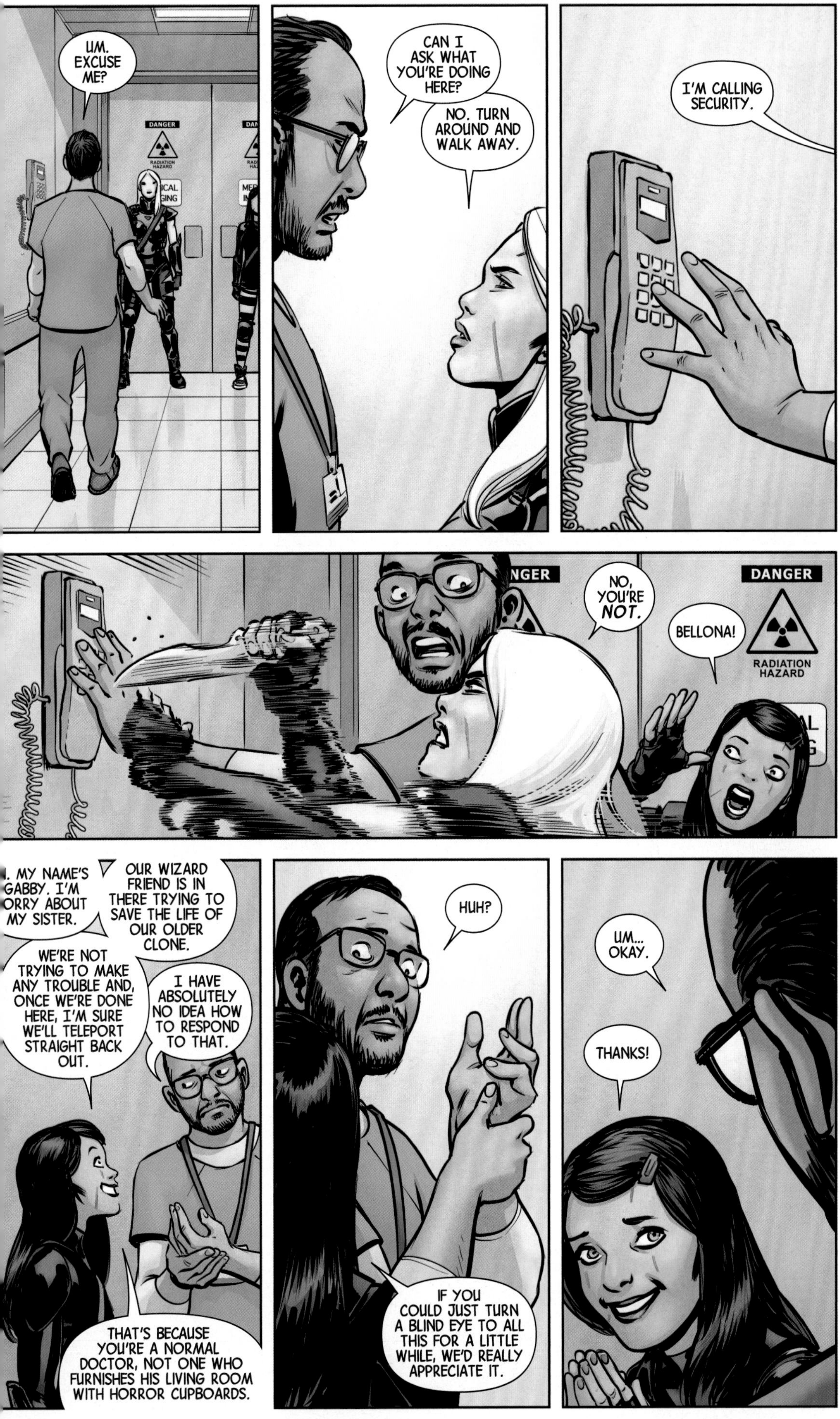
UM. EXCUSE ME?
CAN I ASK WHAT YOU'RE DOING HERE?
NO. TURN AROUND AND WALK AWAY.
I'M CALLING SECURITY.
DANGER
RADIATION HAZARD
NO, YOU'RE NOT.
BELLONA!
DANGER
RADIATION HAZARD
. MY NAME'S GABBY. I'M ORRY ABOUT MY SISTER.
OUR WIZARD FRIEND IS IN THERE TRYING TO SAVE THE LIFE OF OUR OLDER CLONE.
WE'RE NOT TRYING TO MAKE ANY TROUBLE AND, ONCE WE'RE DONE HERE, I'M SURE WE'LL TELEPORT STRAIGHT BACK OUT.
I HAVE ABSOLUTELY NO IDEA HOW TO RESPOND TO THAT.
THAT'S BECAUSE YOU'RE A NORMAL DOCTOR, NOT ONE WHO FURNISHES HIS LIVING ROOM WITH HORROR CUPBOARDS.
HUH?
IF YOU COULD JUST TURN A BLIND EYE TO ALL THIS FOR A LITTLE WHILE, WE'D REALLY APPRECIATE IT.
UM... OKAY.
THANKS!

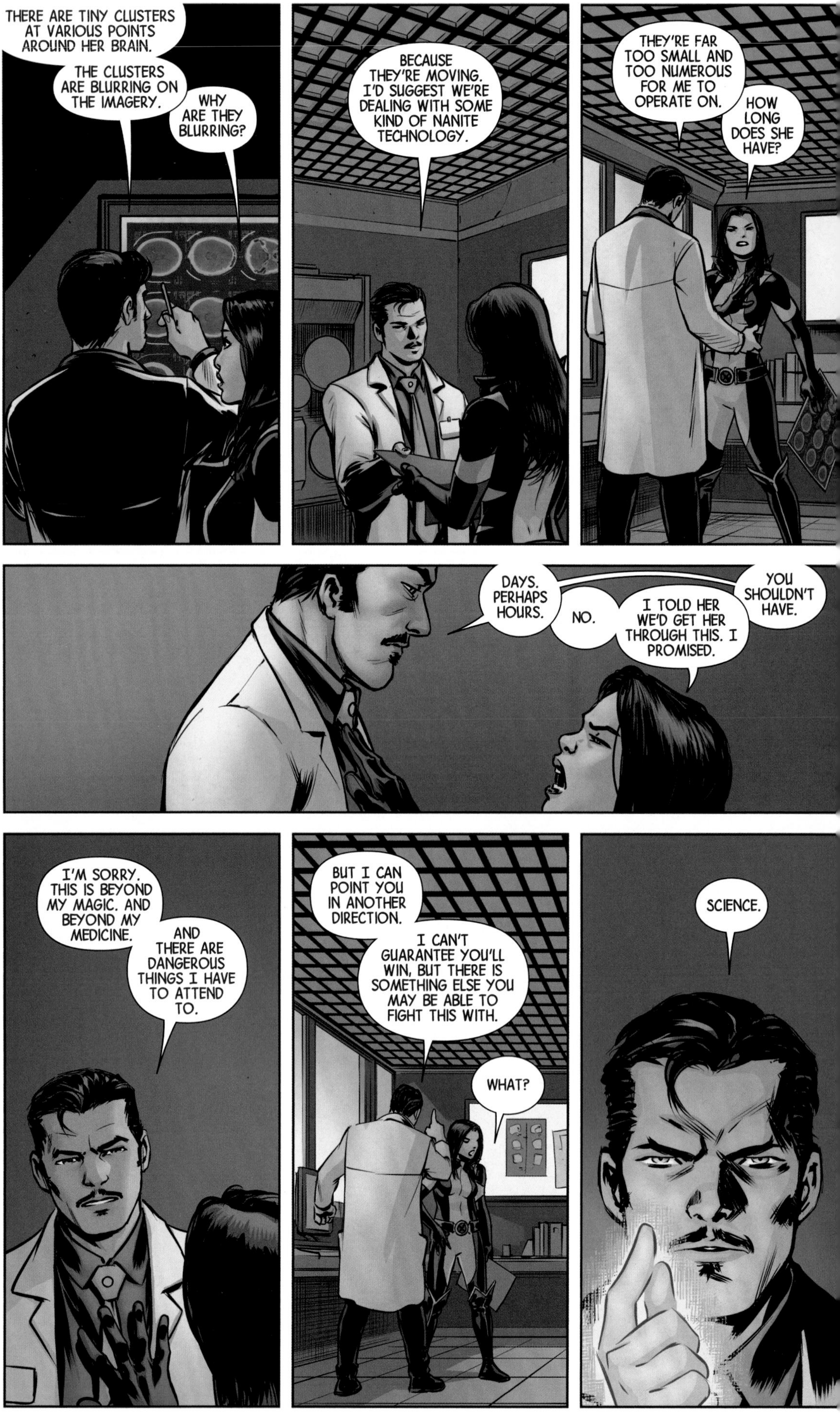
THERE ARE TINY CLUSTERS AT VARIOUS POINTS AROUND HER BRAIN.
THE CLUSTERS ARE BLURRING ON THE IMAGERY.
WHY ARE THEY BLURRING?
BECAUSE THEY'RE MOVING. I'D SUGGEST WE'RE DEALING WITH SOME KIND OF NANITE TECHNOLOGY.
THEY'RE FAR TOO SMALL AND TOO NUMEROUS FOR ME TO OPERATE ON.
HOW LONG DOES SHE HAVE?
DAYS. PERHAPS HOURS.
NO.
I TOLD HER WE'D GET HER THROUGH THIS. I PROMISED.
YOU SHOULDN'T HAVE.
I'M SORRY. THIS IS BEYOND MY MAGIC. AND BEYOND MY MEDICINE.
AND THERE ARE DANGEROUS THINGS I HAVE TO ATTEND TO.
BUT I CAN POINT YOU IN ANOTHER DIRECTION.
I CAN'T GUARANTEE YOU'LL WIN, BUT THERE IS SOMETHING ELSE YOU MAY BE ABLE TO FIGHT THIS WITH.
WHAT?
SCIENCE.

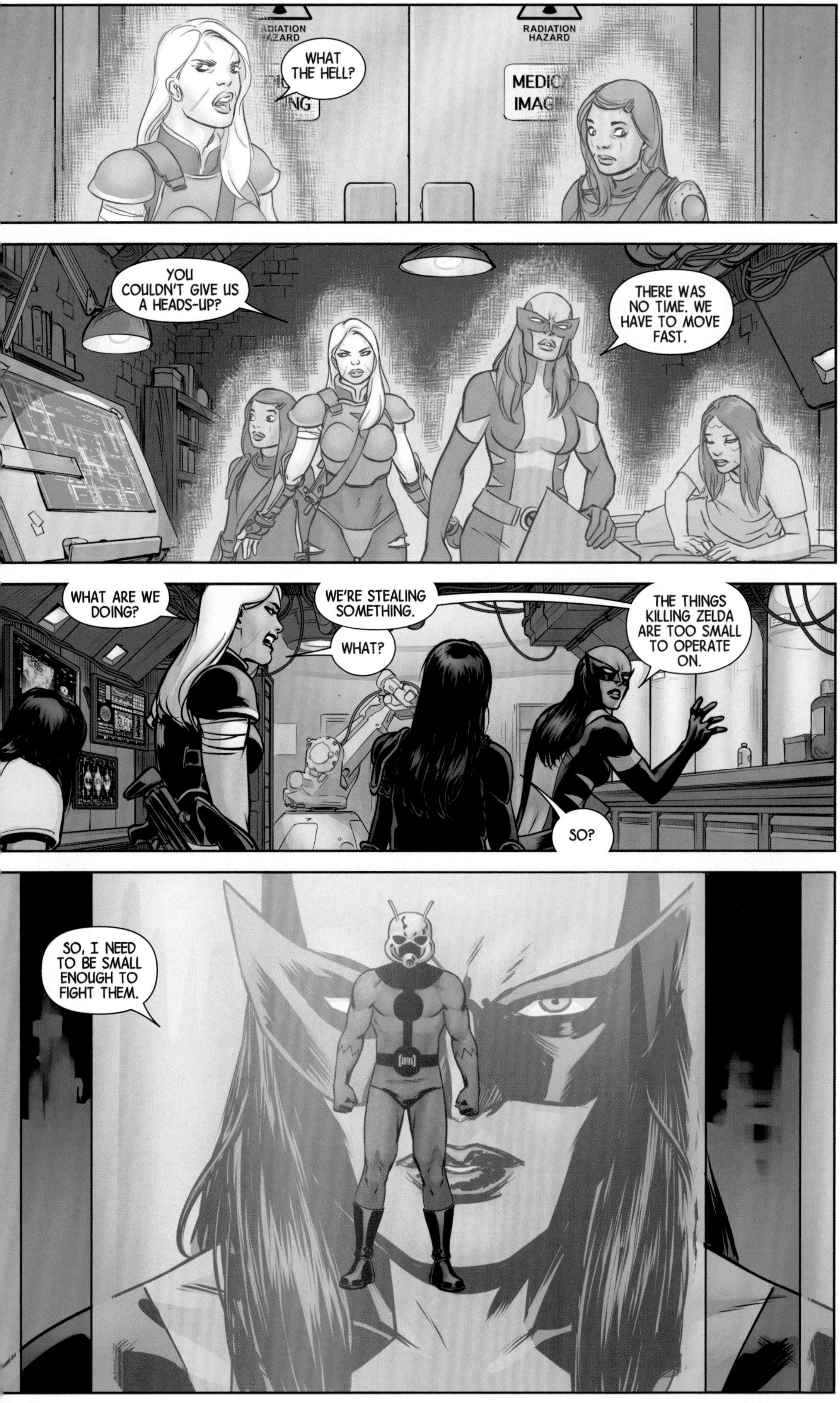
RADIATION HAZARD
RADIATION HAZARD
WHAT THE HELL?
MEDIC
IMAG
YOU COULDN'T GIVE US A HEADS-UP?
THERE WAS NO TIME. WE HAVE TO MOVE FAST.
WHAT ARE WE DOING?
WE'RE STEALING SOMETHING.
WHAT?
THE THINGS KILLING ZELDA ARE TOO SMALL TO OPERATE ON.
SO?
SO, I NEED TO BE SMALL ENOUGH TO FIGHT THEM.

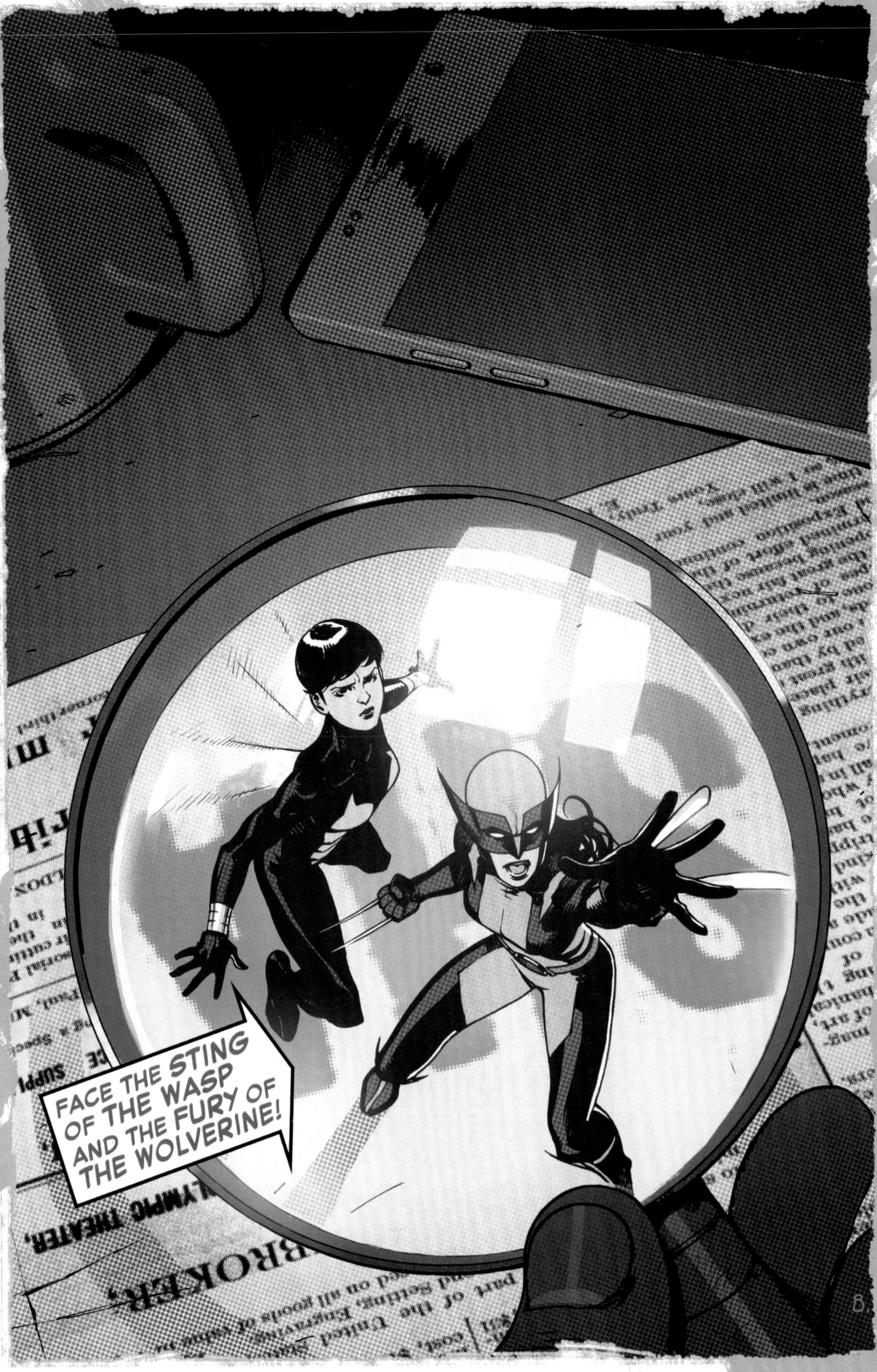
FACE THE STING OF THE WASP AND THE FURY OF THE WOLVERINE!

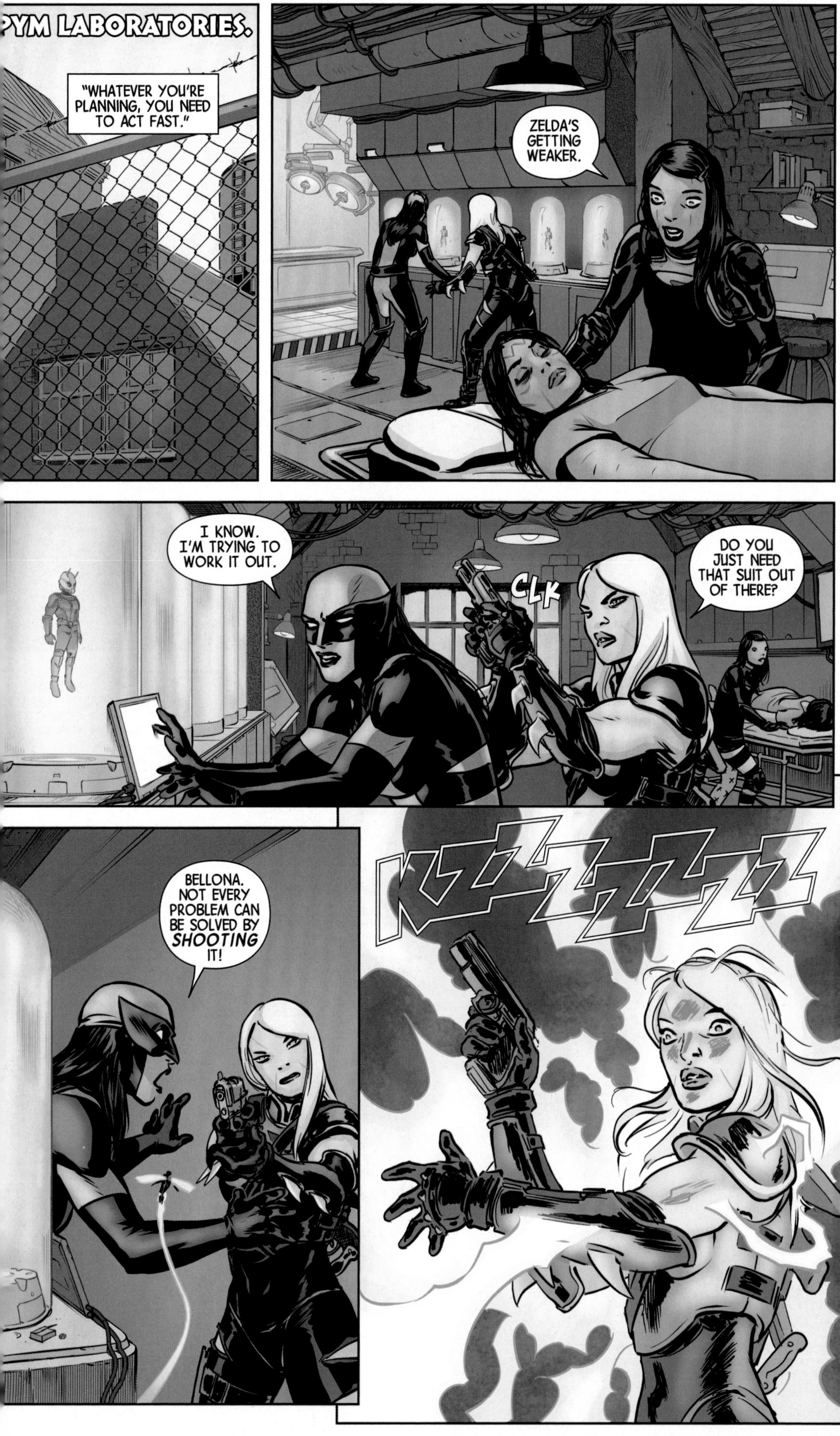

PYM LABORATORIES.
"WHATEVER YOU'RE PLANNING, YOU NEED TO ACT FAST."
ZELDA'S GETTING WEAKER.
I KNOW. I'M TRYING TO WORK IT OUT.
CLK
DO YOU JUST NEED THAT SUIT OUT OF THERE?
BELLONA. NOT EVERY PROBLEM CAN BE SOLVED BY SHOOTING IT!
KZZZZZZZ

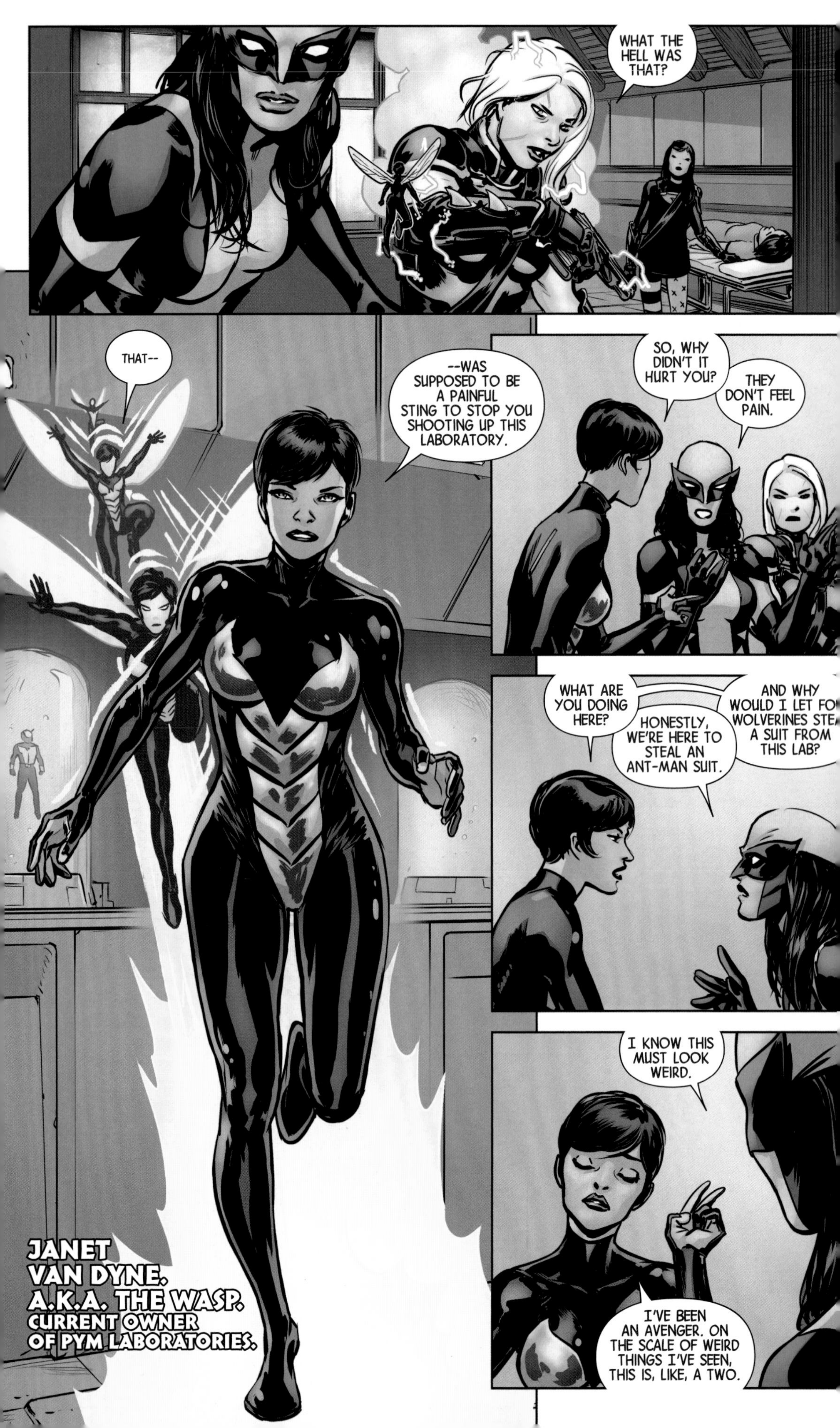
WHAT THE HELL WAS THAT?
THAT--
--WAS SUPPOSED TO BE A PAINFUL STING TO STOP YOU SHOOTING UP THIS LABORATORY.
JANET VAN DYNE. A.K.A. THE WASP. CURRENT OWNER OF PYM LABORATORIES.
SO, WHY DIDN'T IT HURT YOU?
THEY DON'T FEEL PAIN.
WHAT ARE YOU DOING HERE?
AND WHY WOULD I LET FO WOLVERINES STE A SUIT FROM THIS LAB?
HONESTLY, WE'RE HERE TO STEAL AN ANT-MAN SUIT.
I KNOW THIS MUST LOOK WEIRD.
I'VE BEEN AN AVENGER. ON THE SCALE OF WEIRD THINGS I'VE SEEN, THIS IS, LIKE, A TWO.

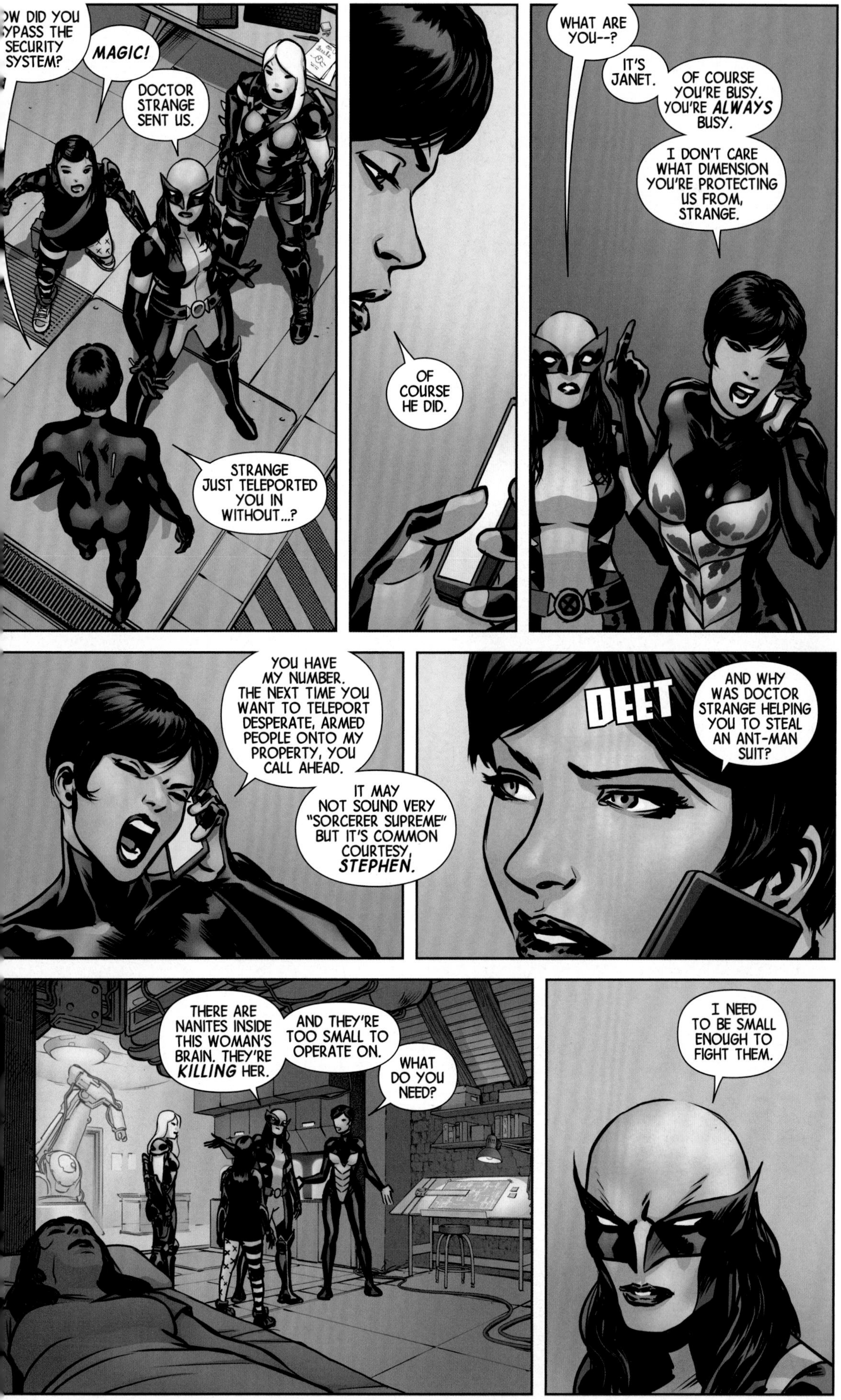

OW DID YOU YPASS THE SECURITY SYSTEM?
MAGIC!
DOCTOR STRANGE SENT US.
STRANGE JUST TELEPORTED YOU IN WITHOUT...?
OF COURSE HE DID.
WHAT ARE YOU--?
IT'S JANET.
OF COURSE YOU'RE BUSY. YOU'RE ALWAYS BUSY.
I DON'T CARE WHAT DIMENSION YOU'RE PROTECTING US FROM, STRANGE.
YOU HAVE MY NUMBER. THE NEXT TIME YOU WANT TO TELEPORT DESPERATE, ARMED PEOPLE ONTO MY PROPERTY, YOU CALL AHEAD.
IT MAY NOT SOUND VERY "SORCERER SUPREME" BUT IT'S COMMON COURTESY, STEPHEN.
DEET
AND WHY WAS DOCTOR STRANGE HELPING YOU TO STEAL AN ANT-MAN SUIT?
THERE ARE NANITES INSIDE THIS WOMAN'S BRAIN. THEY'RE KILLING HER.
AND THEY'RE TOO SMALL TO OPERATE ON.
WHAT DO YOU NEED?
I NEED TO BE SMALL ENOUGH TO FIGHT THEM.

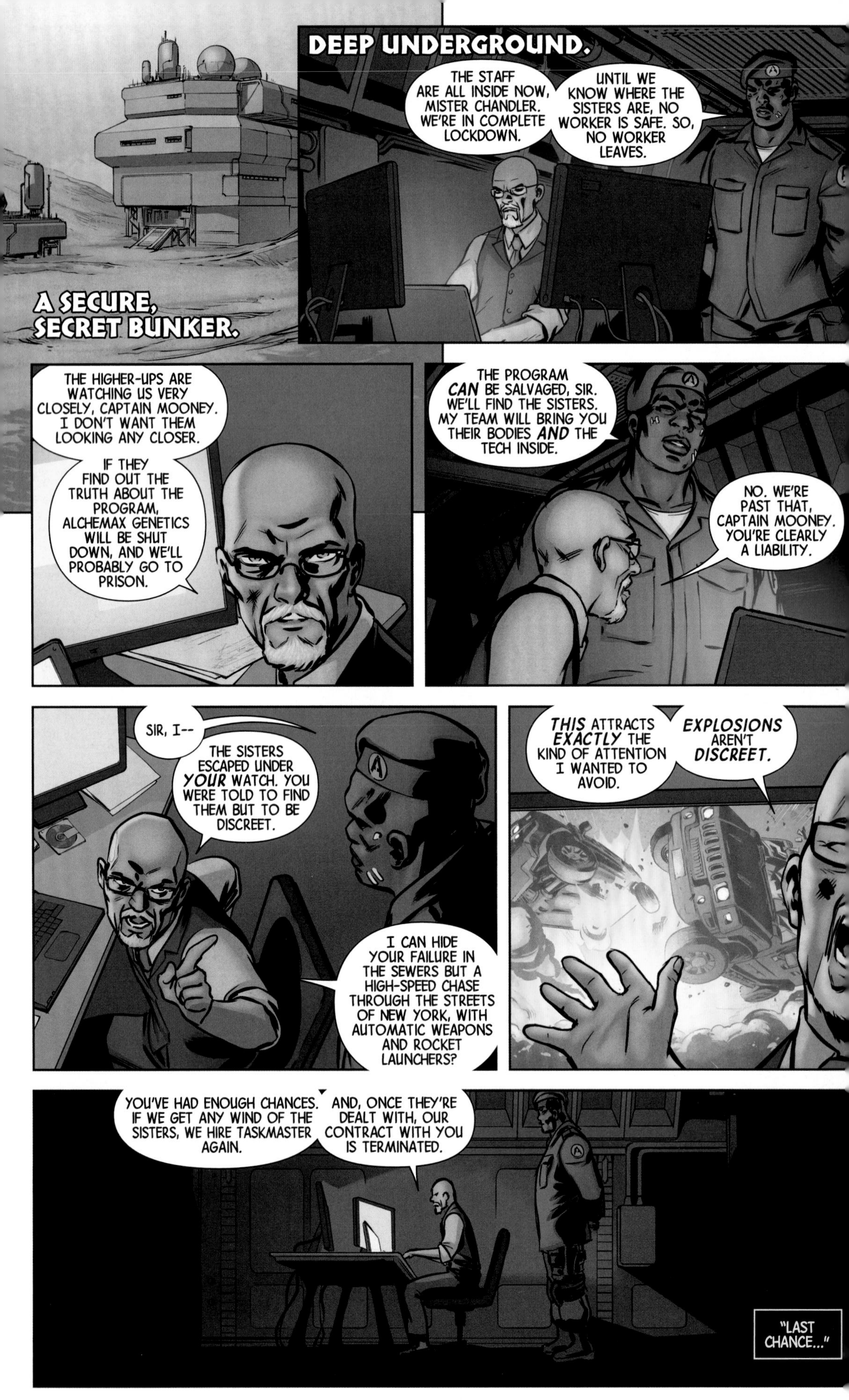
A SECURE, SECRET BUNKER.
DEEP UNDERGROUND.
THE STAFF ARE ALL INSIDE NOW, MISTER CHANDLER. WE'RE IN COMPLETE LOCKDOWN.
UNTIL WE KNOW WHERE THE SISTERS ARE, NO WORKER IS SAFE. SO, NO WORKER LEAVES.
THE HIGHER-UPS ARE WATCHING US VERY CLOSELY, CAPTAIN MOONEY. I DON'T WANT THEM LOOKING ANY CLOSER.
IF THEY FIND OUT THE TRUTH ABOUT THE PROGRAM, ALCHEMAX GENETICS WILL BE SHUT DOWN, AND WE'LL PROBABLY GO TO PRISON.
THE PROGRAM CAN BE SALVAGED, SIR. WE'LL FIND THE SISTERS. MY TEAM WILL BRING YOU THEIR BODIES AND THE TECH INSIDE.
NO. WE'RE PAST THAT, CAPTAIN MOONEY. YOU'RE CLEARLY A LIABILITY.
SIR, I--
THE SISTERS ESCAPED UNDER YOUR WATCH. YOU WERE TOLD TO FIND THEM BUT TO BE DISCREET.
I CAN HIDE YOUR FAILURE IN THE SEWERS BUT A HIGH-SPEED CHASE THROUGH THE STREETS OF NEW YORK, WITH AUTOMATIC WEAPONS AND ROCKET LAUNCHERS?
THIS ATTRACTS EXACTLY THE KIND OF ATTENTION I WANTED TO AVOID.
EXPLOSIONS AREN'T DISCREET.
YOU'VE HAD ENOUGH CHANCES. IF WE GET ANY WIND OF THE SISTERS, WE HIRE TASKMASTER AGAIN.
AND, ONCE THEY'RE DEALT WITH, OUR CONTRACT WITH YOU IS TERMINATED.
"LAST CHANCE..."

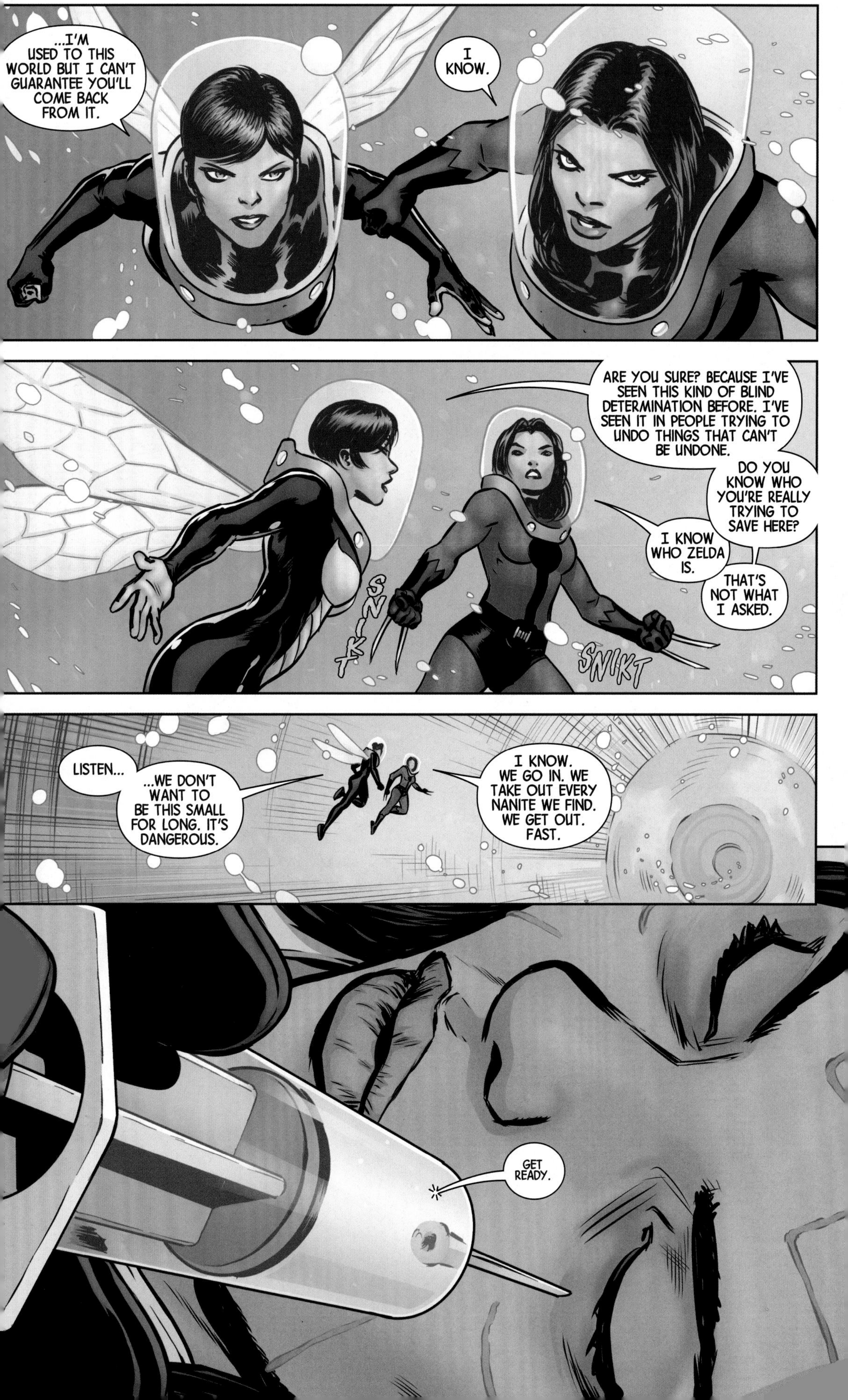
...I'M USED TO THIS WORLD BUT I CAN'T GUARANTEE YOU'LL COME BACK FROM IT.
I KNOW.
ARE YOU SURE? BECAUSE I'VE SEEN THIS KIND OF BLIND DETERMINATION BEFORE. I'VE SEEN IT IN PEOPLE TRYING TO UNDO THINGS THAT CAN'T BE UNDONE.
DO YOU KNOW WHO YOU'RE REALLY TRYING TO SAVE HERE?
I KNOW WHO ZELDA IS.
THAT'S NOT WHAT I ASKED.
SNIKT
SNIKT
LISTEN...
...WE DON'T WANT TO BE THIS SMALL FOR LONG. IT'S DANGEROUS.
I KNOW. WE GO IN. WE TAKE OUT EVERY NANITE WE FIND. WE GET OUT. FAST.
GET READY.

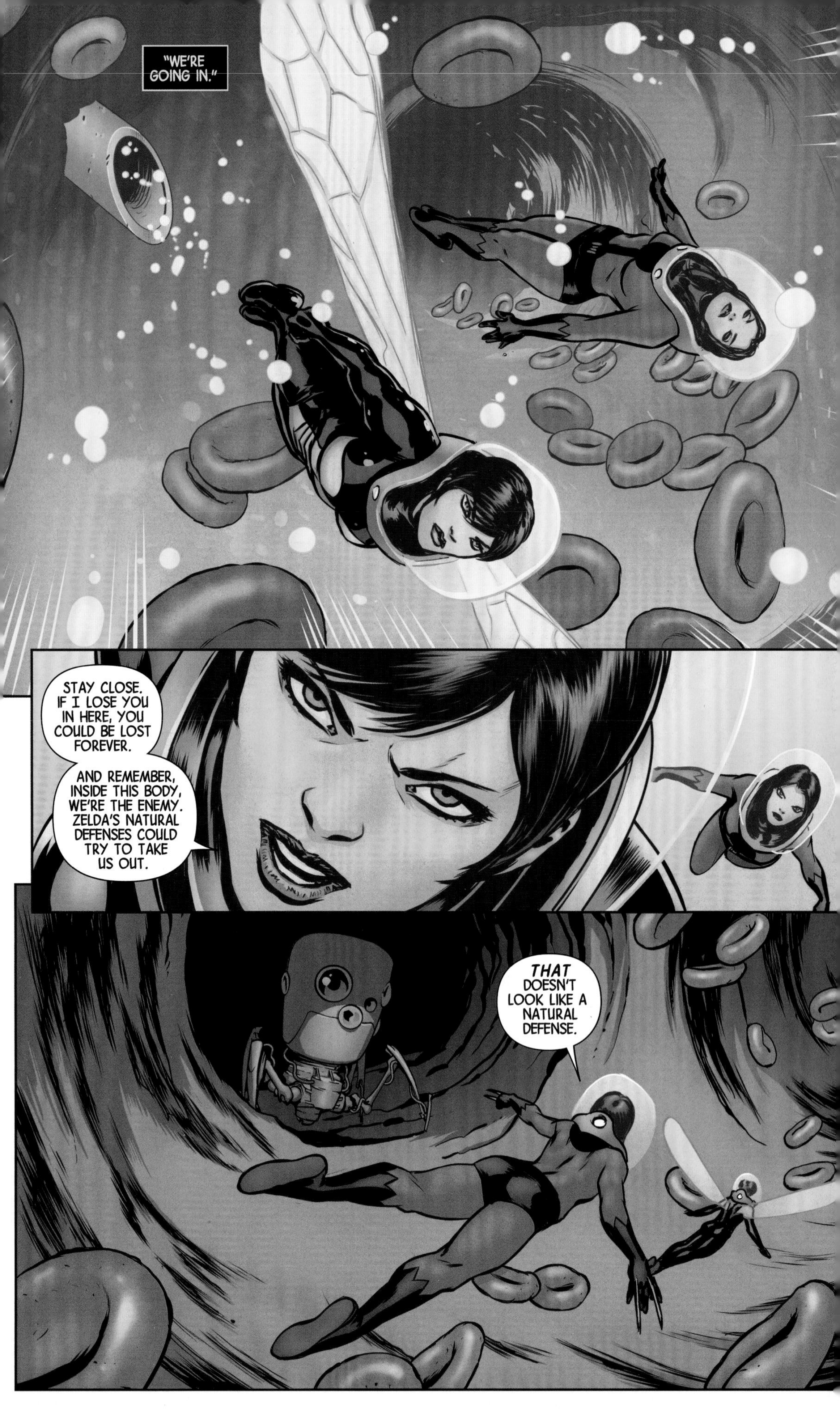
"WE'RE GOING IN."
STAY CLOSE. IF I LOSE YOU IN HERE, YOU COULD BE LOST FOREVER.
AND REMEMBER, INSIDE THIS BODY, WE'RE THE ENEMY. ZELDA'S NATURAL DEFENSES COULD TRY TO TAKE US OUT.
THAT DOESN'T LOOK LIKE A NATURAL DEFENSE.

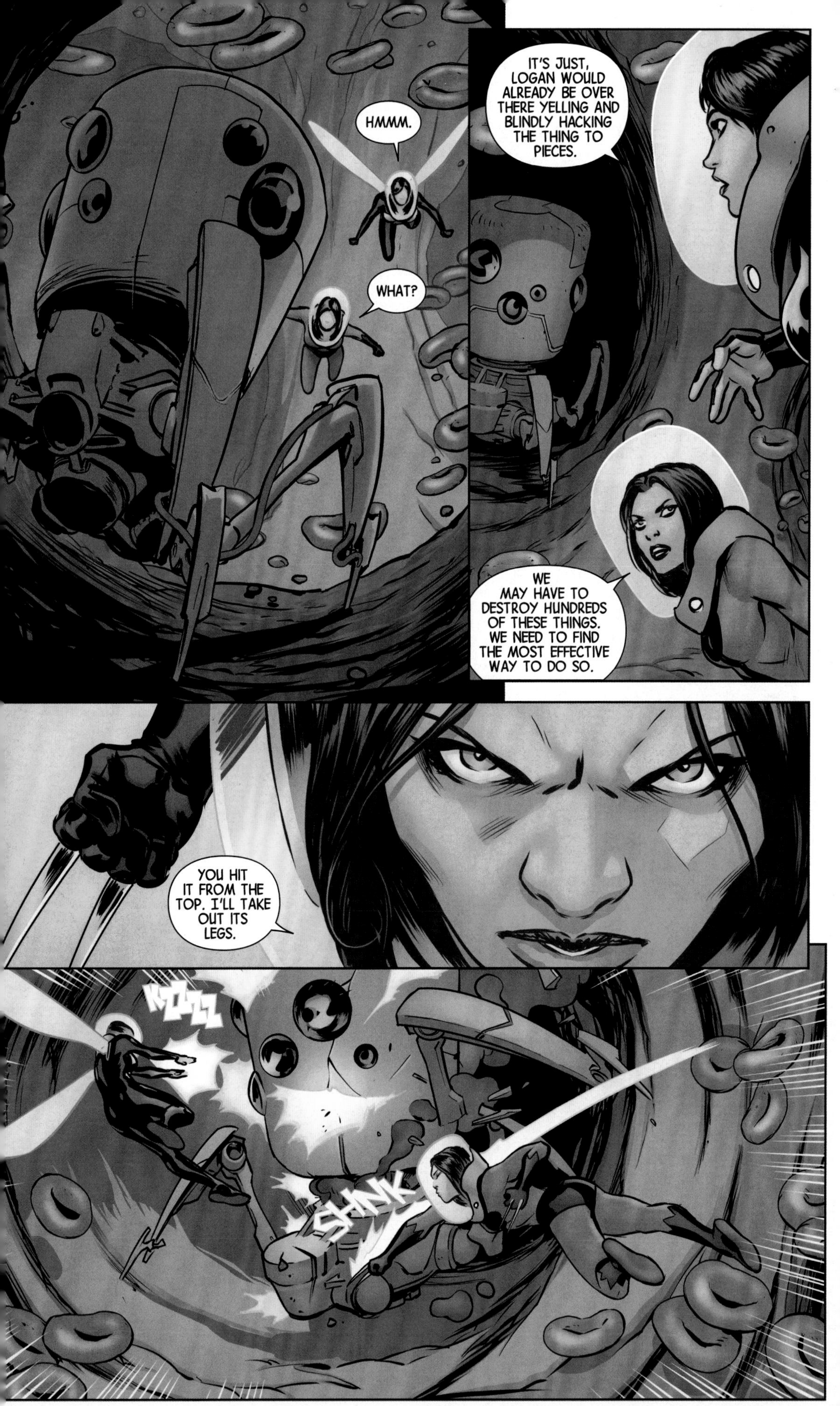
HMMM.
WHAT?
IT'S JUST, LOGAN WOULD ALREADY BE OVER THERE YELLING AND BLINDLY HACKING THE THING TO PIECES.
WE MAY HAVE TO DESTROY HUNDREDS OF THESE THINGS. WE NEED TO FIND THE MOST EFFECTIVE WAY TO DO SO.
YOU HIT IT FROM THE TOP. I'LL TAKE OUT ITS LEGS.
KZZZZ
SHNK

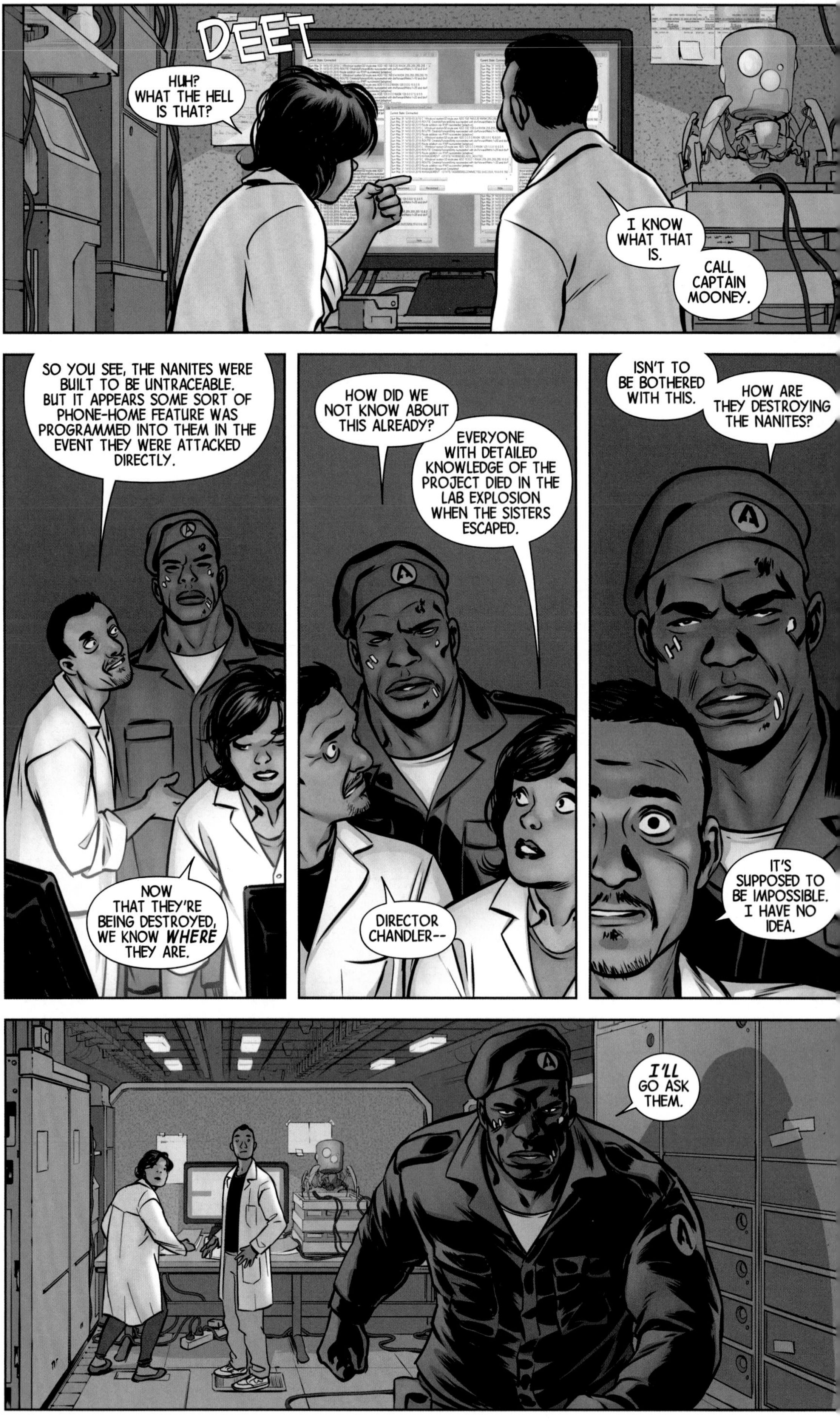
DEET
HUH? WHAT THE HELL IS THAT?
I KNOW WHAT THAT IS.
CALL CAPTAIN MOONEY.
SO YOU SEE, THE NANITES WERE BUILT TO BE UNTRACEABLE. BUT IT APPEARS SOME SORT OF PHONE-HOME FEATURE WAS PROGRAMMED INTO THEM IN THE EVENT THEY WERE ATTACKED DIRECTLY.
NOW THAT THEY'RE BEING DESTROYED, WE KNOW *WHERE* THEY ARE.
HOW DID WE NOT KNOW ABOUT THIS ALREADY?
EVERYONE WITH DETAILED KNOWLEDGE OF THE PROJECT DIED IN THE LAB EXPLOSION WHEN THE SISTERS ESCAPED.
DIRECTOR CHANDLER--
ISN'T TO BE BOTHERED WITH THIS.
HOW ARE THEY DESTROYING THE NANITES?
IT'S SUPPOSED TO BE IMPOSSIBLE. I HAVE NO IDEA.
I'LL GO ASK THEM.

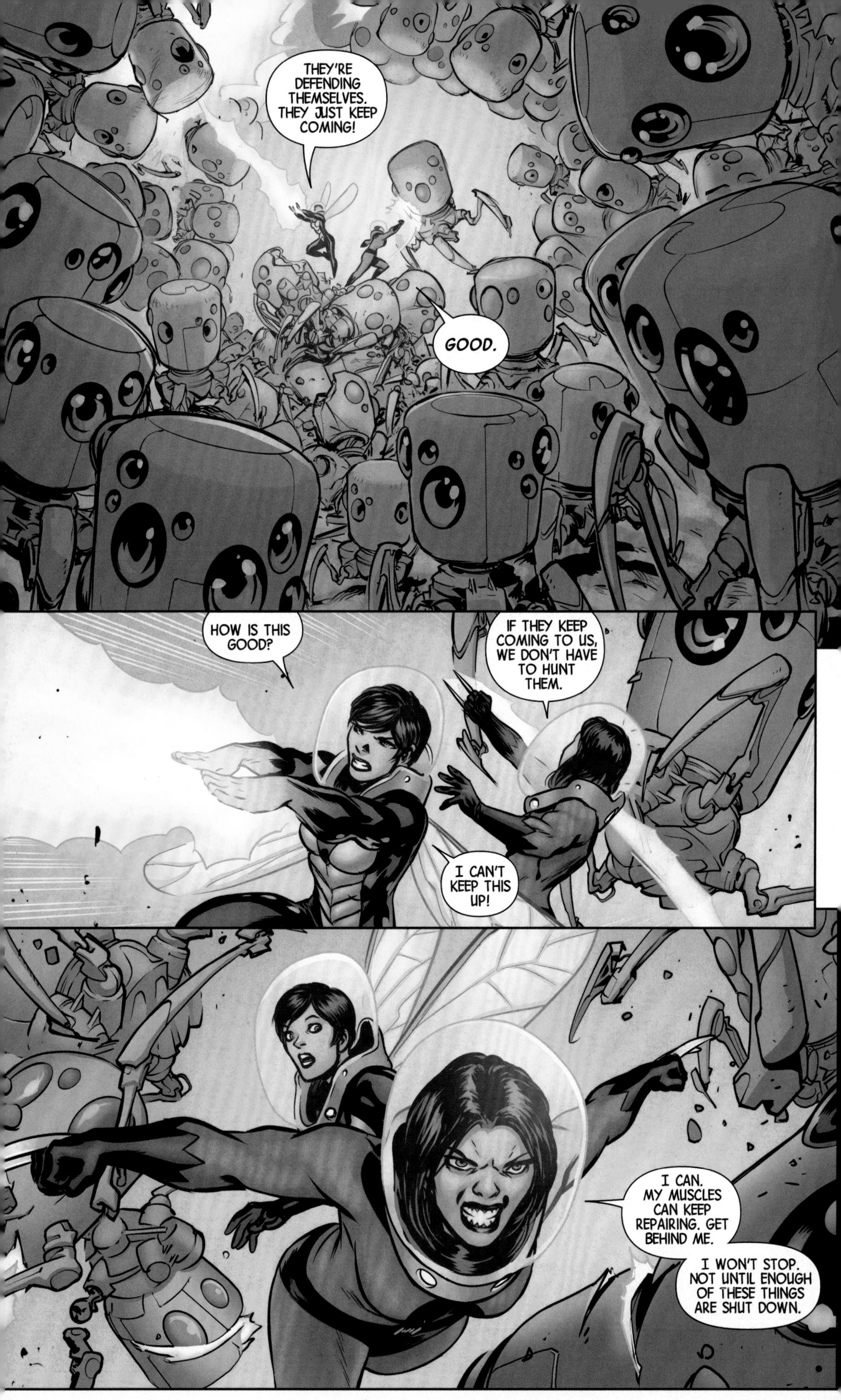
THEY'RE DEFENDING THEMSELVES. THEY JUST KEEP COMING!
GOOD.
HOW IS THIS GOOD?
IF THEY KEEP COMING TO US, WE DON'T HAVE TO HUNT THEM.
I CAN'T KEEP THIS UP!
I CAN. MY MUSCLES CAN KEEP REPAIRING. GET BEHIND ME.
I WON'T STOP. NOT UNTIL ENOUGH OF THESE THINGS ARE SHUT DOWN.

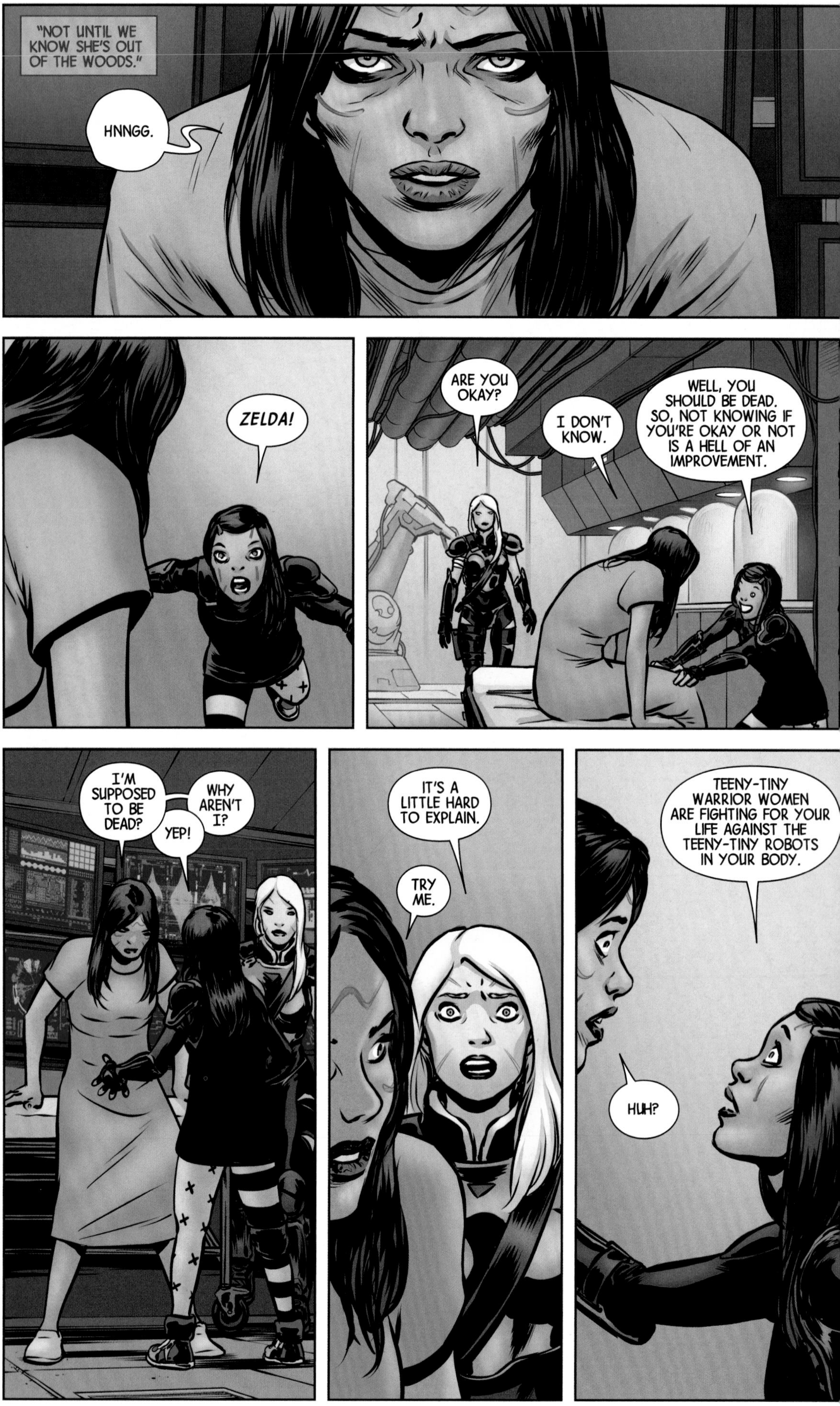
"NOT UNTIL WE KNOW SHE'S OUT OF THE WOODS."
HNNGG.
ZELDA!
ARE YOU OKAY?
I DON'T KNOW.
WELL, YOU SHOULD BE DEAD. SO, NOT KNOWING IF YOU'RE OKAY OR NOT IS A HELL OF AN IMPROVEMENT.
I'M SUPPOSED TO BE DEAD?
YEP!
WHY AREN'T I?
IT'S A LITTLE HARD TO EXPLAIN.
TRY ME.
TEENY-TINY WARRIOR WOMEN ARE FIGHTING FOR YOUR LIFE AGAINST THE TEENY-TINY ROBOTS IN YOUR BODY.
HUH?

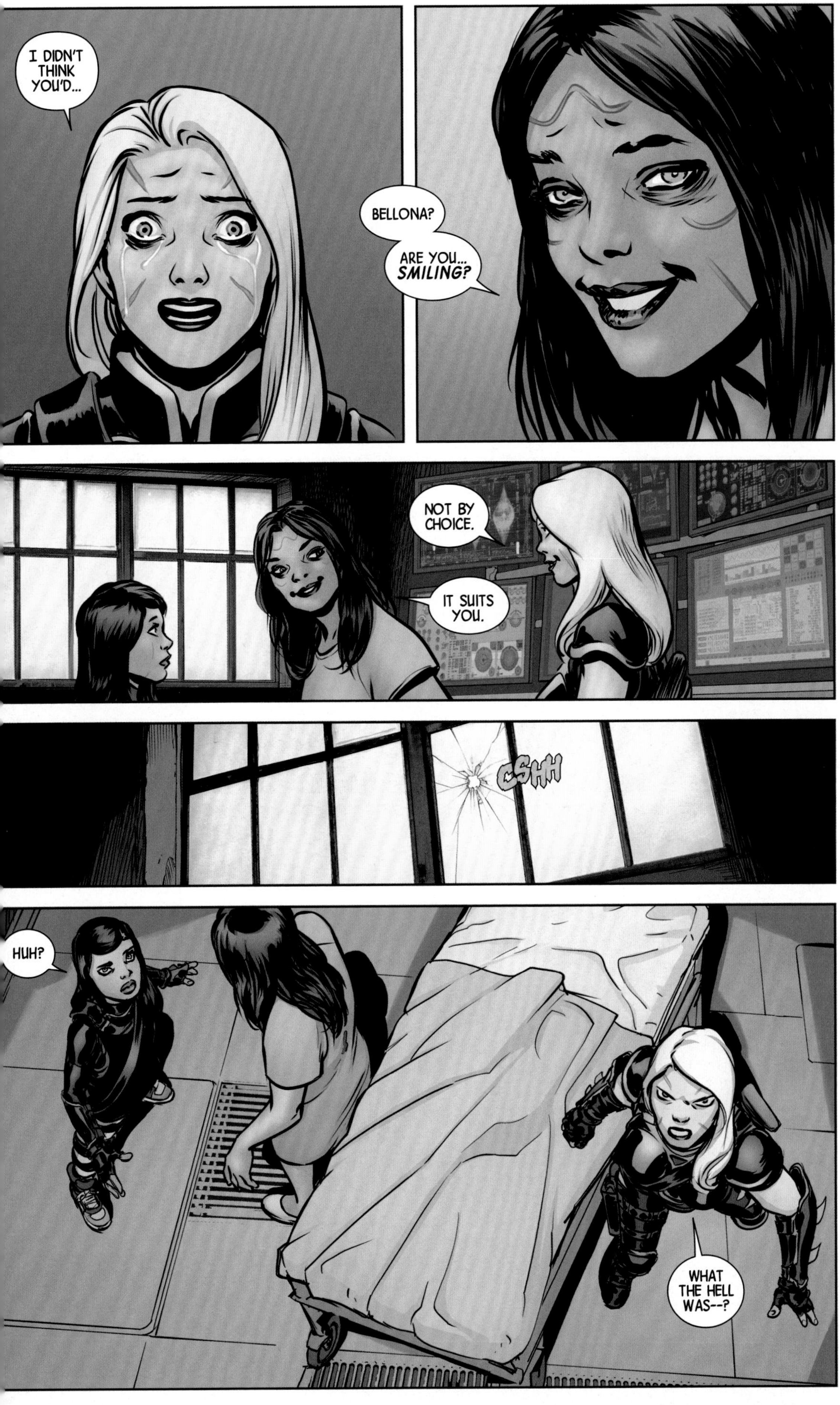

I DIDN'T THINK YOU'D...
BELLONA?
ARE YOU... SMILING?
NOT BY CHOICE.
IT SUITS YOU.
CSHH
HUH?
WHAT THE HELL WAS--?

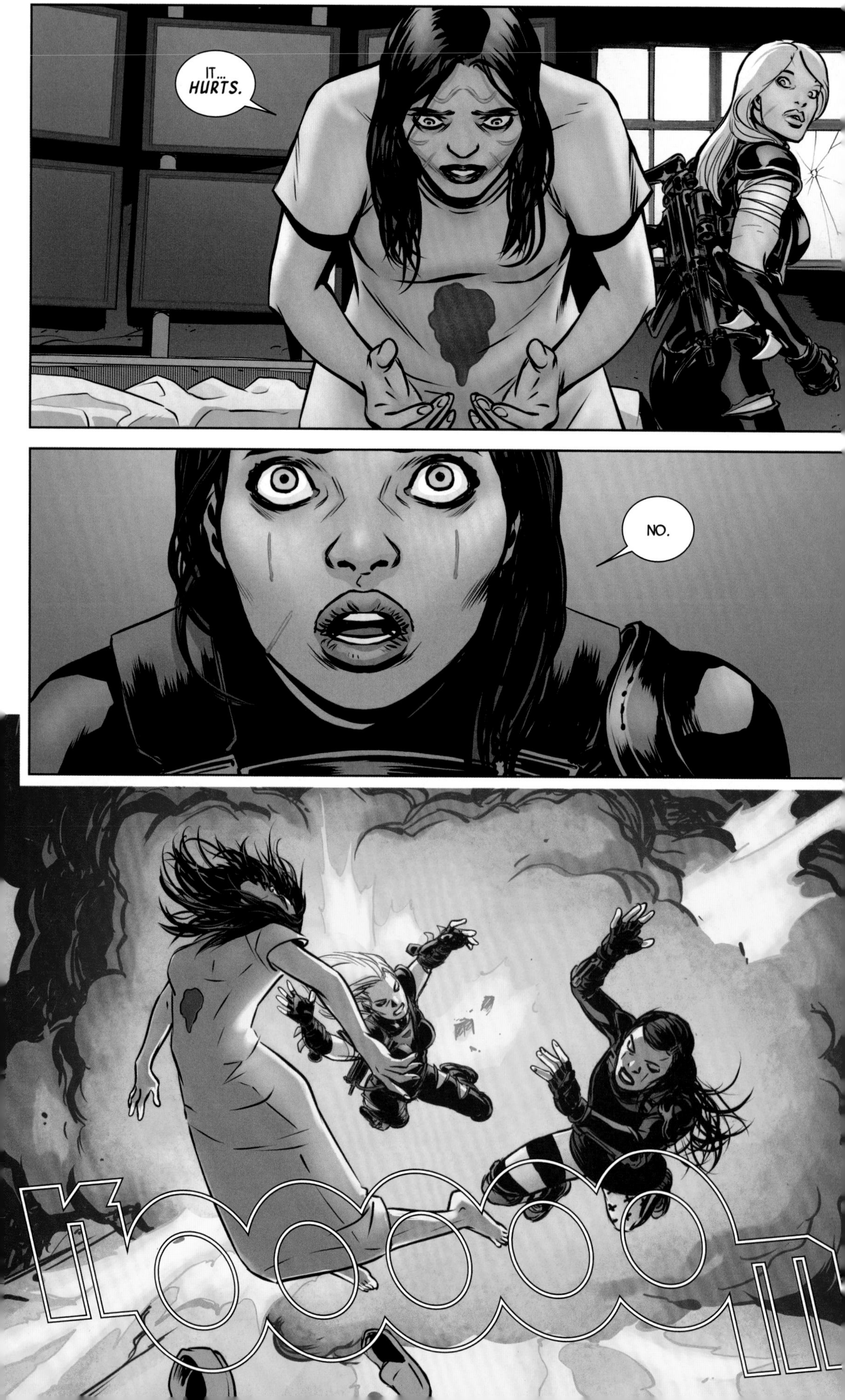
IT... HURTS.
NO.
KOOOOOM

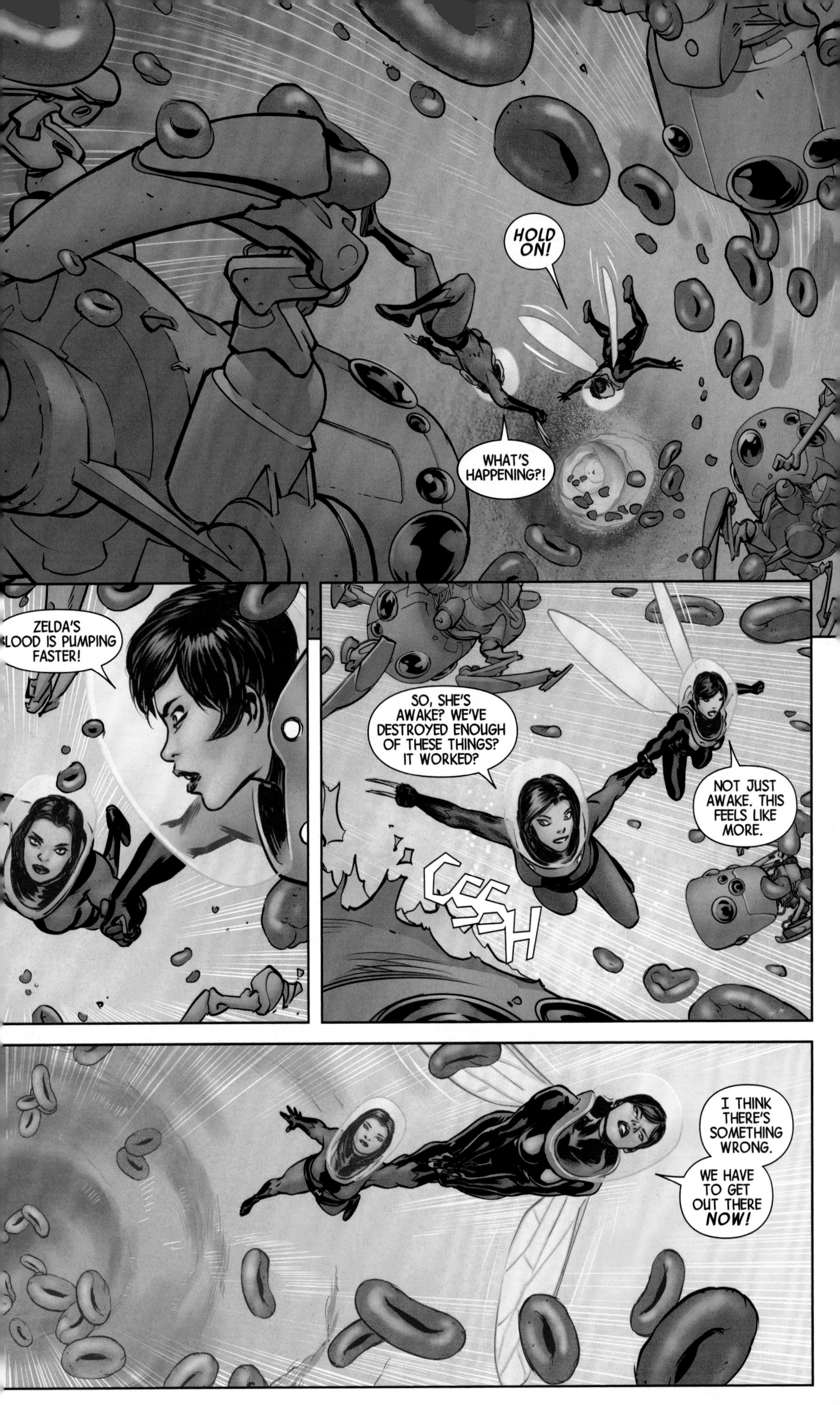
HOLD ON!
WHAT'S HAPPENING?!
ZELDA'S BLOOD IS PUMPING FASTER!
SO, SHE'S AWAKE? WE'VE DESTROYED ENOUGH OF THESE THINGS? IT WORKED?
NOT JUST AWAKE. THIS FEELS LIKE MORE.
CSSSH
I THINK THERE'S SOMETHING WRONG.
WE HAVE TO GET OUT THERE NOW!

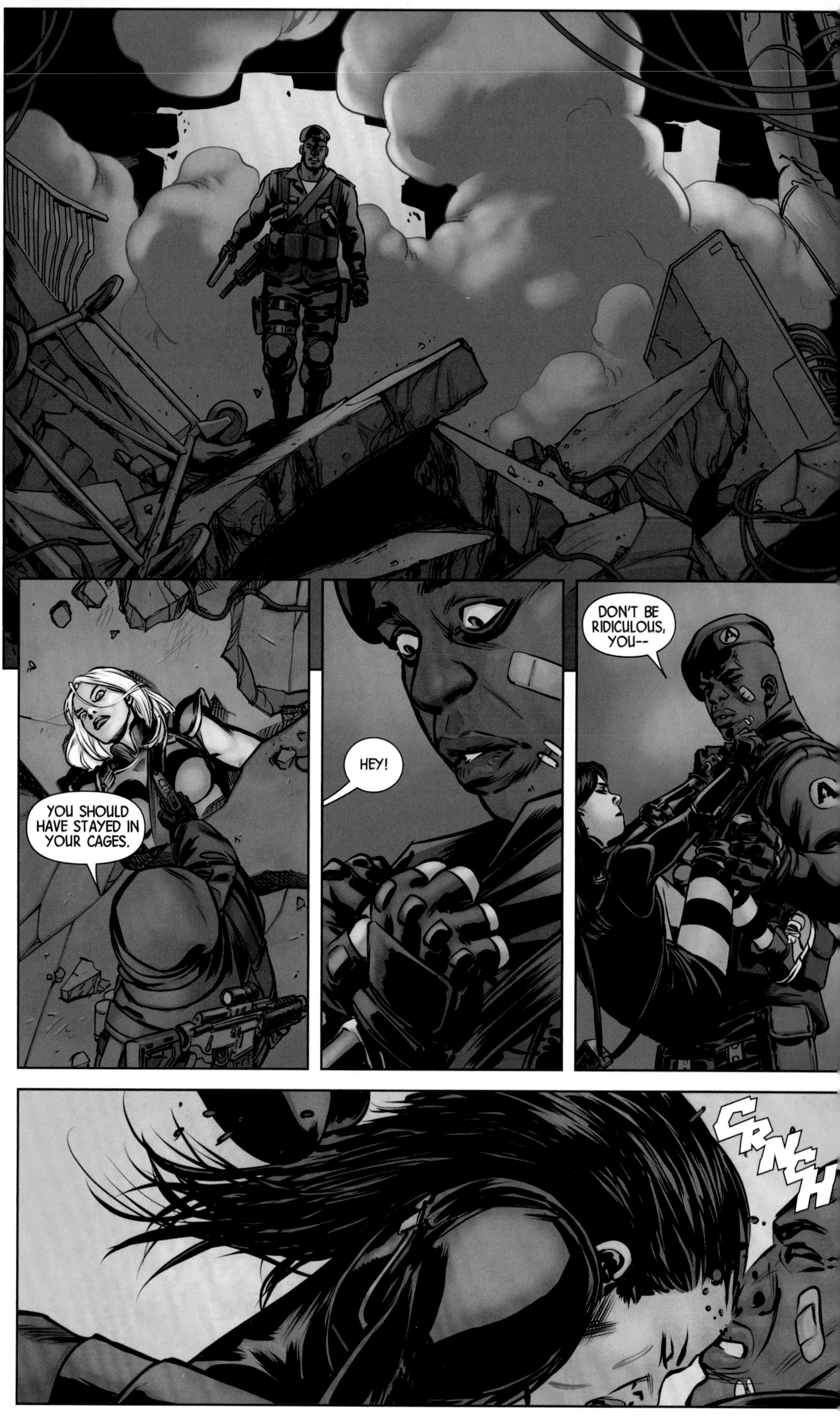
YOU SHOULD HAVE STAYED IN YOUR CAGES.
HEY!
DON'T BE RIDICULOUS, YOU--
CRNCH

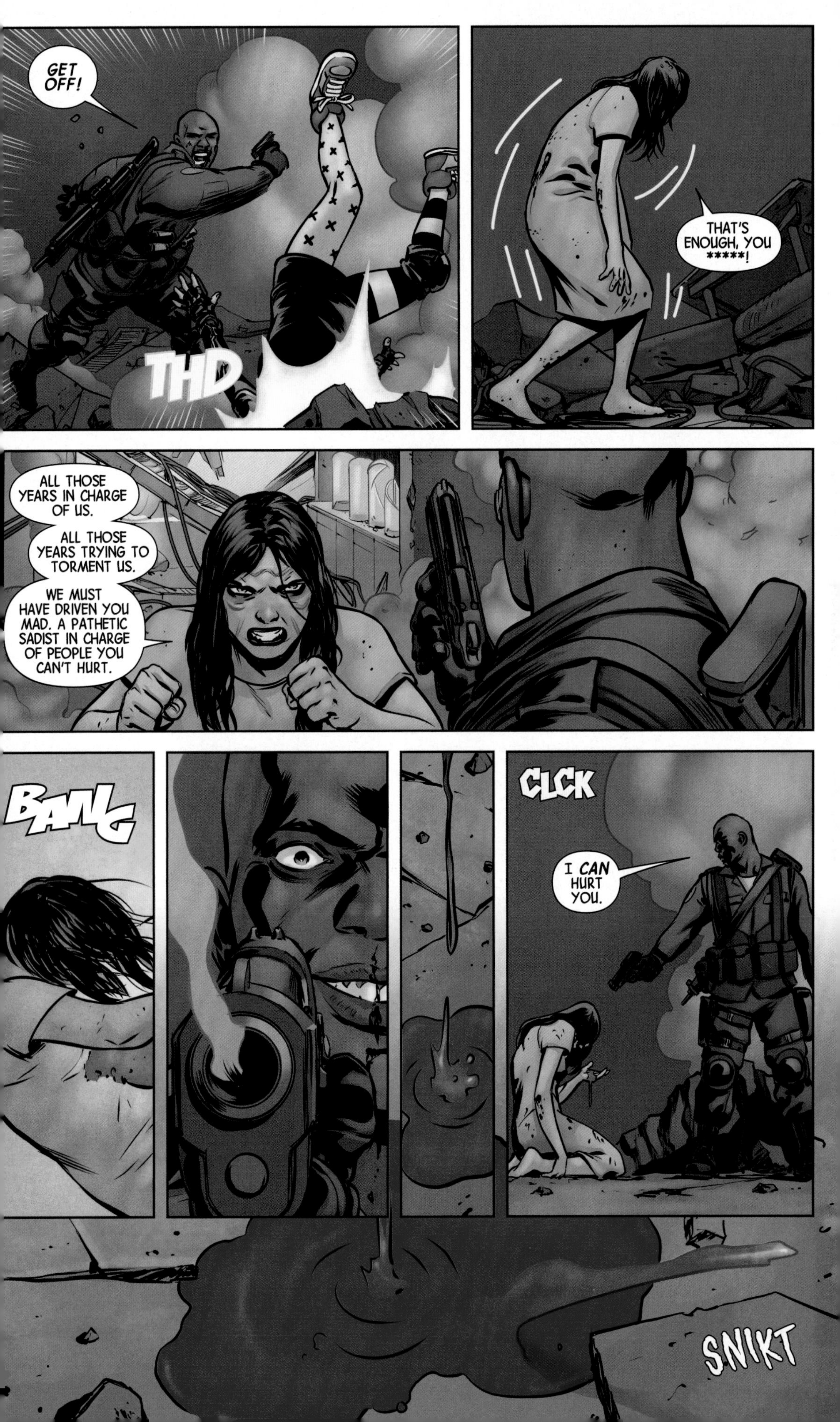
GET OFF!
THD
THAT'S ENOUGH, YOU *****!
ALL THOSE YEARS IN CHARGE OF US.
ALL THOSE YEARS TRYING TO TORMENT US.
WE MUST HAVE DRIVEN YOU MAD. A PATHETIC SADIST IN CHARGE OF PEOPLE YOU CAN'T HURT.
BANG
CLCK
I CAN HURT YOU.
SNIKT

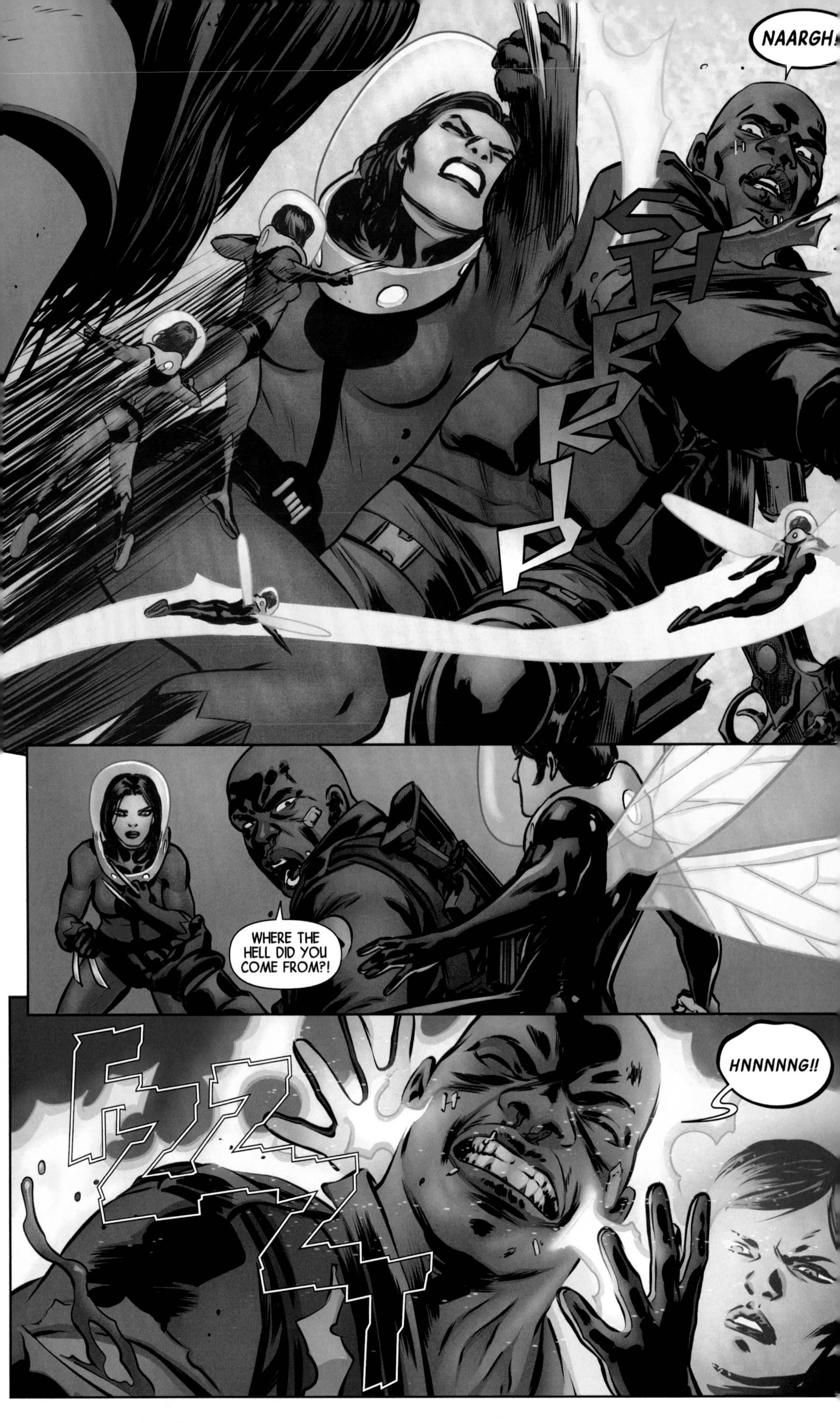
NAARGH!
SHRRRIP
WHERE THE HELL DID YOU COME FROM?!
FZZZT
HNNNNNG!!

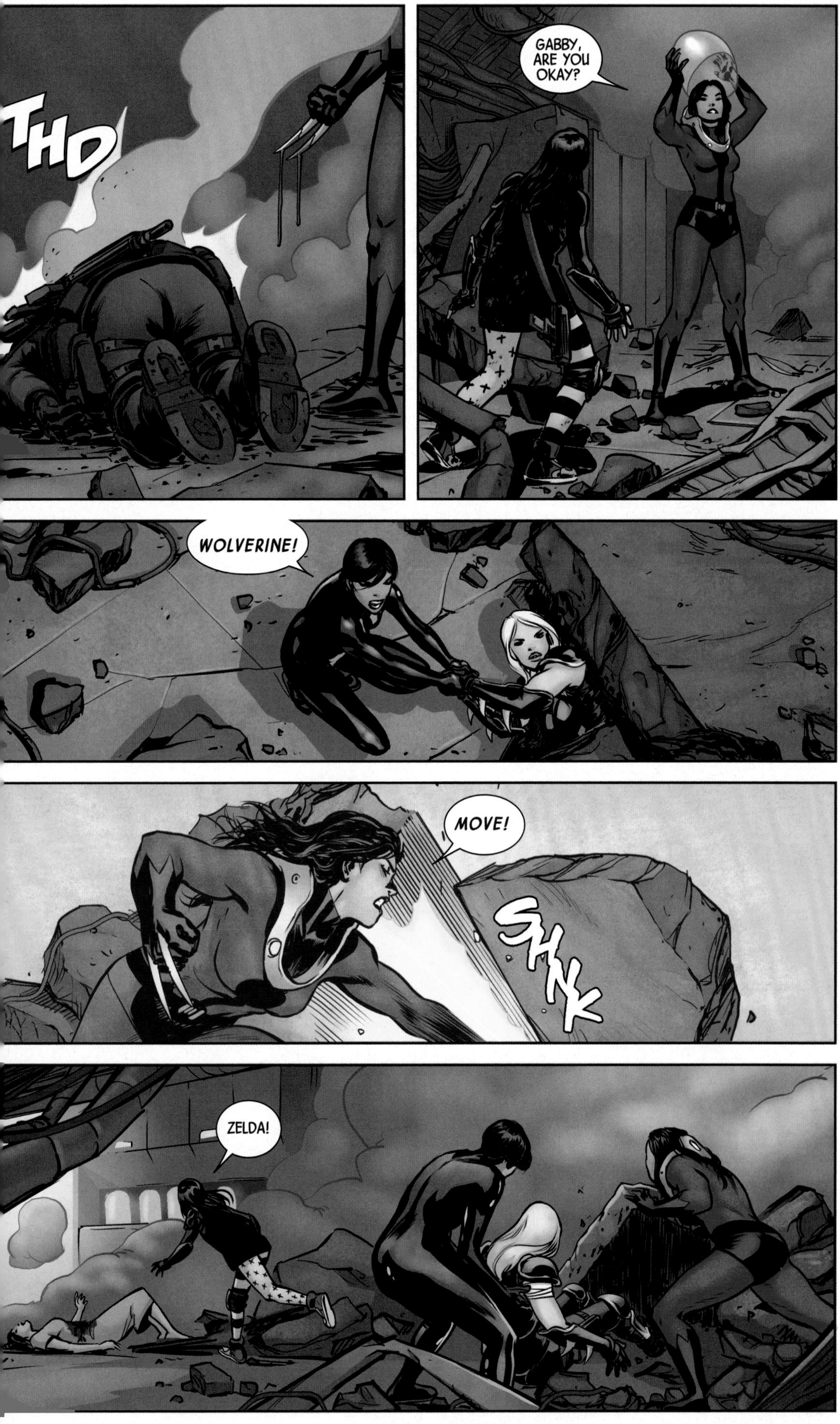
THD
GABBY, ARE YOU OKAY?
WOLVERINE!
MOVE!
SHNK
ZELDA!

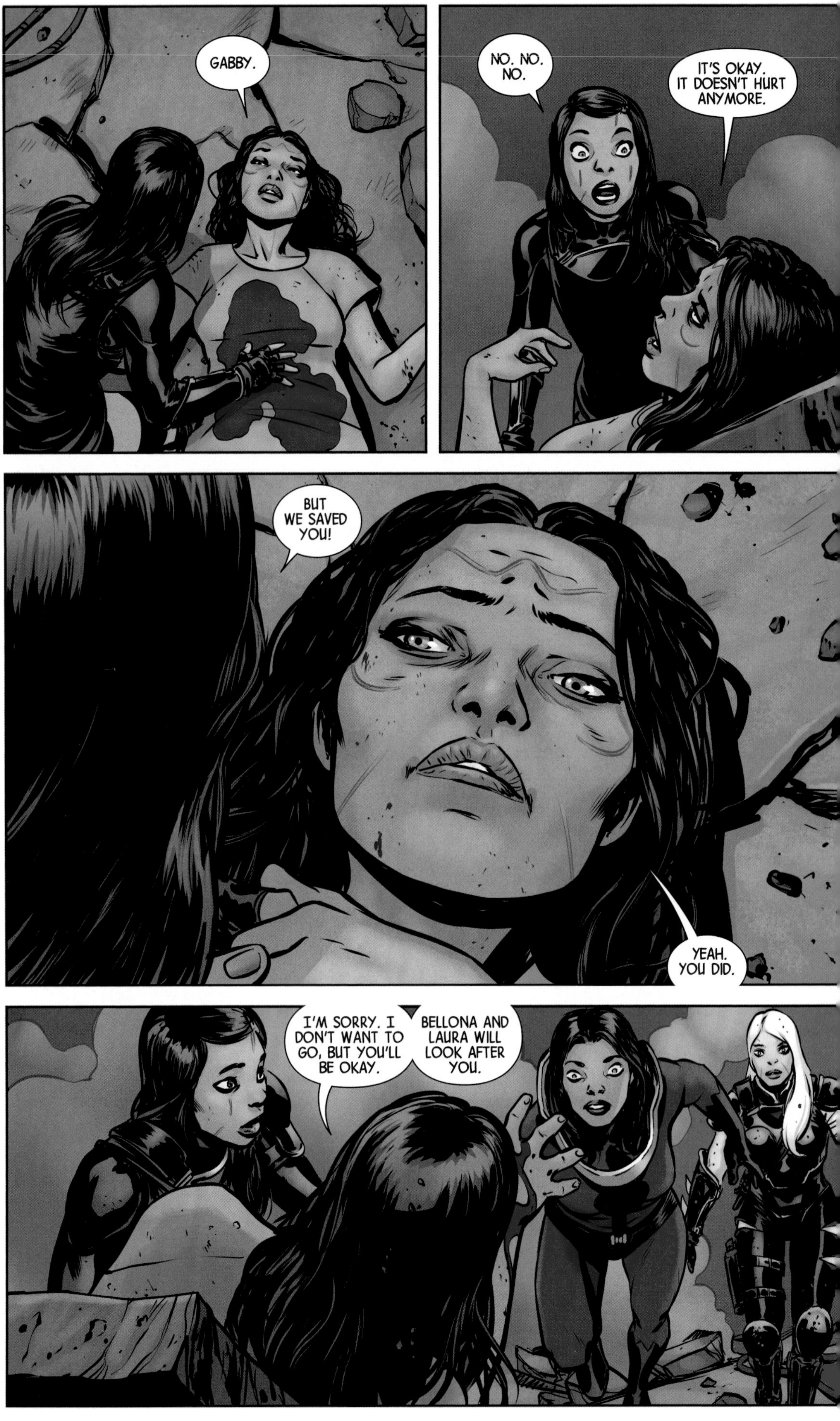
GABBY.
NO. NO. NO.
IT'S OKAY. IT DOESN'T HURT ANYMORE.
BUT WE SAVED YOU!
YEAH. YOU DID.
I'M SORRY. I DON'T WANT TO GO, BUT YOU'LL BE OKAY.
BELLONA AND LAURA WILL LOOK AFTER YOU.

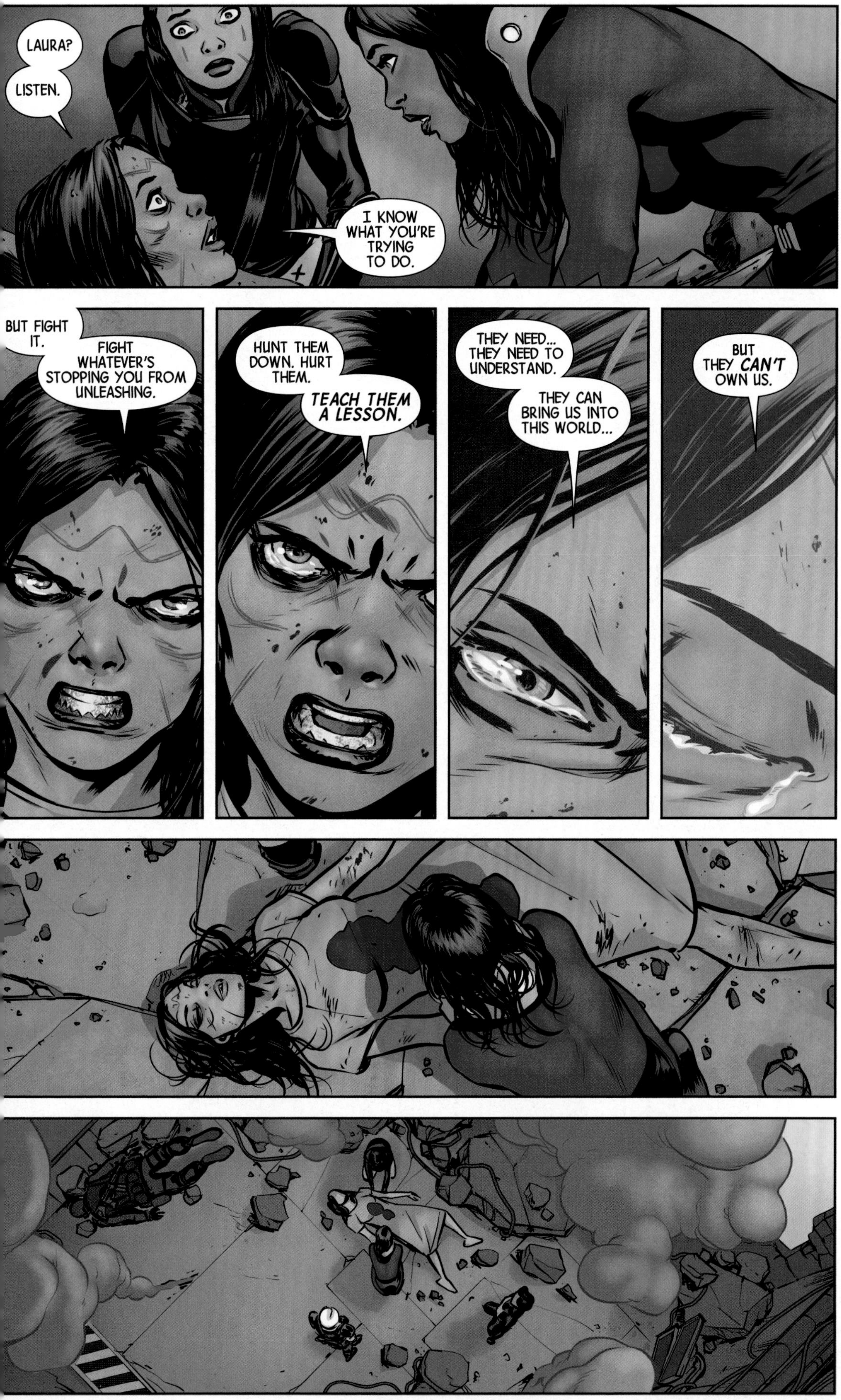

LAURA?
LISTEN.
I KNOW WHAT YOU'RE TRYING TO DO.
BUT FIGHT IT.
FIGHT WHATEVER'S STOPPING YOU FROM UNLEASHING.
HUNT THEM DOWN. HURT THEM.
TEACH THEM A LESSON.
THEY NEED... THEY NEED TO UNDERSTAND.
THEY CAN BRING US INTO THIS WORLD...
BUT THEY *CAN'T* OWN US.

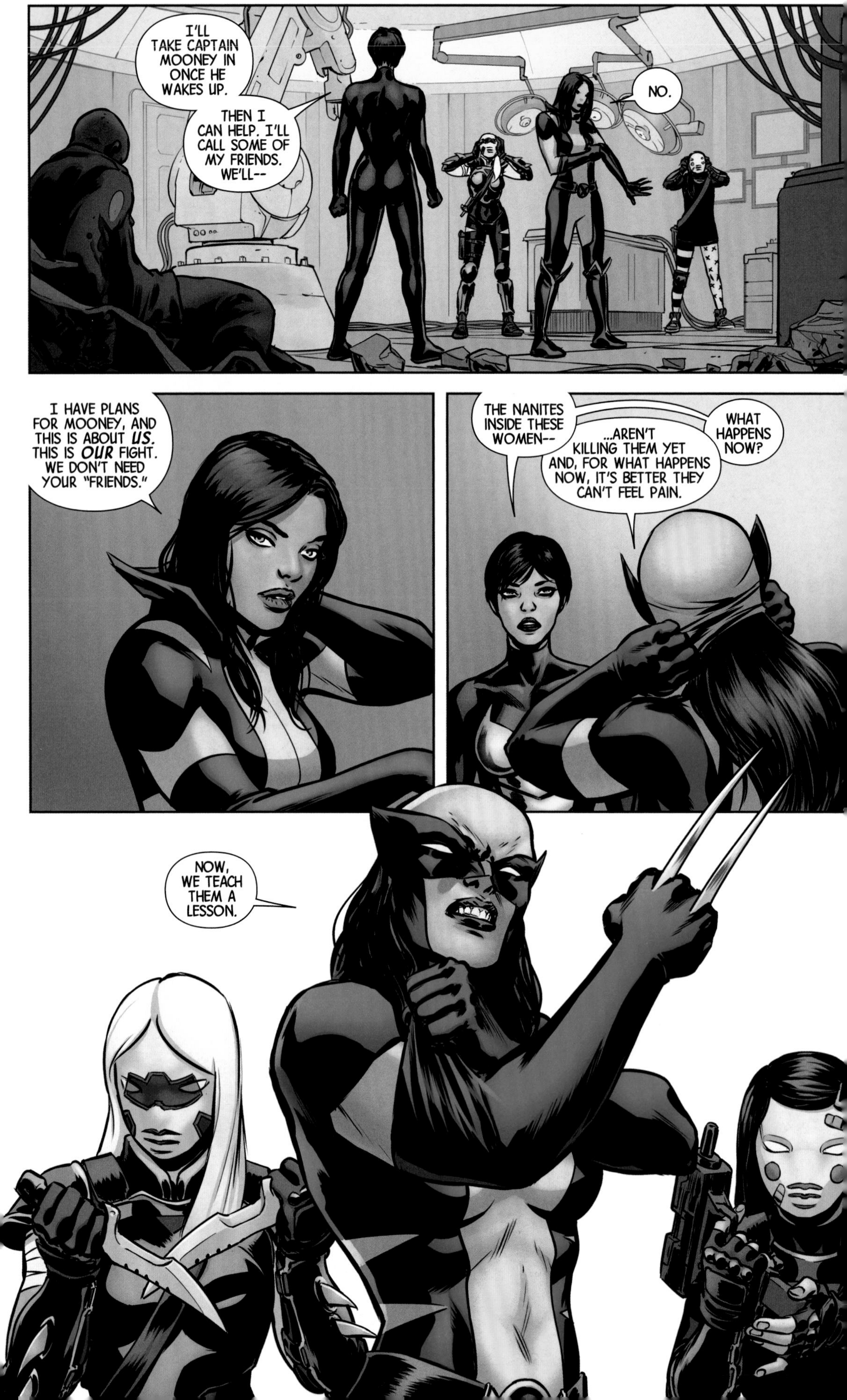
I'LL TAKE CAPTAIN MOONEY IN ONCE HE WAKES UP.
THEN I CAN HELP. I'LL CALL SOME OF MY FRIENDS. WE'LL--
NO.
I HAVE PLANS FOR MOONEY, AND THIS IS ABOUT *US.* THIS IS *OUR* FIGHT. WE DON'T NEED YOUR "FRIENDS."
THE NANITES INSIDE THESE WOMEN--
WHAT HAPPENS NOW?
...AREN'T KILLING THEM YET AND, FOR WHAT HAPPENS NOW, IT'S BETTER THEY CAN'T FEEL PAIN.
NOW, WE TEACH THEM A LESSON.

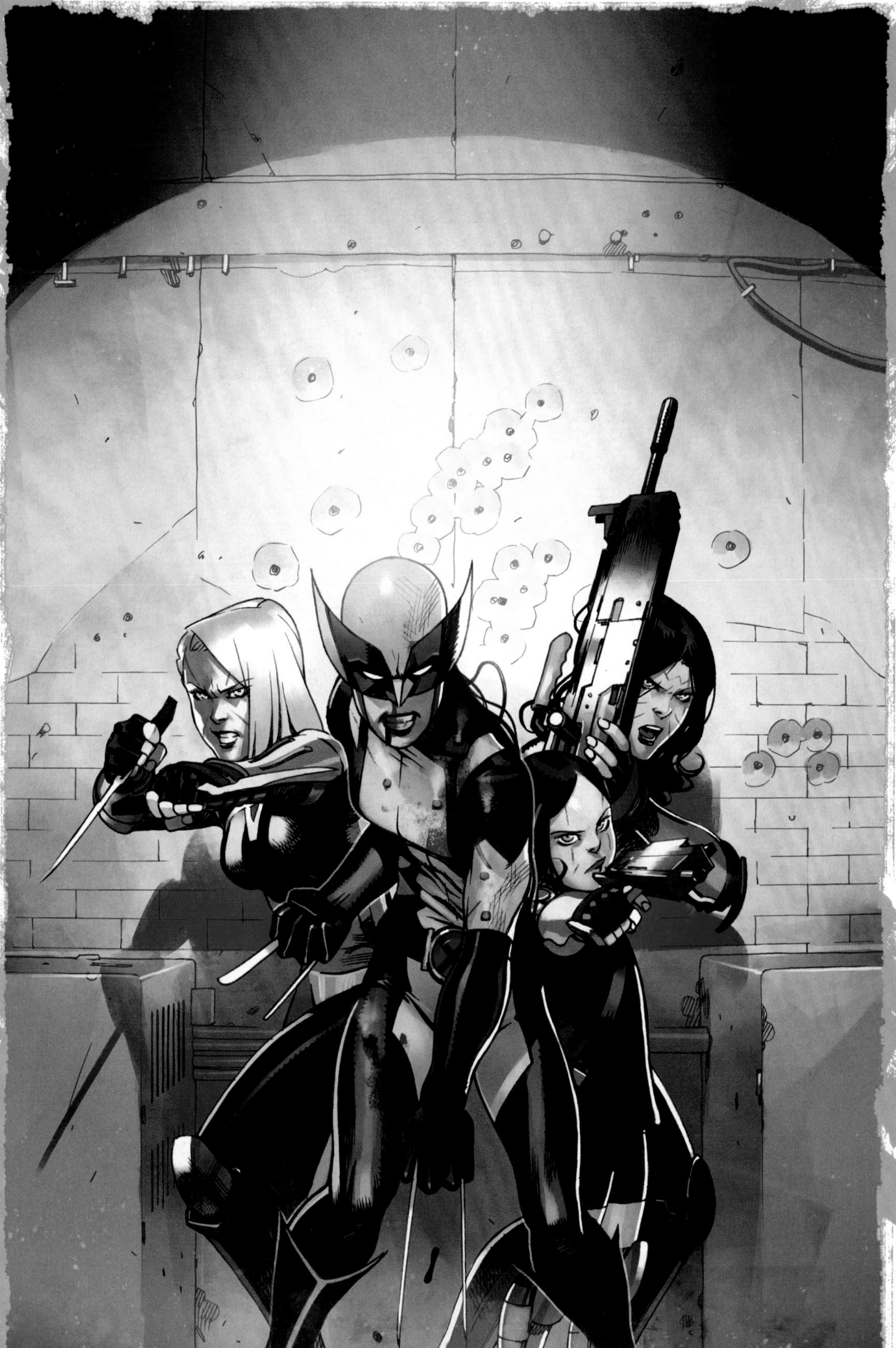

6

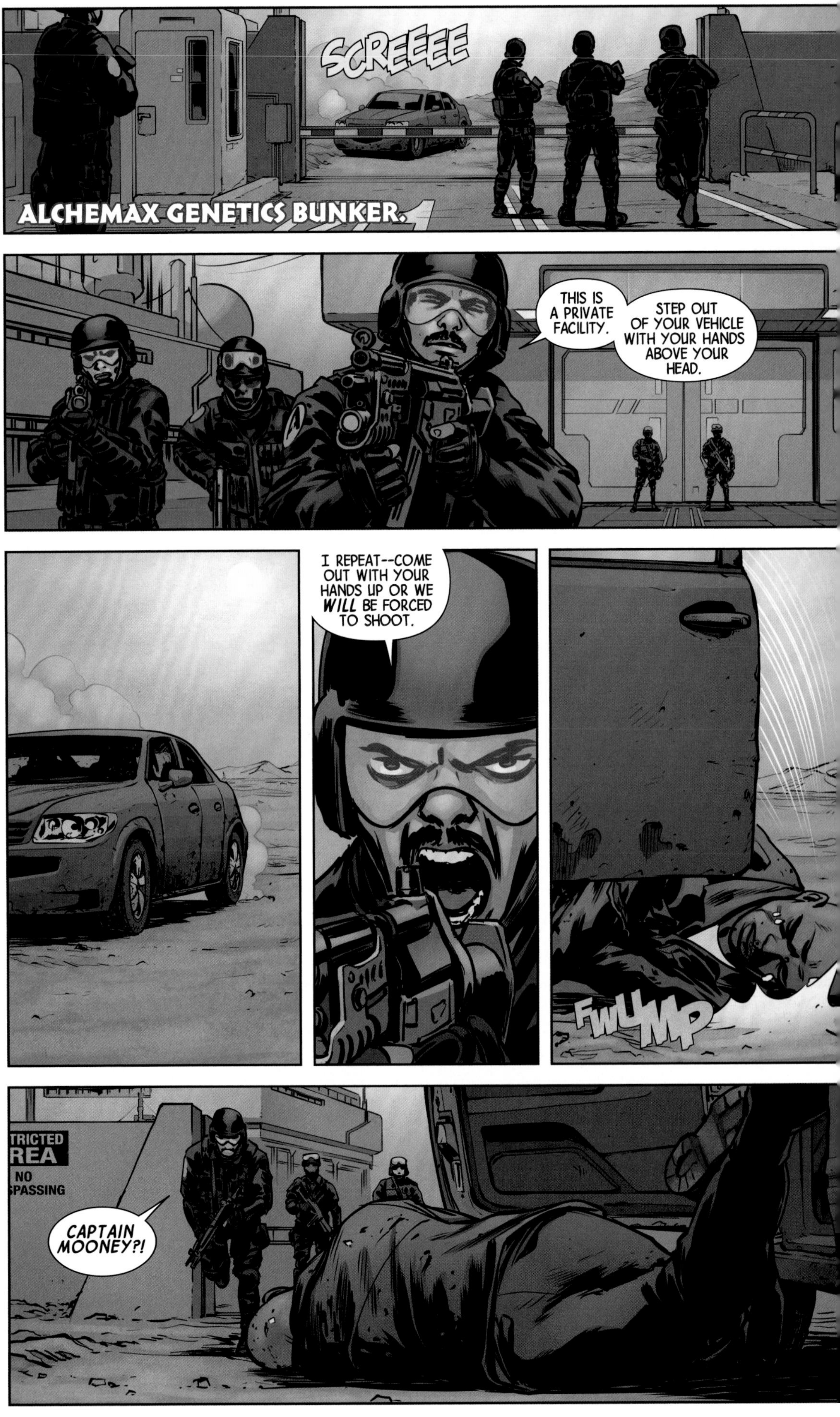
SCREEEE
ALCHEMAX GENETICS BUNKER.
THIS IS A PRIVATE FACILITY.
STEP OUT OF YOUR VEHICLE WITH YOUR HANDS ABOVE YOUR HEAD.
I REPEAT--COME OUT WITH YOUR HANDS UP OR WE *WILL* BE FORCED TO SHOOT.
FWUMP
TRICTED
REA
NO
SPASSING
CAPTAIN MOONEY?!

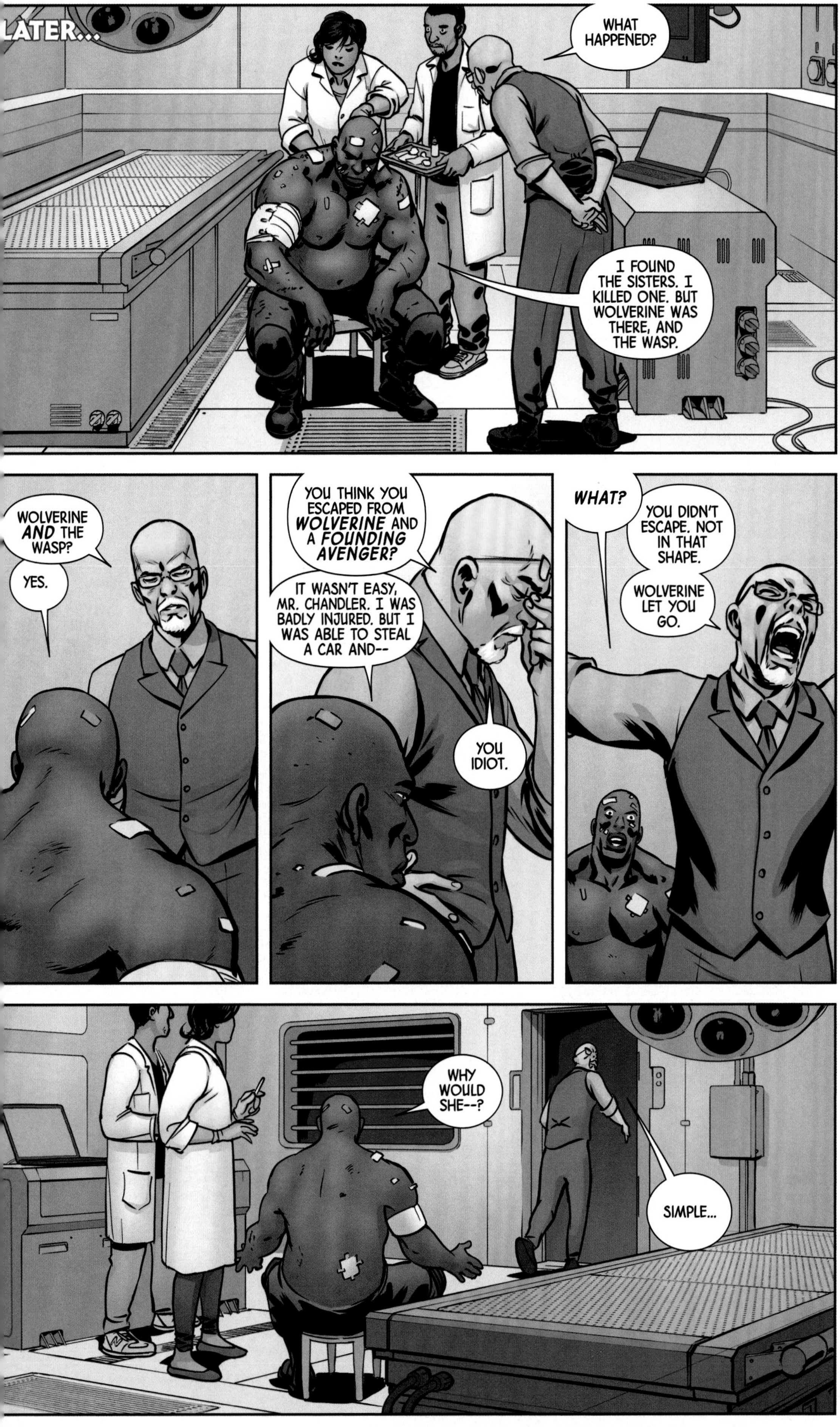
LATER...
WHAT HAPPENED?
I FOUND THE SISTERS. I KILLED ONE. BUT WOLVERINE WAS THERE, AND THE WASP.
WOLVERINE *AND* THE WASP?
YES.
YOU THINK YOU ESCAPED FROM *WOLVERINE* AND A *FOUNDING AVENGER?*
IT WASN'T EASY, MR. CHANDLER. I WAS BADLY INJURED. BUT I WAS ABLE TO STEAL A CAR AND--
YOU IDIOT.
WHAT?
YOU DIDN'T ESCAPE. NOT IN THAT SHAPE.
WOLVERINE LET YOU GO.
WHY WOULD SHE--?
SIMPLE...

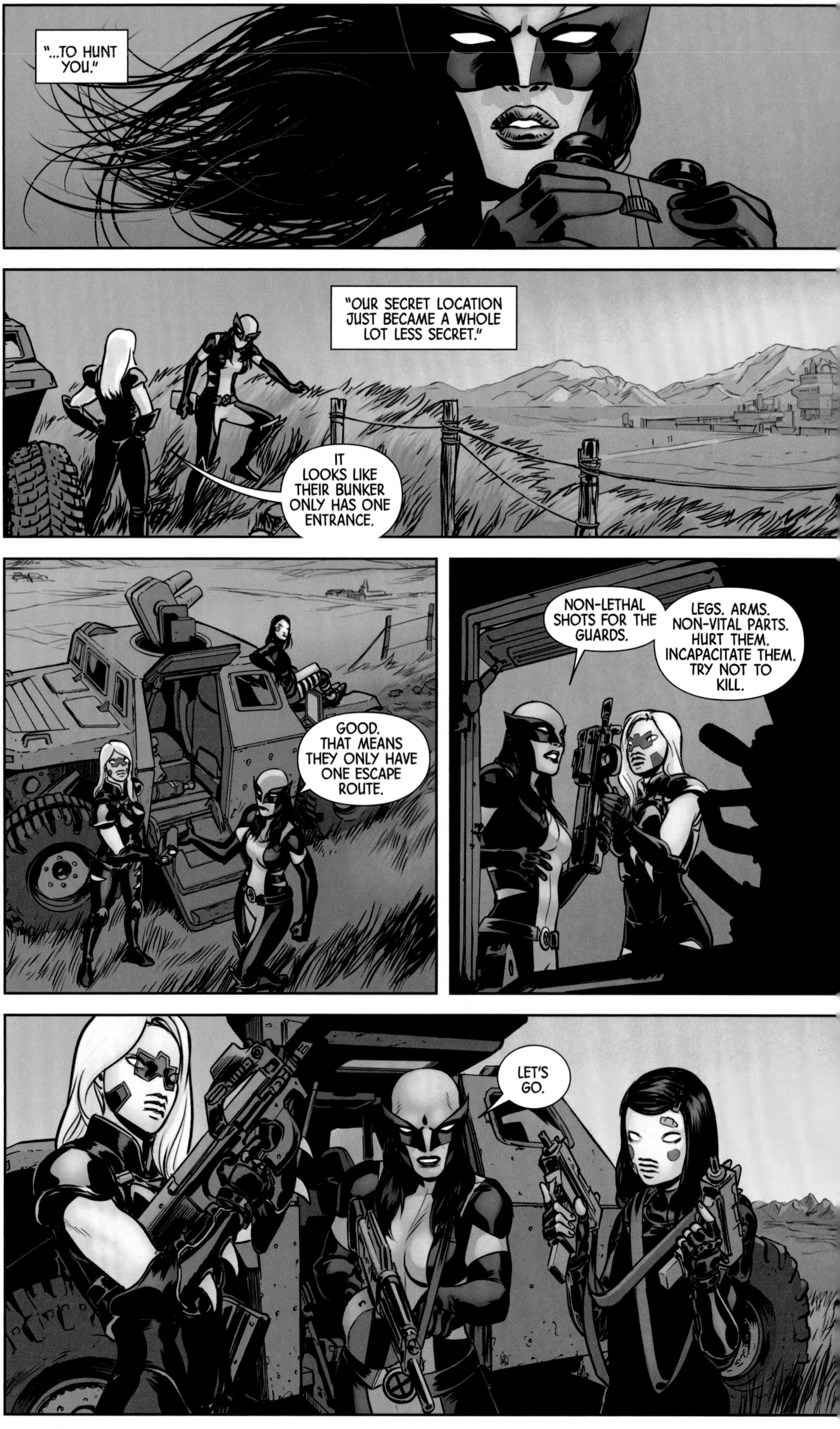
"...TO HUNT YOU."
"OUR SECRET LOCATION JUST BECAME A WHOLE LOT LESS SECRET."
IT LOOKS LIKE THEIR BUNKER ONLY HAS ONE ENTRANCE.
GOOD. THAT MEANS THEY ONLY HAVE ONE ESCAPE ROUTE.
NON-LETHAL SHOTS FOR THE GUARDS.
LEGS. ARMS. NON-VITAL PARTS. HURT THEM. INCAPACITATE THEM. TRY NOT TO KILL.
LET'S GO.

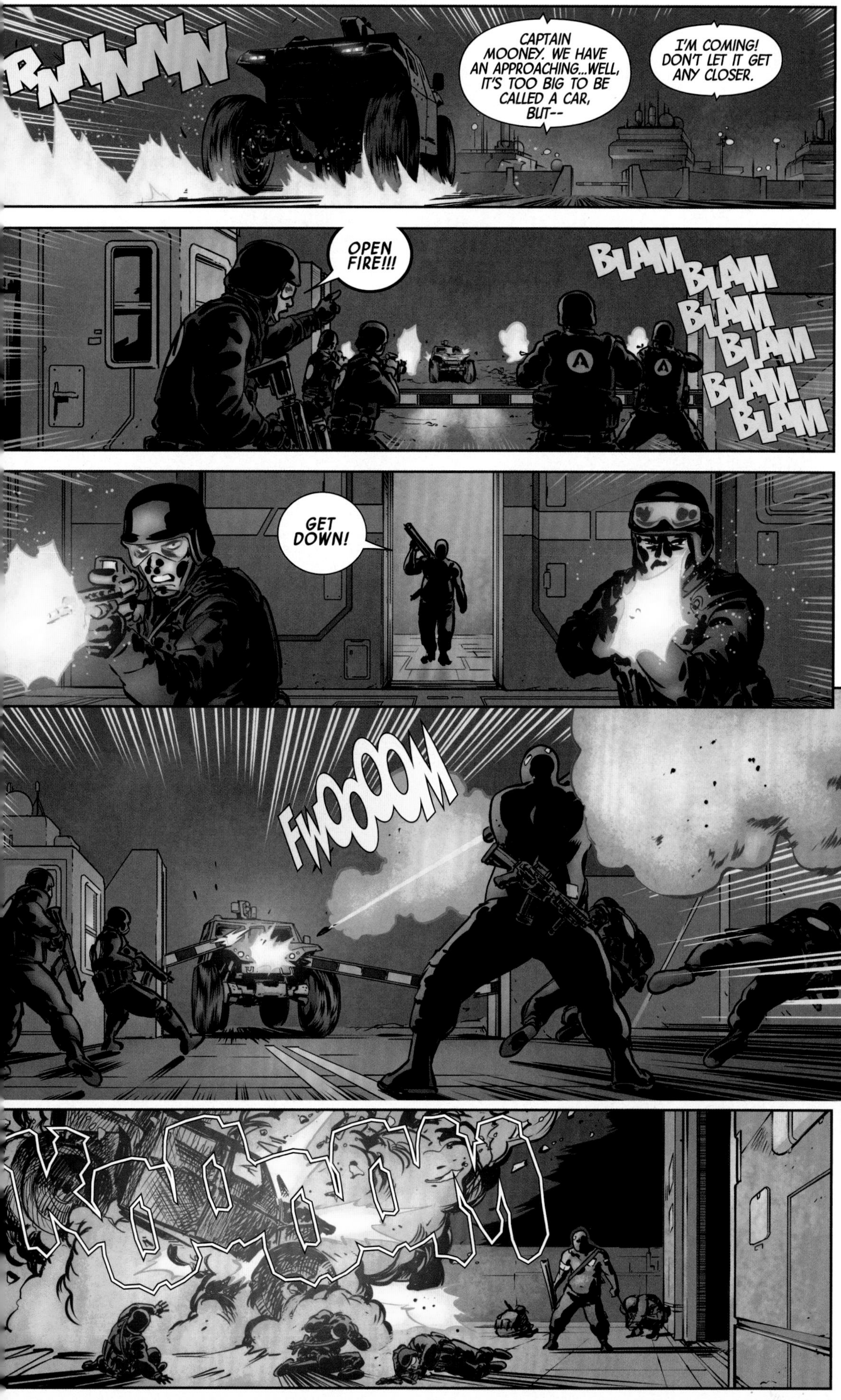

RNNNNN
CAPTAIN MOONEY. WE HAVE AN APPROACHING...WELL, IT'S TOO BIG TO BE CALLED A CAR, BUT--
I'M COMING! DON'T LET IT GET ANY CLOSER.
OPEN FIRE!!!
BLAM BLAM BLAM BLAM BLAM BLAM
GET DOWN!
FWOOOOM
KROOOOOM

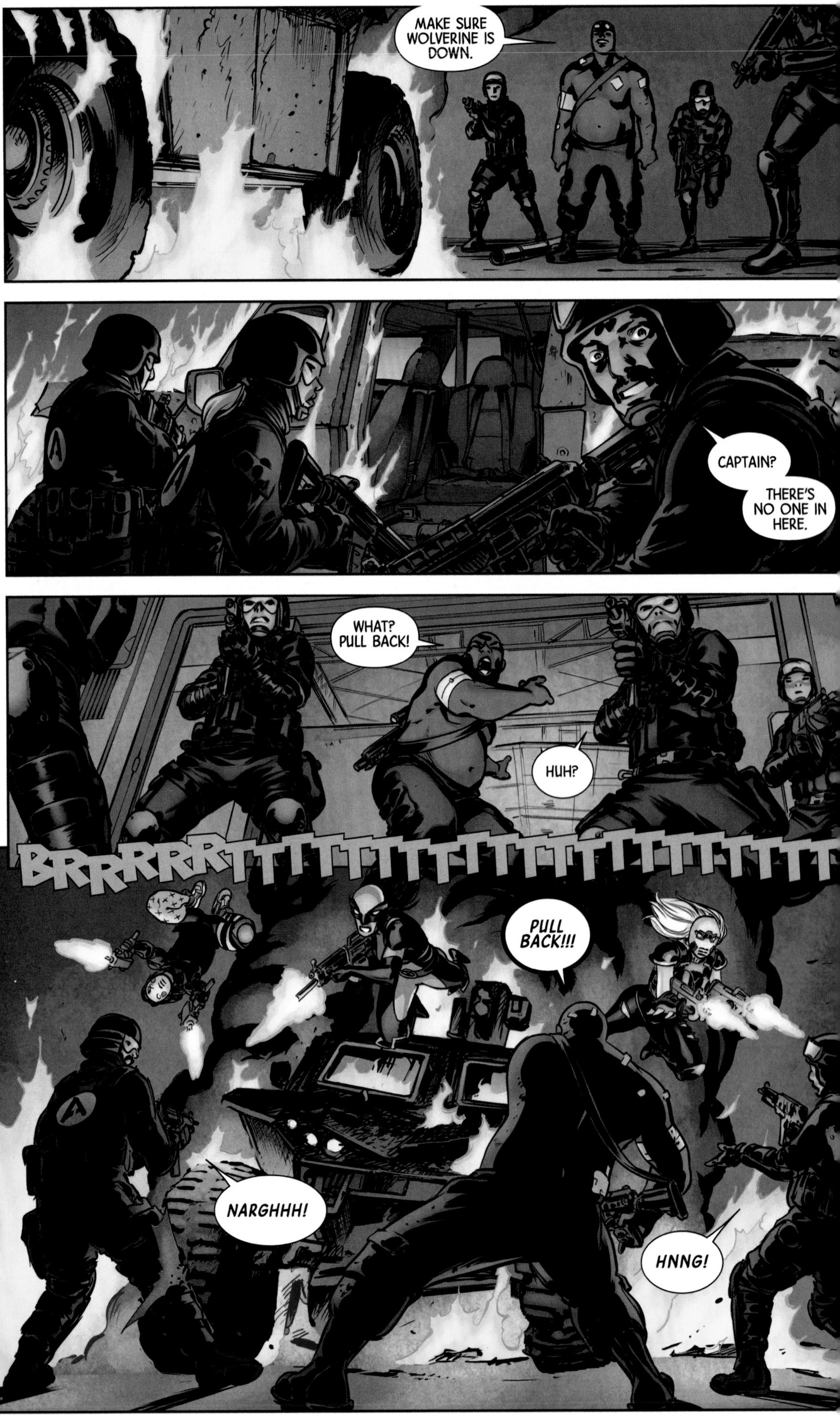
MAKE SURE WOLVERINE IS DOWN.
CAPTAIN?
THERE'S NO ONE IN HERE.
WHAT? PULL BACK!
HUH?
BRRRRRTTTTTTTTTTTTTTTTTTTTT
PULL BACK!!!
NARGHHH!
HNNG!

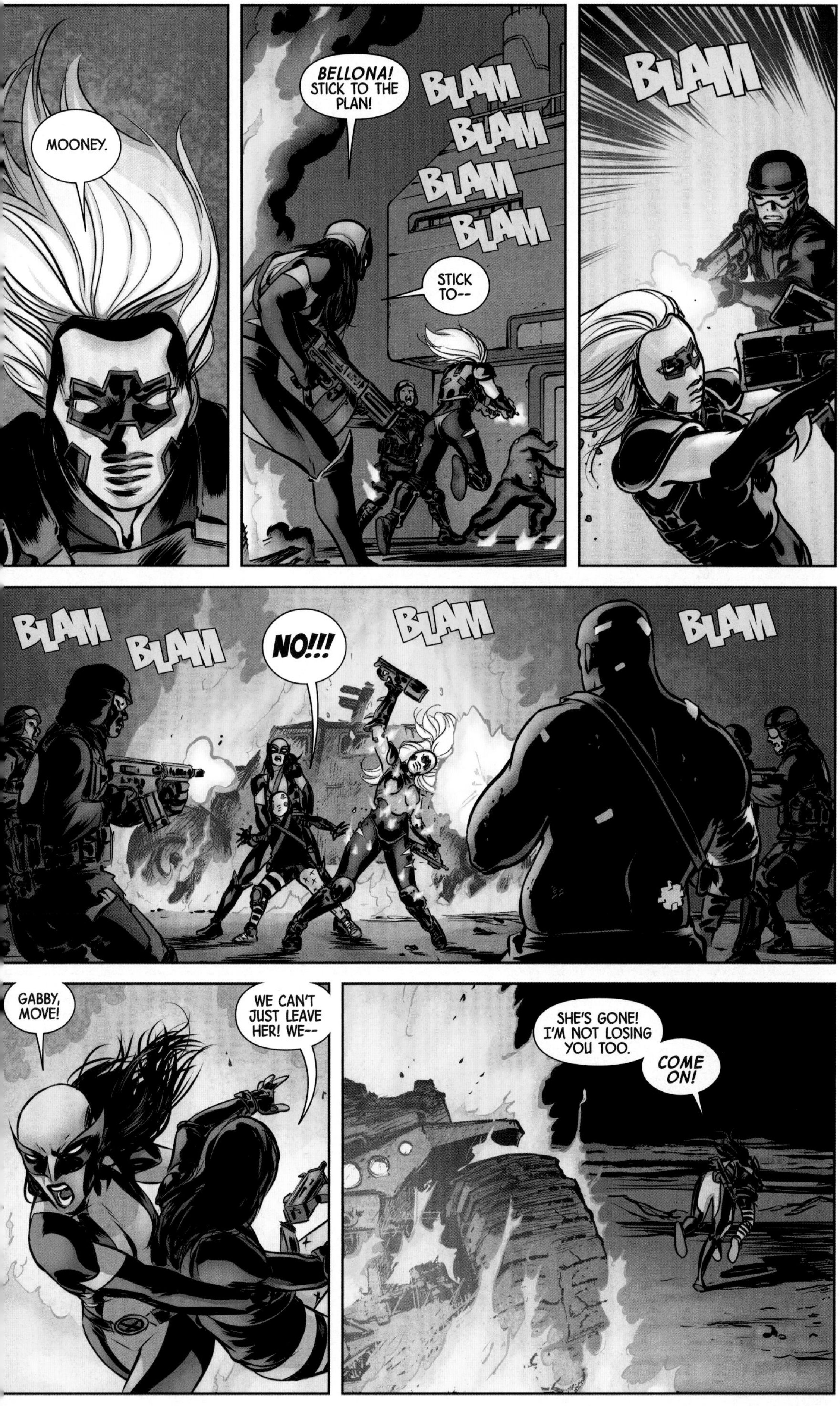

MOONEY.
BELLONA! STICK TO THE PLAN!
BLAM
BLAM
BLAM
BLAM
STICK TO--
BLAM
BLAM
BLAM
NO!!!
BLAM
BLAM
GABBY, MOVE!
WE CAN'T JUST LEAVE HER! WE--
SHE'S GONE! I'M NOT LOSING YOU TOO.
COME ON!

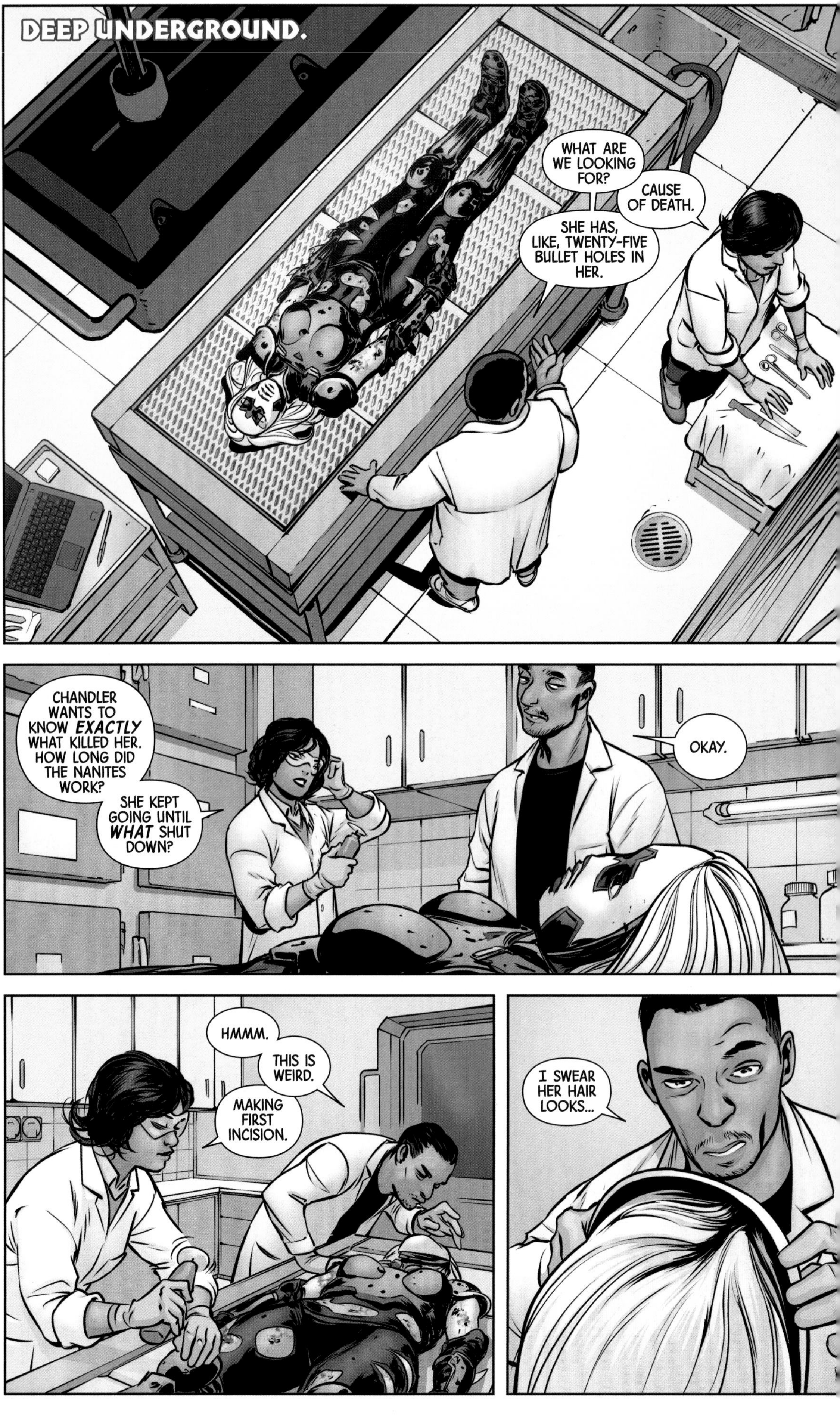
DEEP UNDERGROUND.
WHAT ARE WE LOOKING FOR?
CAUSE OF DEATH.
SHE HAS, LIKE, TWENTY-FIVE BULLET HOLES IN HER.
CHANDLER WANTS TO KNOW EXACTLY WHAT KILLED HER. HOW LONG DID THE NANITES WORK?
SHE KEPT GOING UNTIL WHAT SHUT DOWN?
OKAY.
HMMM.
THIS IS WEIRD.
MAKING FIRST INCISION.
I SWEAR HER HAIR LOOKS...

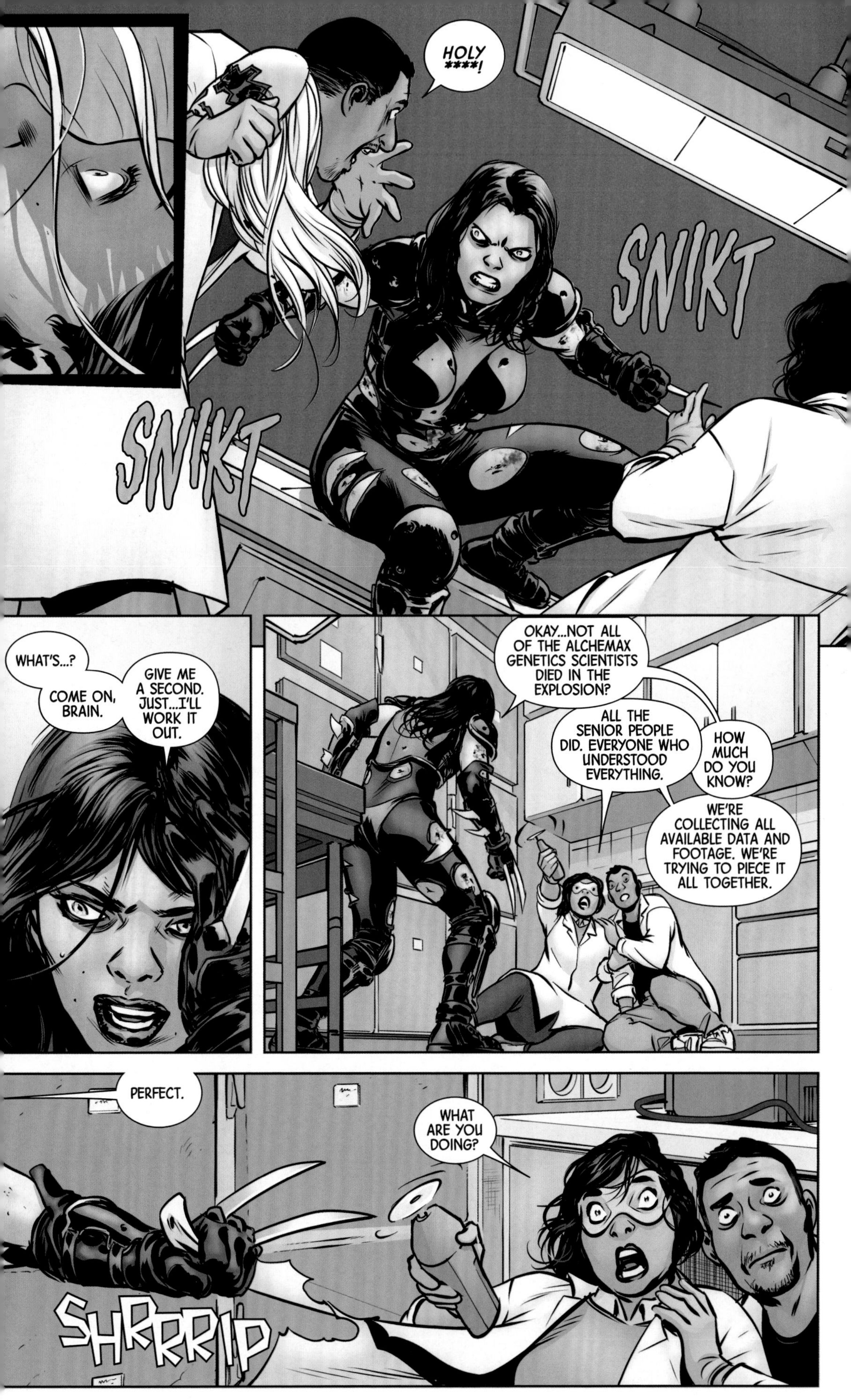

HOLY ****!
SNIKT
SNIKT
WHAT'S...?
COME ON, BRAIN.
GIVE ME A SECOND. JUST...I'LL WORK IT OUT.
OKAY...NOT ALL OF THE ALCHEMAX GENETICS SCIENTISTS DIED IN THE EXPLOSION?
ALL THE SENIOR PEOPLE DID. EVERYONE WHO UNDERSTOOD EVERYTHING.
HOW MUCH DO YOU KNOW?
WE'RE COLLECTING ALL AVAILABLE DATA AND FOOTAGE. WE'RE TRYING TO PIECE IT ALL TOGETHER.
PERFECT.
WHAT ARE YOU DOING?
SHRRRIP

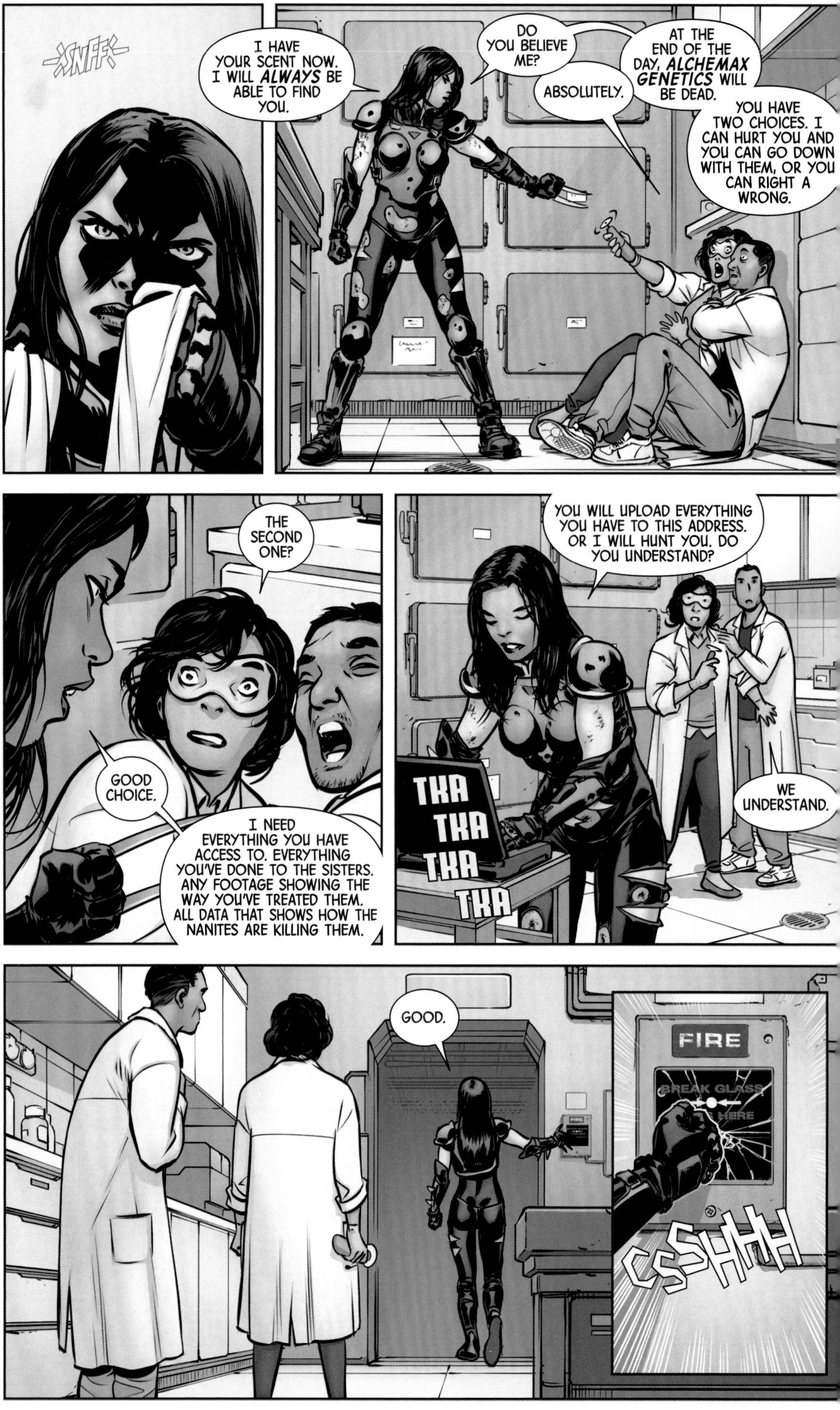
SNFF
I HAVE YOUR SCENT NOW. I WILL ALWAYS BE ABLE TO FIND YOU.
DO YOU BELIEVE ME?
ABSOLUTELY.
AT THE END OF THE DAY, ALCHEMAX GENETICS WILL BE DEAD.
YOU HAVE TWO CHOICES. I CAN HURT YOU AND YOU CAN GO DOWN WITH THEM, OR YOU CAN RIGHT A WRONG.
THE SECOND ONE?
GOOD CHOICE.
I NEED EVERYTHING YOU HAVE ACCESS TO. EVERYTHING YOU'VE DONE TO THE SISTERS. ANY FOOTAGE SHOWING THE WAY YOU'VE TREATED THEM. ALL DATA THAT SHOWS HOW THE NANITES ARE KILLING THEM.
YOU WILL UPLOAD EVERYTHING YOU HAVE TO THIS ADDRESS. OR I WILL HUNT YOU. DO YOU UNDERSTAND?
TKA TKA TKA TKA
WE UNDERSTAND.
GOOD.
FIRE
BREAK GLASS
CSHHH

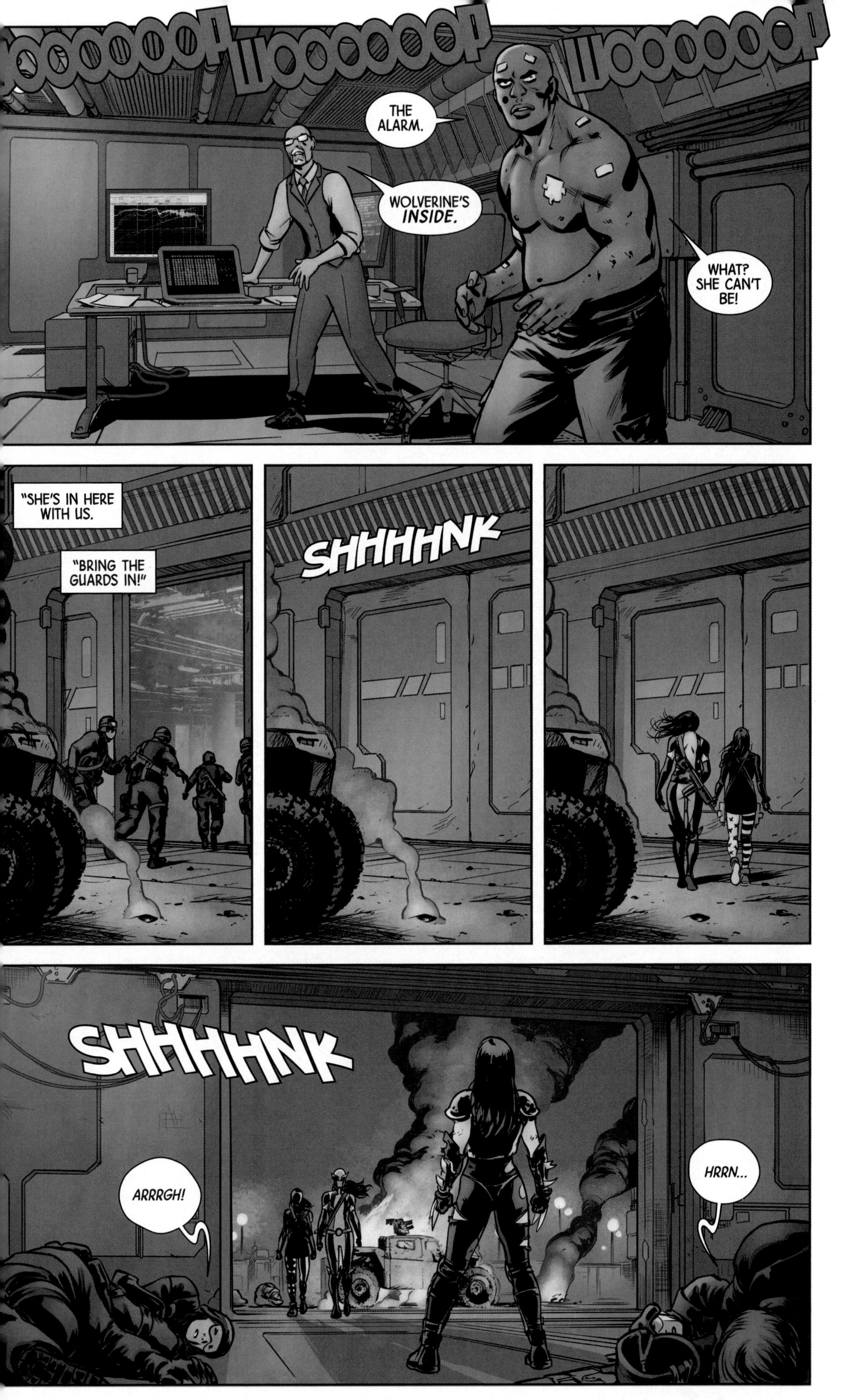
WOOOOOOP WOOOOOOP WOOOOOOP
THE ALARM.
WOLVERINE'S *INSIDE.*
WHAT? SHE CAN'T BE!
"SHE'S IN HERE WITH US.
"BRING THE GUARDS IN!"
SHHHHNK
SHHHHNK
ARRRGH!
HRRN...

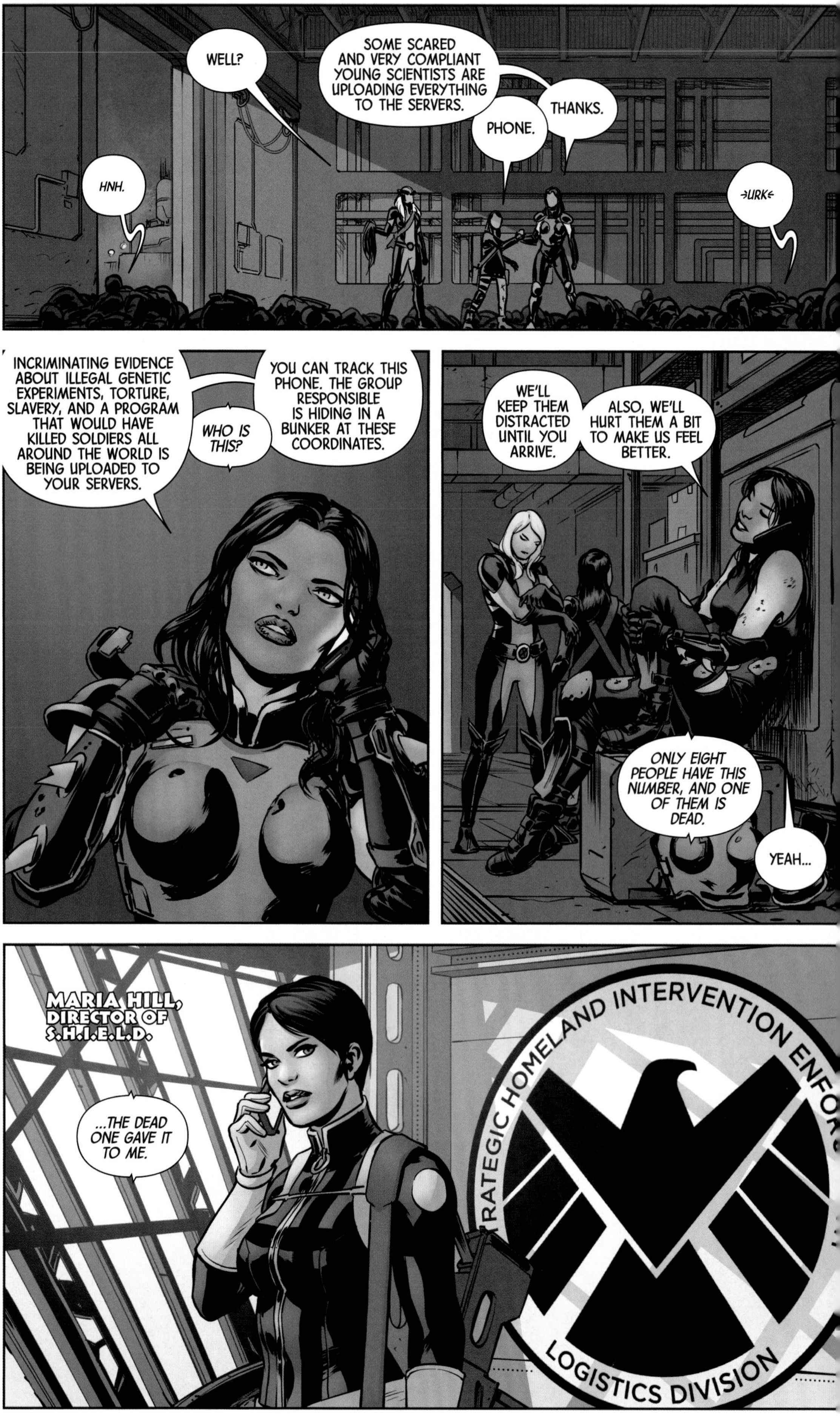
WELL?
SOME SCARED AND VERY COMPLIANT YOUNG SCIENTISTS ARE UPLOADING EVERYTHING TO THE SERVERS.
THANKS.
PHONE.
HNH.
URK
INCRIMINATING EVIDENCE ABOUT ILLEGAL GENETIC EXPERIMENTS, TORTURE, SLAVERY, AND A PROGRAM THAT WOULD HAVE KILLED SOLDIERS ALL AROUND THE WORLD IS BEING UPLOADED TO YOUR SERVERS.
WHO IS THIS?
YOU CAN TRACK THIS PHONE. THE GROUP RESPONSIBLE IS HIDING IN A BUNKER AT THESE COORDINATES.
WE'LL KEEP THEM DISTRACTED UNTIL YOU ARRIVE.
ALSO, WE'LL HURT THEM A BIT TO MAKE US FEEL BETTER.
ONLY EIGHT PEOPLE HAVE THIS NUMBER, AND ONE OF THEM IS DEAD.
YEAH...
MARIA HILL, DIRECTOR OF S.H.I.E.L.D.
...THE DEAD ONE GAVE IT TO ME.
STRATEGIC HOMELAND INTERVENTION ENFO
LOGISTICS DIVISION

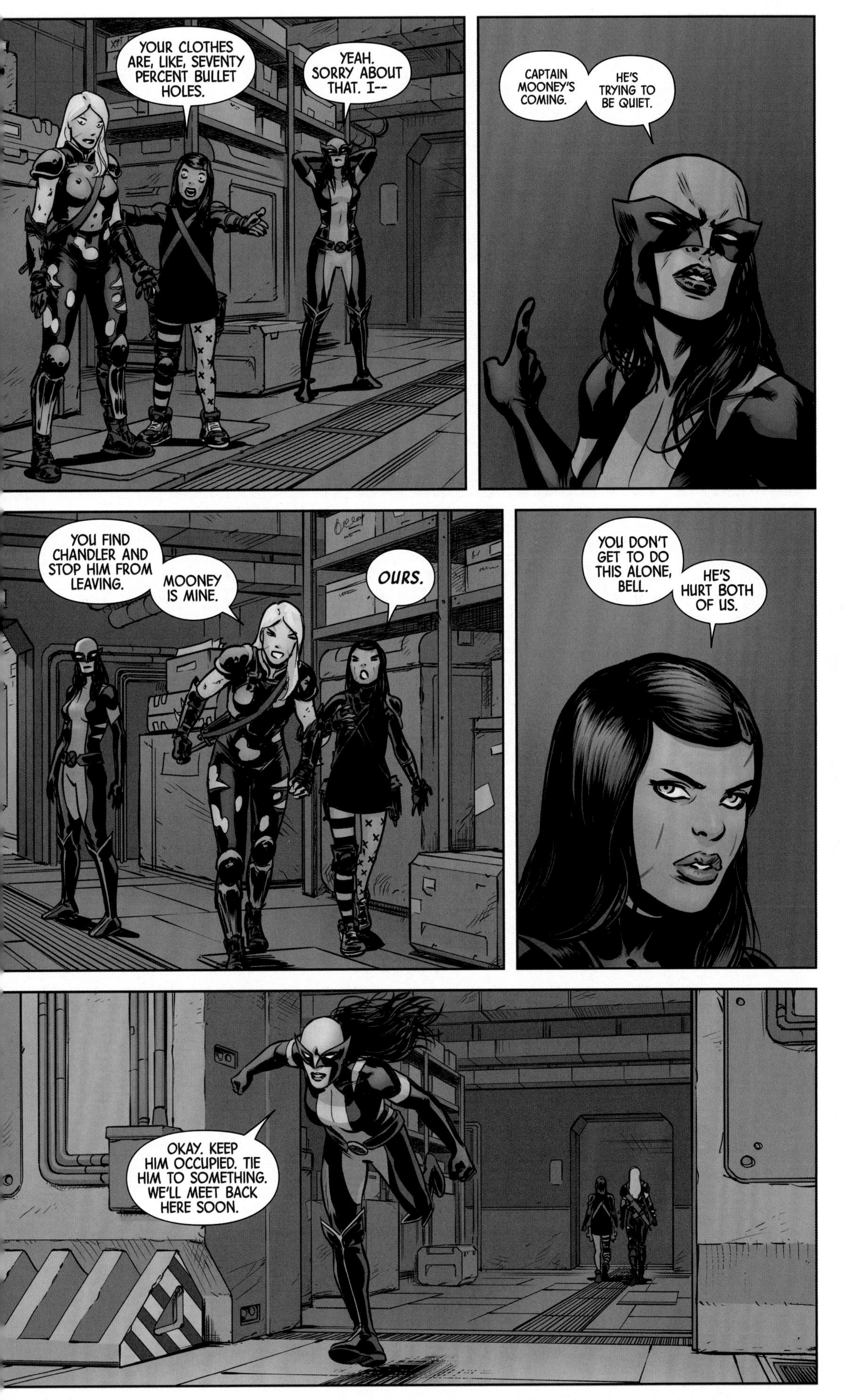
YOUR CLOTHES ARE, LIKE, SEVENTY PERCENT BULLET HOLES.
YEAH. SORRY ABOUT THAT. I--
CAPTAIN MOONEY'S COMING.
HE'S TRYING TO BE QUIET.
YOU FIND CHANDLER AND STOP HIM FROM LEAVING.
MOONEY IS MINE.
OURS.
YOU DON'T GET TO DO THIS ALONE, BELL.
HE'S HURT BOTH OF US.
OKAY. KEEP HIM OCCUPIED. TIE HIM TO SOMETHING. WE'LL MEET BACK HERE SOON.

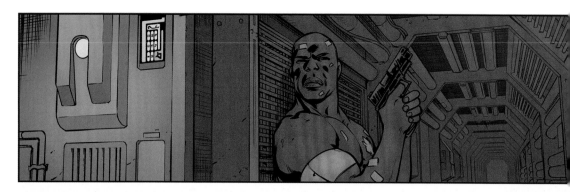

UNF!

I WANT YOU TO KNOW, THIS IS ALL YOUR FAULT.

YOU HURT US. YOU TRAINED US TO *KILL*.

HNF!

WE WOULDN'T BE CAPABLE OF THIS WITHOUT YOU.

I WOULDN'T *WANT* TO DO THIS WITHOUT YOU.

IF YOU DIDN'T HATE US SO MUCH FOR ALL THOSE YEARS IN OUR CAGE, MAYBE WE WOULD HAVE JUST WALKED AWAY.

GABBY. WAIT AROUND THE CORNER.

BELL. HE'S GOING TO JAIL. WE CAN JUST--

WAIT. AROUND. THE CORNER.

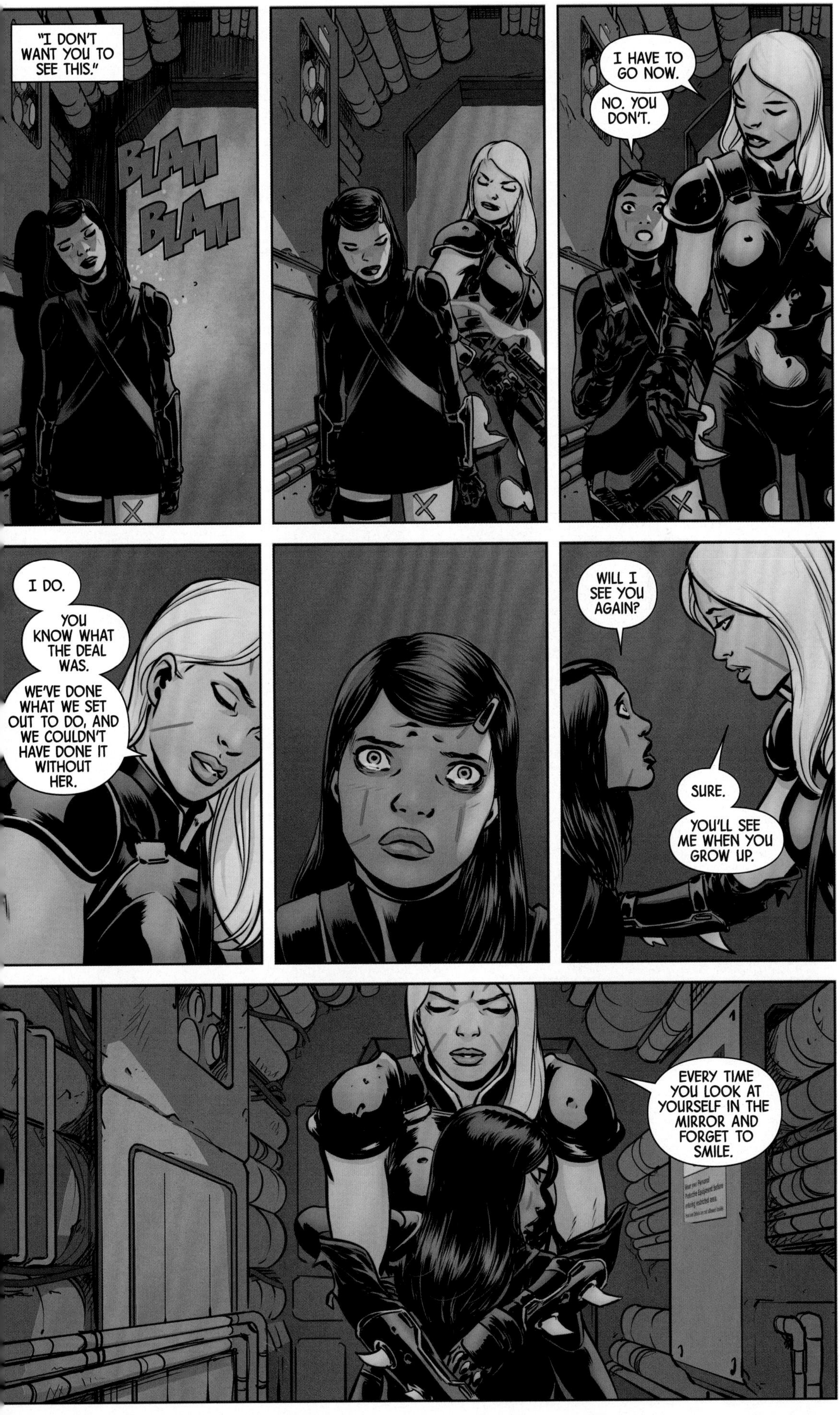
"I DON'T WANT YOU TO SEE THIS."
BLAM BLAM
I HAVE TO GO NOW.
NO. YOU DON'T.
I DO.
YOU KNOW WHAT THE DEAL WAS.
WE'VE DONE WHAT WE SET OUT TO DO, AND WE COULDN'T HAVE DONE IT WITHOUT HER.
WILL I SEE YOU AGAIN?
SURE.
YOU'LL SEE ME WHEN YOU GROW UP.
EVERY TIME YOU LOOK AT YOURSELF IN THE MIRROR AND FORGET TO SMILE.

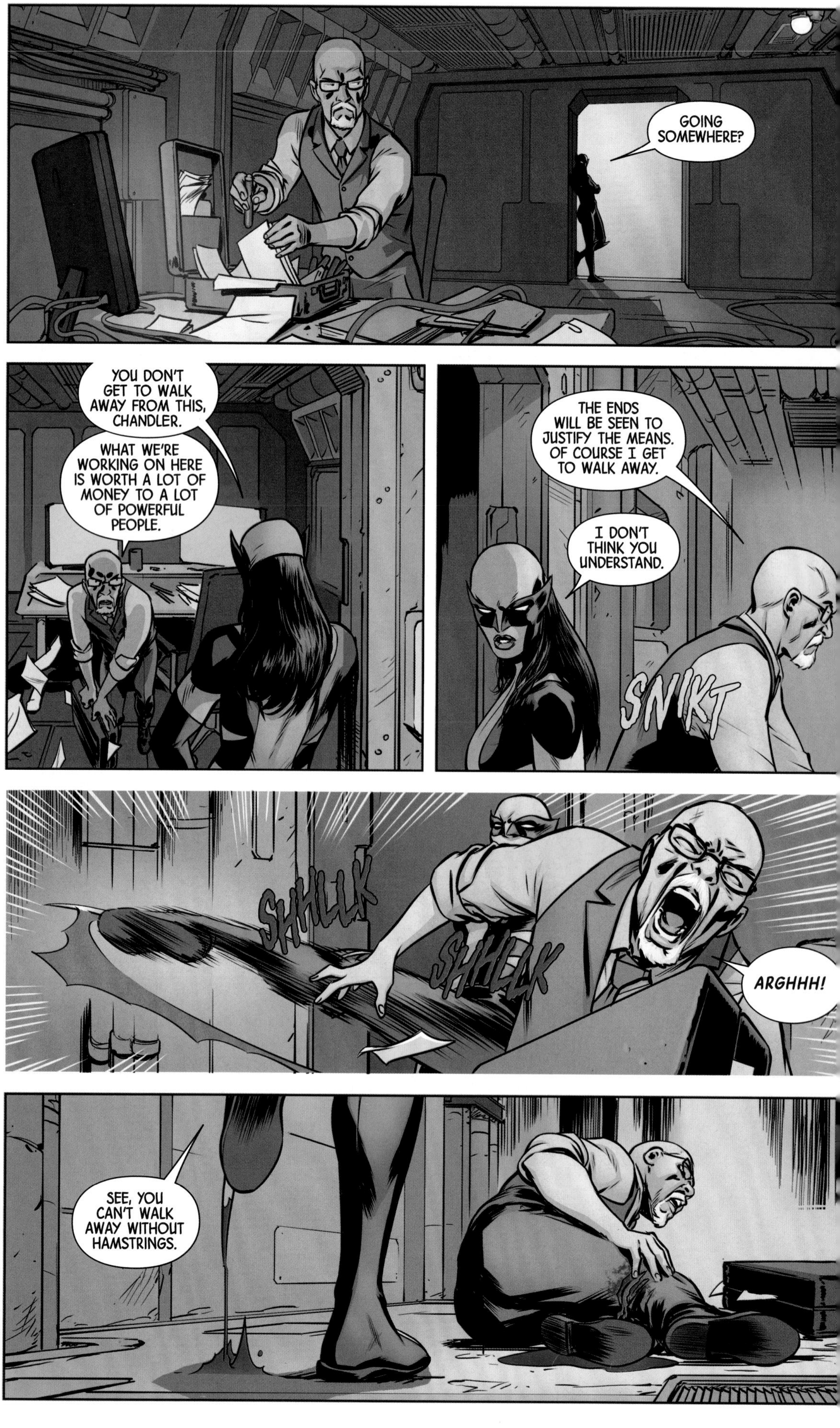
GOING SOMEWHERE?
YOU DON'T GET TO WALK AWAY FROM THIS, CHANDLER.
WHAT WE'RE WORKING ON HERE IS WORTH A LOT OF MONEY TO A LOT OF POWERFUL PEOPLE.
THE ENDS WILL BE SEEN TO JUSTIFY THE MEANS. OF COURSE I GET TO WALK AWAY.
I DON'T THINK YOU UNDERSTAND.
SNIKT
SHHLLK
SHHLLK
ARGHHH!
SEE, YOU CAN'T WALK AWAY WITHOUT HAMSTRINGS.

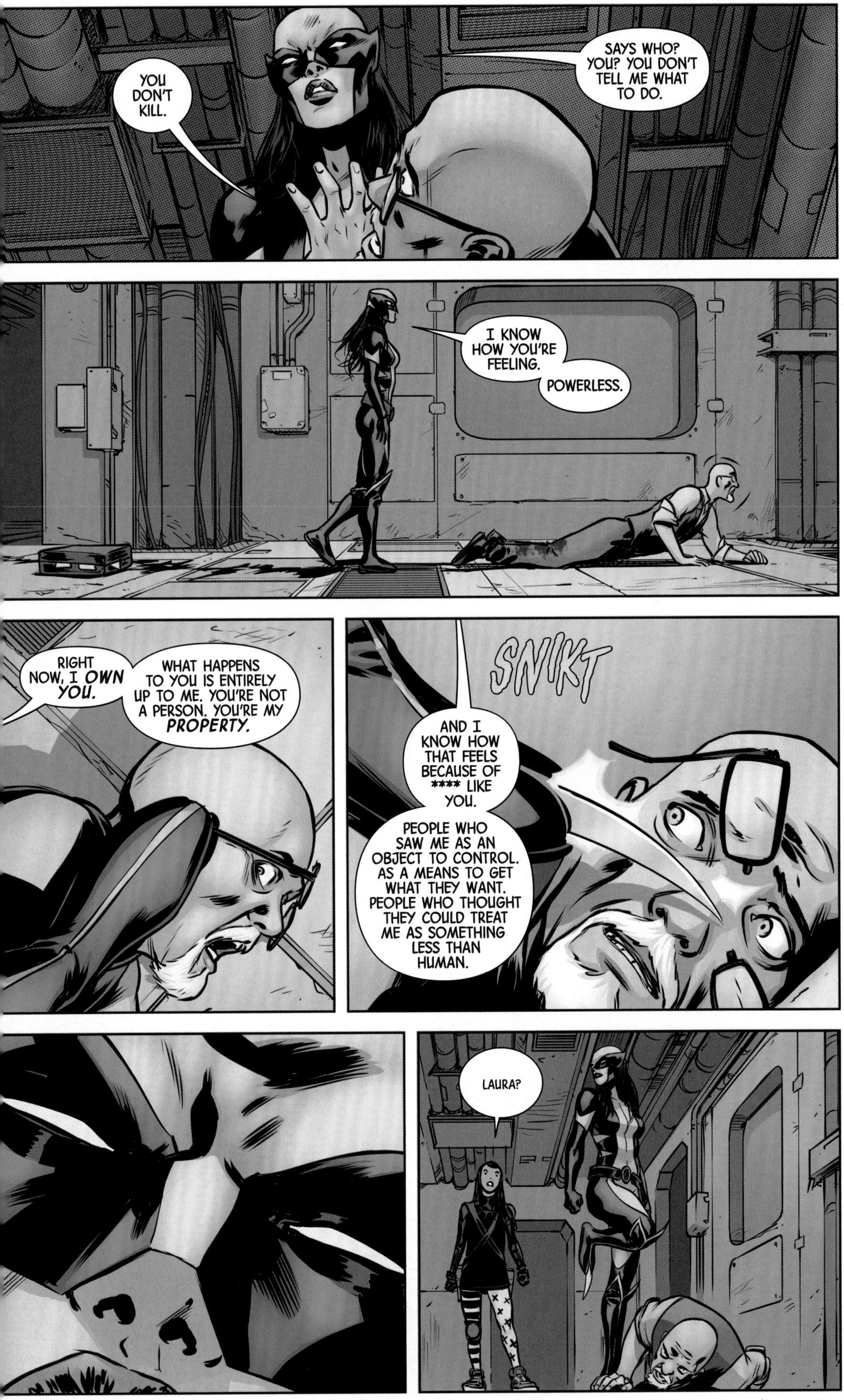
YOU DON'T KILL.
SAYS WHO? YOU? YOU DON'T TELL ME WHAT TO DO.
I KNOW HOW YOU'RE FEELING.
POWERLESS.
RIGHT NOW, I *OWN YOU.*
WHAT HAPPENS TO YOU IS ENTIRELY UP TO ME. YOU'RE NOT A PERSON. YOU'RE MY *PROPERTY.*
SNIKT
AND I KNOW HOW THAT FEELS BECAUSE OF **** LIKE YOU.
PEOPLE WHO SAW ME AS AN OBJECT TO CONTROL. AS A MEANS TO GET WHAT THEY WANT. PEOPLE WHO THOUGHT THEY COULD TREAT ME AS SOMETHING LESS THAN HUMAN.
LAURA?

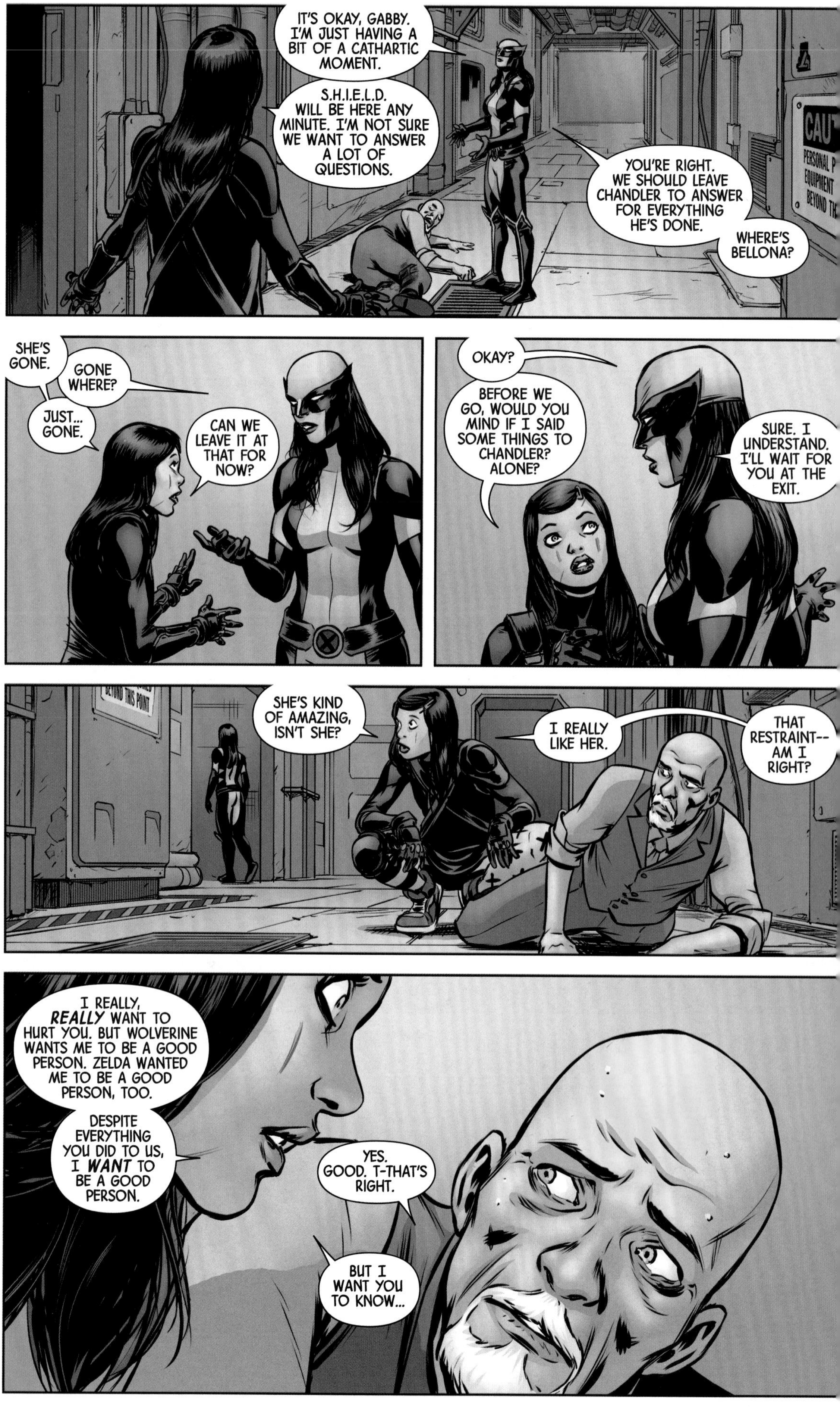
IT'S OKAY, GABBY. I'M JUST HAVING A BIT OF A CATHARTIC MOMENT.
S.H.I.E.L.D. WILL BE HERE ANY MINUTE. I'M NOT SURE WE WANT TO ANSWER A LOT OF QUESTIONS.
YOU'RE RIGHT. WE SHOULD LEAVE CHANDLER TO ANSWER FOR EVERYTHING HE'S DONE.
WHERE'S BELLONA?
CAU
PERSONAL P EQUIPMENT BEYOND TH
SHE'S GONE.
GONE WHERE?
JUST... GONE.
CAN WE LEAVE IT AT THAT FOR NOW?
OKAY?
BEFORE WE GO, WOULD YOU MIND IF I SAID SOME THINGS TO CHANDLER? ALONE?
SURE. I UNDERSTAND. I'LL WAIT FOR YOU AT THE EXIT.
BEYOND THIS POINT
SHE'S KIND OF AMAZING, ISN'T SHE?
I REALLY LIKE HER.
THAT RESTRAINT-- AM I RIGHT?
I REALLY, ***REALLY*** WANT TO HURT YOU. BUT WOLVERINE WANTS ME TO BE A GOOD PERSON. ZELDA WANTED ME TO BE A GOOD PERSON, TOO.
DESPITE EVERYTHING YOU DID TO US, I ***WANT*** TO BE A GOOD PERSON.
YES. GOOD. T-THAT'S RIGHT.
BUT I WANT YOU TO KNOW...

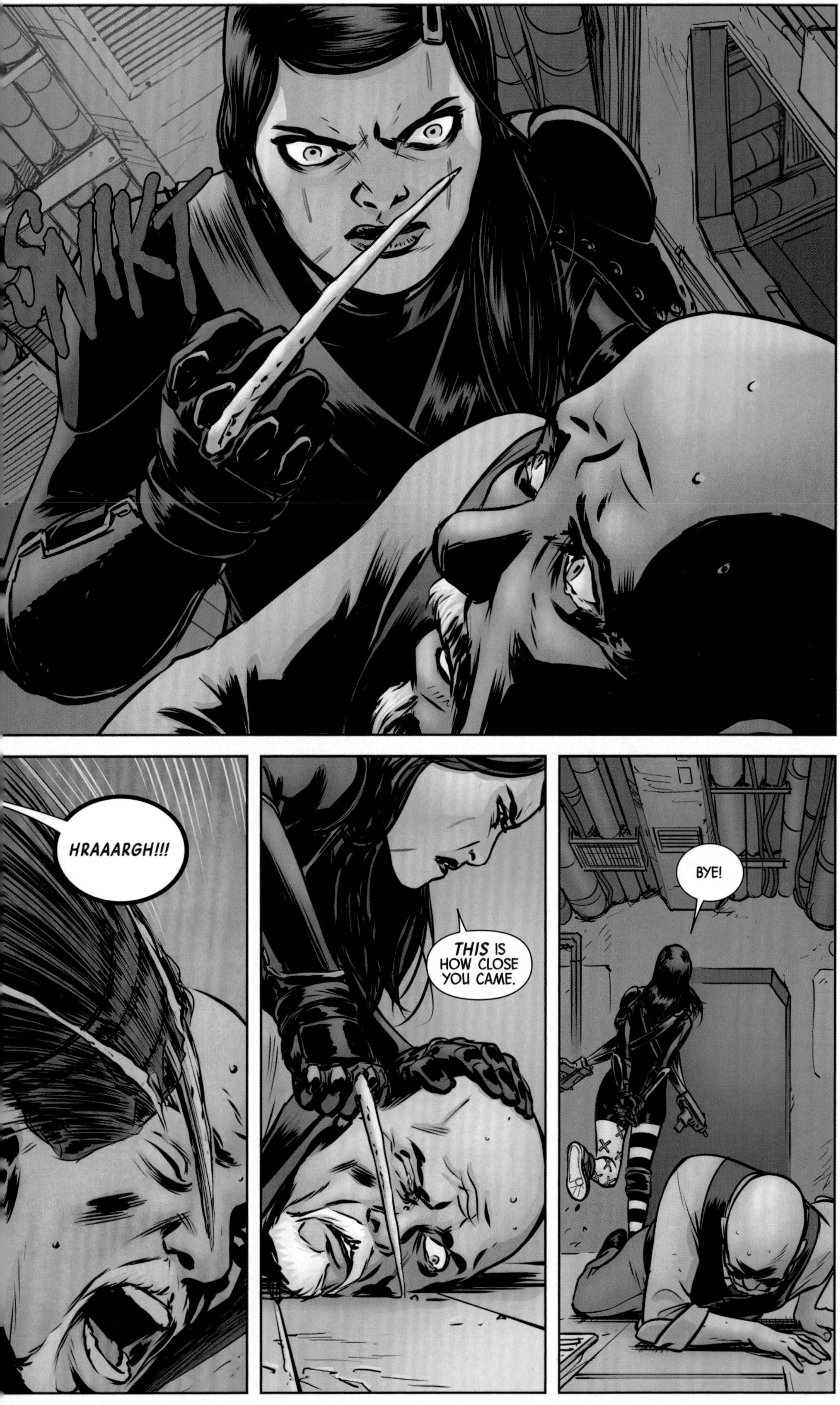
SNIKT
HRAAARGH!!!
THIS IS HOW CLOSE YOU CAME.
BYE!

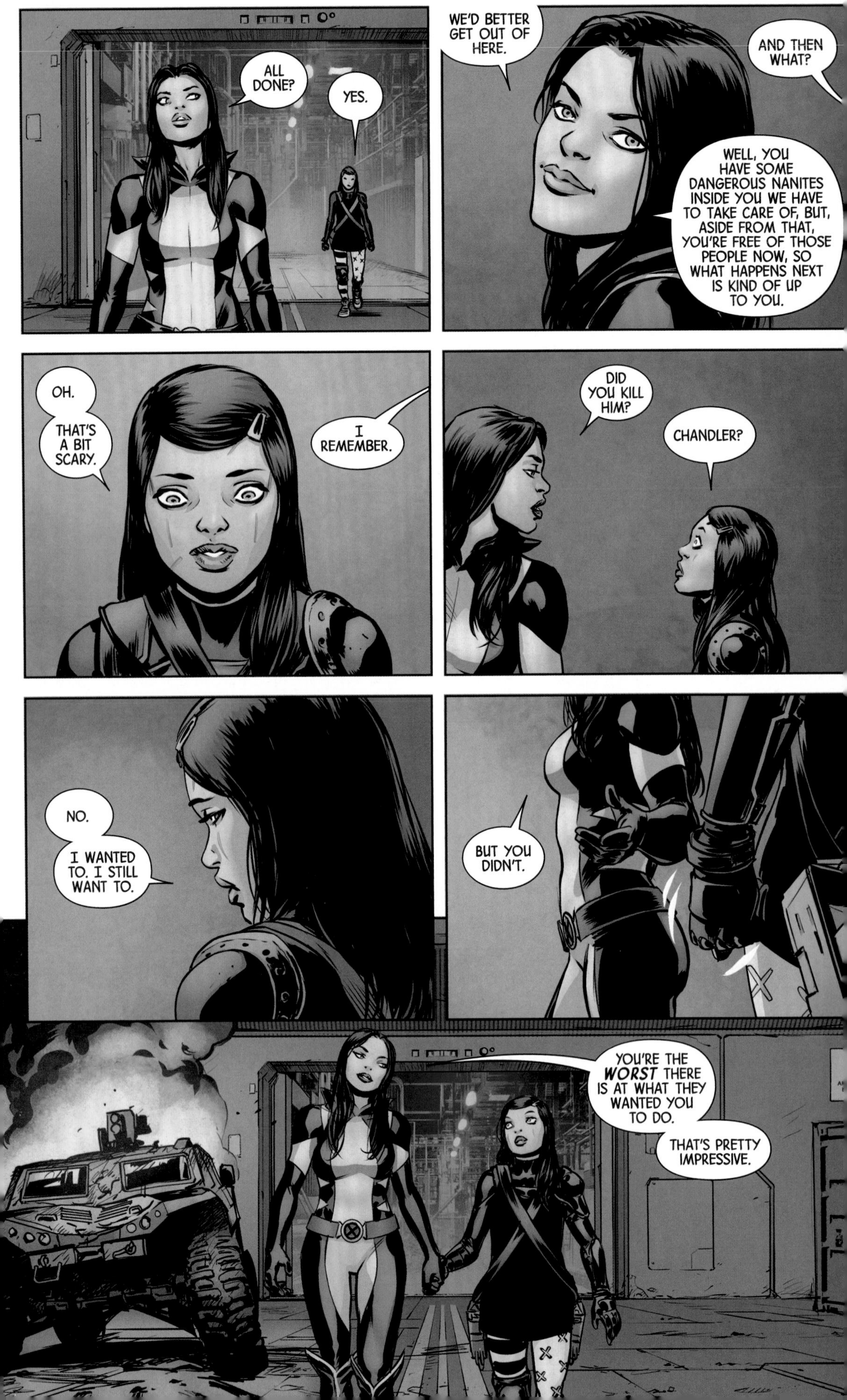

ALL DONE?
YES.
WE'D BETTER GET OUT OF HERE.
AND THEN WHAT?
WELL, YOU HAVE SOME DANGEROUS NANITES INSIDE YOU WE HAVE TO TAKE CARE OF, BUT, ASIDE FROM THAT, YOU'RE FREE OF THOSE PEOPLE NOW, SO WHAT HAPPENS NEXT IS KIND OF UP TO YOU.
OH.
THAT'S A BIT SCARY.
I REMEMBER.
DID YOU KILL HIM?
CHANDLER?
NO.
I WANTED TO. I STILL WANT TO.
BUT YOU DIDN'T.
YOU'RE THE *WORST* THERE IS AT WHAT THEY WANTED YOU TO DO.
THAT'S PRETTY IMPRESSIVE.

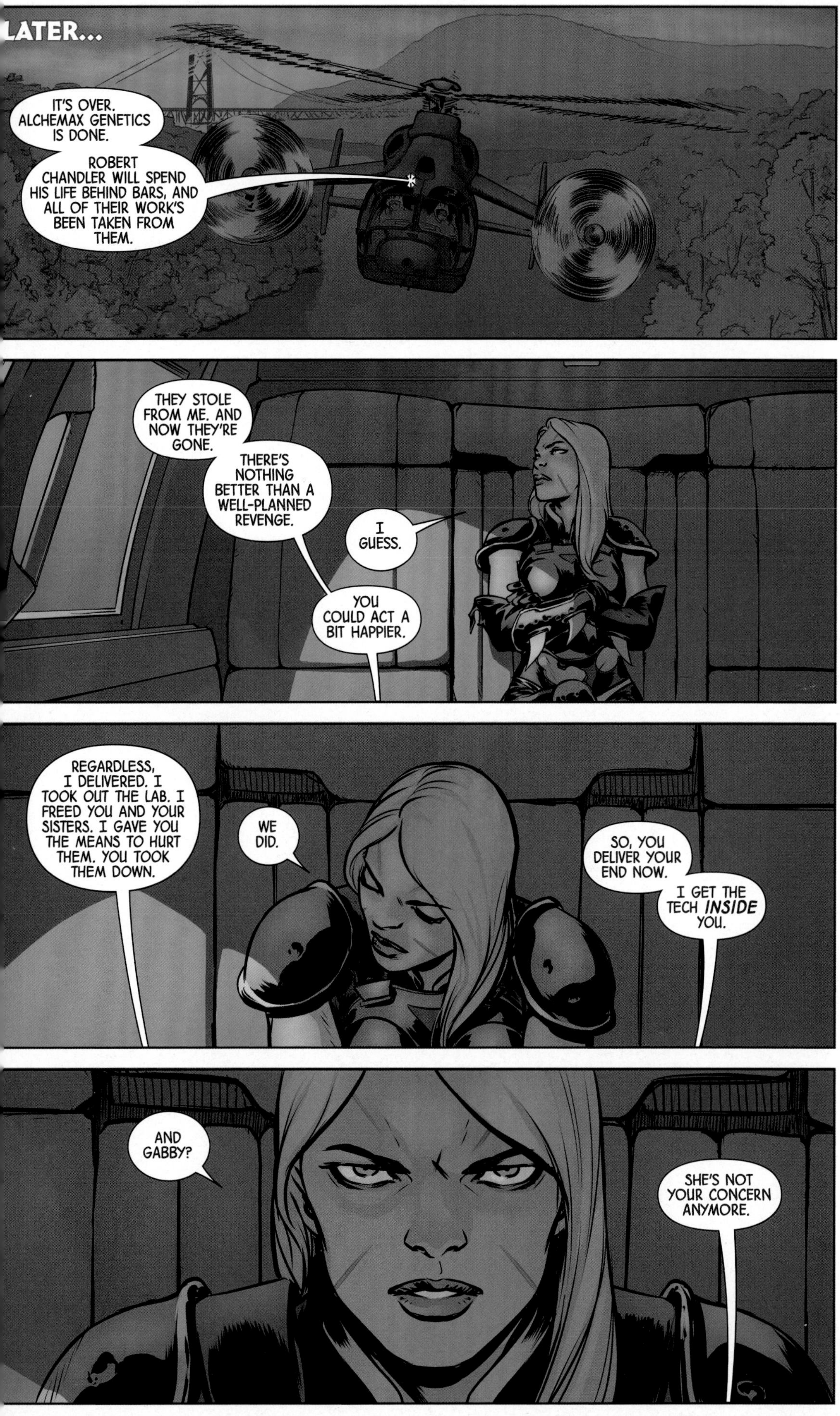
LATER...
IT'S OVER. ALCHEMAX GENETICS IS DONE.
ROBERT CHANDLER WILL SPEND HIS LIFE BEHIND BARS, AND ALL OF THEIR WORK'S BEEN TAKEN FROM THEM.
THEY STOLE FROM ME. AND NOW THEY'RE GONE.
THERE'S NOTHING BETTER THAN A WELL-PLANNED REVENGE.
I GUESS.
YOU COULD ACT A BIT HAPPIER.
REGARDLESS, I DELIVERED. I TOOK OUT THE LAB. I FREED YOU AND YOUR SISTERS. I GAVE YOU THE MEANS TO HURT THEM. YOU TOOK THEM DOWN.
WE DID.
SO, YOU DELIVER YOUR END NOW.
I GET THE TECH *INSIDE* YOU.
AND GABBY?
SHE'S NOT YOUR CONCERN ANYMORE.

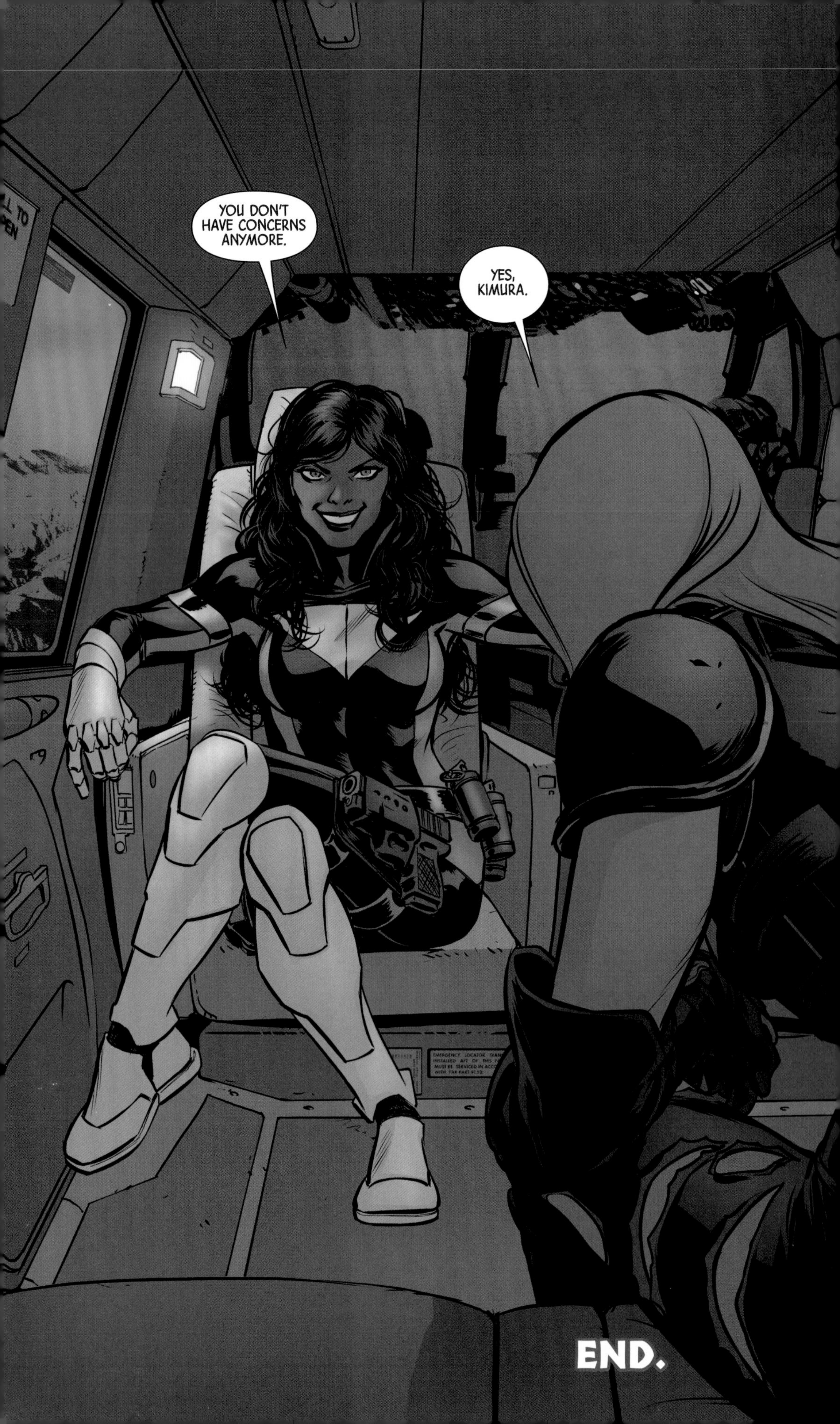
YOU DON'T HAVE CONCERNS ANYMORE.
YES, KIMURA.
END.

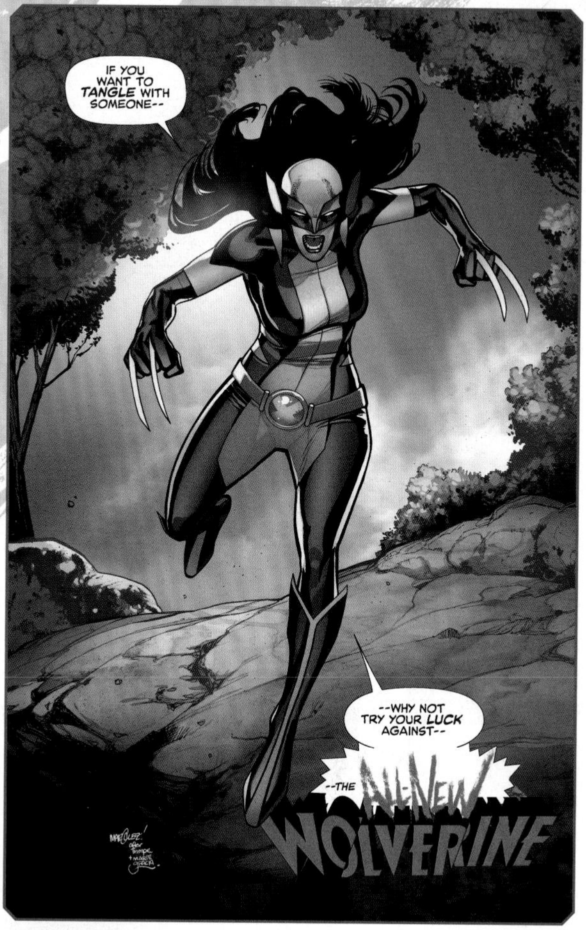
IF YOU WANT TO TANGLE WITH SOMEONE--
--WHY NOT TRY YOUR LUCK AGAINST--
--THE ALL-NEW WOLVERINE

#1 variant by
DAVID MARQUEZ &
MARTE GRACIA

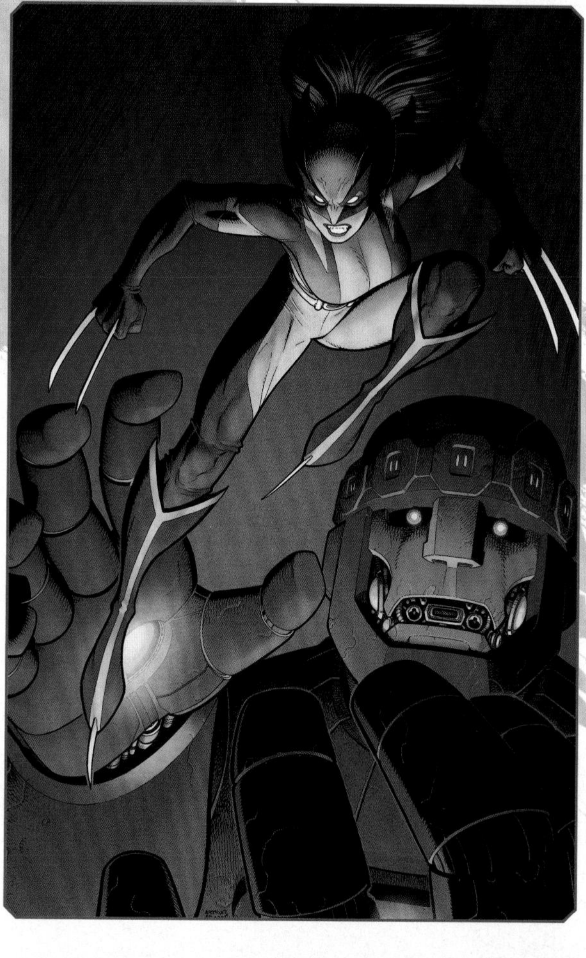

#1 variant by
ART ADAMS &
PETER STEIGERWALD

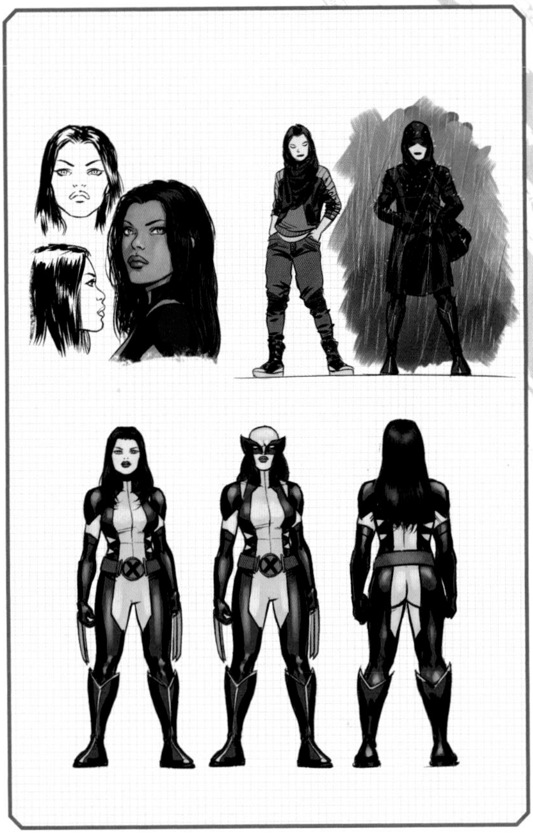

#1 design variant by
DAVID LOPEZ & DAVID NAVARROT

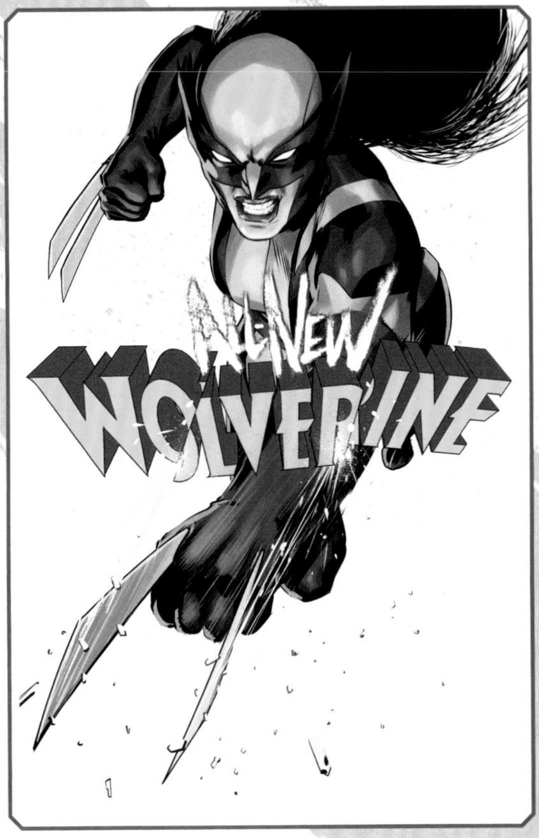

ALL-NEW
WOLVERINE

#1 variant by
DAVID LOPEZ

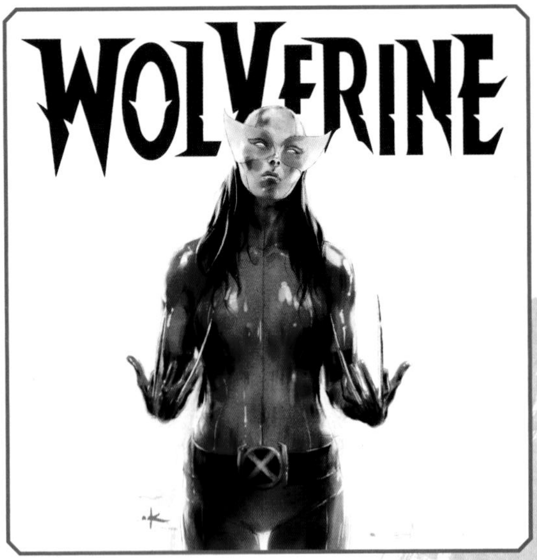

WOLVERINE

#1 hip-hop variant by
KERON GRANT

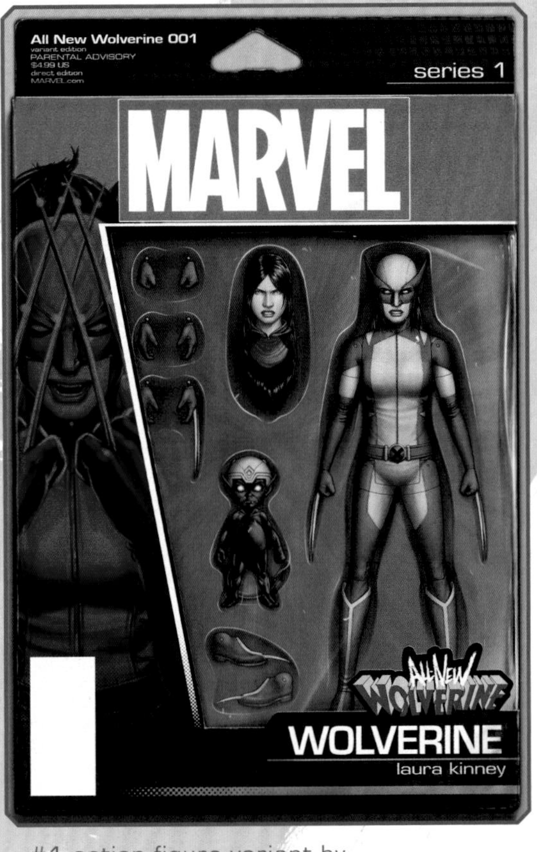

All New Wolverine 001
variant edition
PARENTAL ADVISORY
$4.99 US
direct edition
MARVEL.com
series 1
MARVEL
ALL-NEW
WOLVERINE
WOLVERINE
laura kinney

#1 action figure variant by
JOHN TYLER CHRISTOPHER

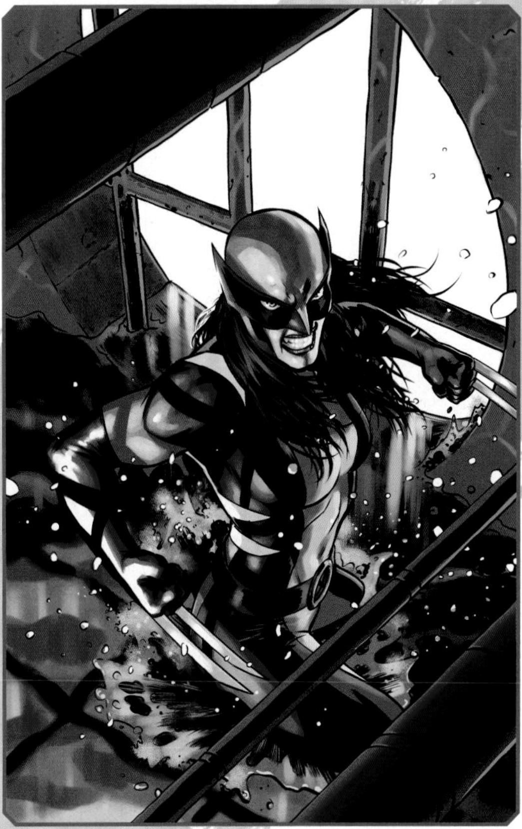

#2 variant by
DAVID LOPEZ

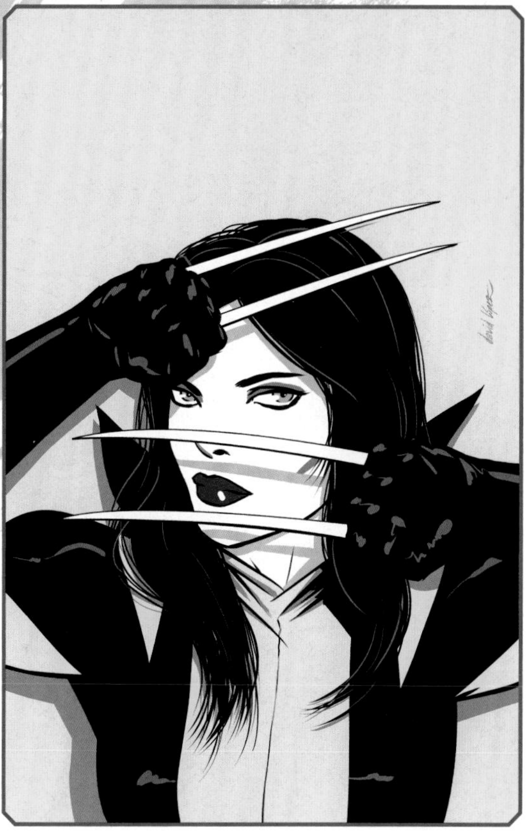

#3 variant by
DAVID LOPEZ

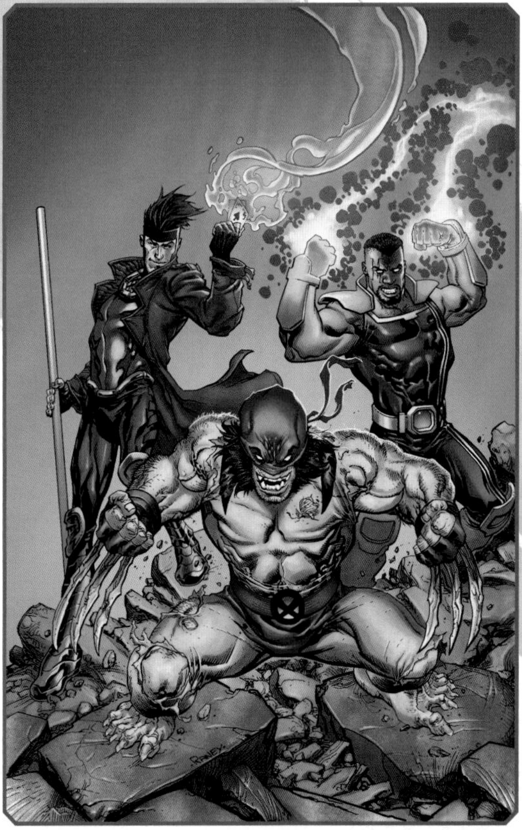

#3 Marvel '92 variant by
TOM RANEY & **CHRIS SOTOMAYOR**

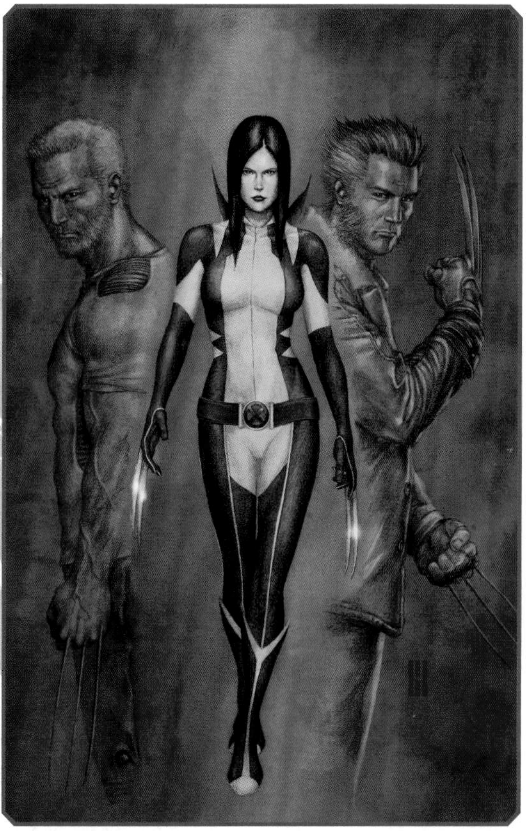

#3 variant by
MIKE CHOI

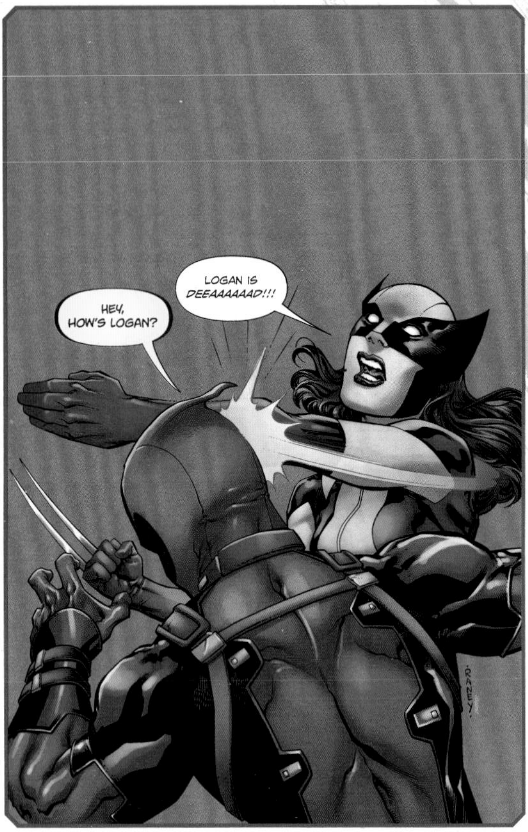
HEY, HOW'S LOGAN?
LOGAN IS DEEAAAAAAD!!!
RANEY

#4 Deadpool variant by
TOM RANEY & **CHRIS SOTOMAYOR**

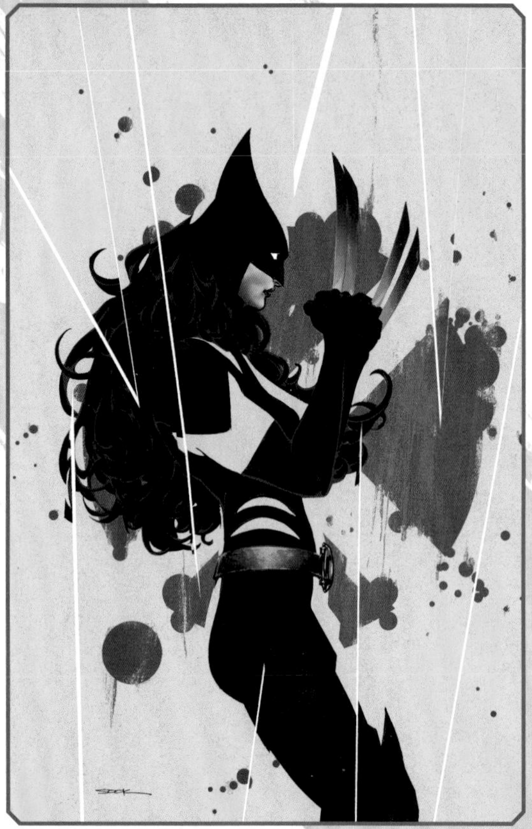

#4 variant by
RYAN SOOK

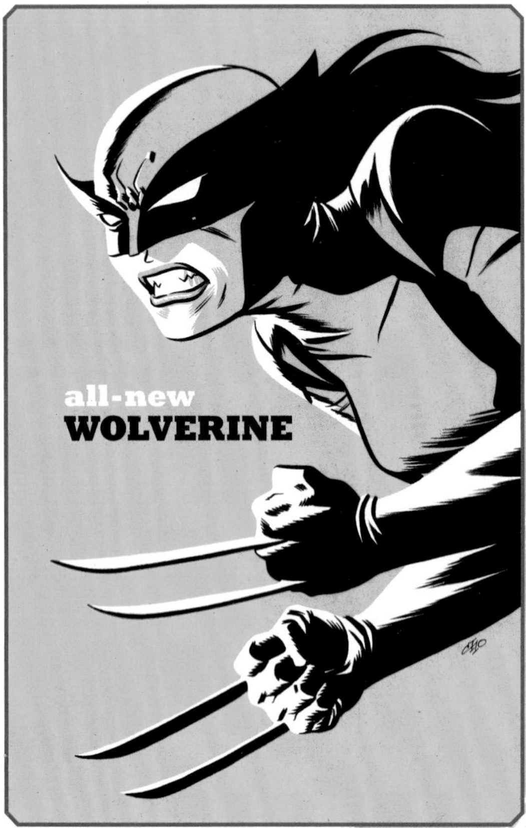
all-new
WOLVERINE

#5 variant by
MICHAEL CHO

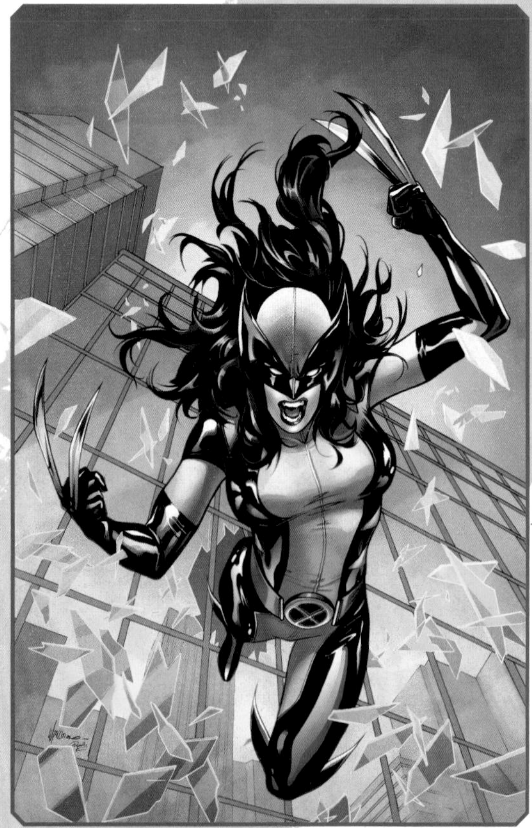

#6 women of power variant by
EMA LUPACCHINO &
RACHELLE ROSENBERG